More praise for *In, and Of*

"...the voice crying out in the wilderness, bravely, madly, tenderly, ironically. ...the very thickness, wit and wonder of it, tumbling page over page exposing the wretchedness, the rapture...bewilderment, confusion, redemption and realization so densely, so wondrously well. The sense of vertigo, of pain, of tearful joy bowls me over ...the phantasmagoric, whirling vortex of meaning /understanding /spirit-surging, thought whirling, abstract-into manifest realization and also, at the other end of the scale, such witty economical evocations of quirky characters; and lush description of place. ...penetrating characterizations that always left me wanting to hear more more more about the words exchanged, the scene, the texture of the encounter." Jonathon Kerslake (editor, *Lived Experience*)

"...one man's journey toward self-understanding, of trying to find one's place not only in his small portion of the world, but in the universe as well. Haas has penned an intensely personal journal... His writing style snares the reader into this journey he has taken until one can literally feel the damp fog and the harshness of the street beneath his back. His ideas are will written, helping the reader to visualize his points as they accompany him along the road taken for the ten long years he spent searching for that ever-elusive 'mystery of life'." Denise M. Clark (*Denise's Pieces Book Reviews*)

Copyright© 2002 Jack Haas

All rights reserved. No part of this publication may be reproduced or transmitted in any form or by any means, electronic or mechanical, including photocopying, recording, or by any information storage or retrieval system, without written permission from the Publisher, except in quoting brief passages.

Thanks to Maggie McGhee and Tanis Mager for their valuable editing comments.

Library of Canada Cataloguing in Publication data:

Haas, Jack, 1966-
    In, and Of

ISBN 0-9731007-1-0

1. Haas, Jack, 1966- 2. Pacific Coast (B.C.)-Biography I. Title.
FC3829.1.H32A3 2002   971.1'092   C2002-910611-7
F1089.P2H32 2002

Published by Iconoclast Press:
Suite 144
3495 Cambie St.
Vancouver, BC.
V5Z 4R3
Canada
admin@iconoclastpress.com

Cover photo by Tanis Mager.

For Larry Edwards, Götz Hanisch, and Bob Liptrot: men of the earth, upon whose soil my seed began to grow.

PART 1

The Way of Sin

"It was a phantom dance of souls, baffled by these deceptive blends, yet still seeking permanence in the midst of what was only perpetually evanescent, or eternally lost. Or it was a dance of the seeker and his goal, here pursuing still the gay colors he did not know he had assumed, there striving to identify the finer scene of which he might never realize he was already a part."
Malcolm Lowry

"The spirit-child is an unwilling adventurer into chaos and sunlight, into the dreams of the living and the dead. Things that are not ready, not willing to be born or become, things for which adequate preparations have not been made to sustain their momentous births, things that are not resolved, things bound up with failure and with fear of being, they all keep recurring, keep coming back, and in themselves partake of the spirit-child's condition. They keep coming and going till their time is right."
Ben Okri

"Separateness is the mystical event of oneness."
Matt Haas

chapter one

    Once you have eaten of the flesh, so to speak, you must ride it out completely.
    Of course everyone's journey is different, but if you give yourself away to life, things cannot avoid falling implausibly into place around you, and an existence you never thought possible eventually swells instinctively up from within, and devours you whole.
    It's all so subtle, unexpected, absurd, and indisputable, that when an epoch ends- when the drama of 'being' comes to one of its cyclic, fabulous crescendos- and the spirit fully emerges, the whole holocaust and rapture of life dissolves back into itself, into you, and you into it, the two sides blend into one, the universe is fulfilled for an instant, time evaporates, distance vanishes, the light mingles and ...we are gone.
    I am speaking of nexus points, unifications, grand synchronicities, and convergences in the hidden patterns of the cosmos, from which sublime realities become conspicuously manifest in the lives of persons chosen or willing to act out the universe's karmic evolution; momentary windows of a deeper vision, leaps of understanding, and etheric mutations in the blueprint of our chimerical beings, such that there are profound times and places in the somnambulistic imagination of the great and dancing Imaginer, when the veil of causality lifts blatantly away to reveal its eternal marriage with effect, the continuum becomes apparent, the Creator finally awakens within and as the Creation, and yet still no one, not even the Maker, can understand how the marvelous making is made.
    It is all very strange, obscure and ineffable, as it were. But to be sure- it happens. Every now and then, due, as it were, to the course of our forgotten, sublime affinities, a cohesion of disparate forces fuse into One, life takes on mythical proportions, the Gods awaken from their slumber, the devil gets his due, and the lone individual, bent awkwardly upon the fulfillment of his or her impossible and unavoidable destiny, breaks loose from the world's hold, resuscitates the old breath, finds the living Life, curses the anguish, weeps for the children, drinks, dances, goes mad with love, and then vanishes into the sky with all those brave or free enough to follow.
    Let me tell you, it happens. Rarely, perhaps very rarely, but by god it comes about. And when it does, the Heavens float down like a warm deluge through the frost of Hell, the veneer of our horrid separation lifts for a blessed instant, the *I* in each one of us untangles itself, and all those ready, strong, innocent, or bored enough, slip quietly away, out into the gentle flow, merging with eternity, and then drifting off into God without going anywhere; they simply float away

without leaving; they stand still and fall apart into everything. That is what happens.

But perhaps I am starting off here too fast. Let me sum it all up, so as to be done with the story, and then we can get on with the meat of this text. It goes like this: when you are born you are not yet born- first you must descend, die, rise from the ashes, forget every idea of right and wrong, lose yourself completely, gain yourself again, and become the All. There you have it, in brief synoptic fashion. What follows are merely the details.

*

two

I can't say precisely when understandings such as these began to smolder within me. It was sometime in my mid twenties, after I had begun to awaken to the folly and immaturity of mankind's ways; after I had finally broken free from the futility and indoctrination of the whole education fiasco; after the collapse of a corrupt business I had owned and operated with one of the devil's own minions; after I had traveled aimlessly in the world for a while, had become disillusioned and confused from the apparent meaninglessness of it all, and had moved away from Ontario, where I was raised, heading west, penniless, possessionless, notionless, and finally free to begin again on my own, to forget all that I had learned, experienced, and lost, and to start again from square one.

I needed a new beginning, a complete change, a resurrection.

Indeed there is little in life of more value to the transformation of the self than to one day uproot your whole existence, cut away the gnarled mass that has grown in and around you, scythe the wheat that has grown from your soil, and take up the rhizome of your soul, away from its homeland, away from all it has known of sunlight and season, away from the forces which watered and fed it and pruned it along, and go to another place, find another patch of earth, and then lay down your tuber in the mud and watch it blossom and grow.

To change dramatic sets is to change roles. New buds grow on old branches, but it is a different fruit which comes forth. The old skin of identity molts away, and the nouvelle vintage is poured within.

I understand now why so many ancient epics are filled with tales of exile, exploration, destiny, and destination, because the inevitable tests and trials which beset a person's existence are quickened when the flow of life bursts through the encumbering form, and the individual breaks away from their old and worn out norm.

Had Odysseus never left Ithaca, Homer would have been forced to write cookbooks. Had Moses not walked out of Egypt and wandered forty years in the desert, the reign of Babylon would never have been broken. Had Lao Tzu not turned away from his homeland in disgust and scorn, the gatekeeper would never have heard his wisdom, and the Tao would never have been born.

It is the breaking away from the confines of context which first liberate the spirit into the subtle life, where all that shifts and moves is hidden from all that stands still.

When I took up my tunic and sack, and walked into the sunset without any idea of what lay ahead, I had, without realizing it, joined in with the great dance of creation, and I was now creating what lay ahead of me.

Knowing nothing of such things back then, I ended up falling to earth on the hallowed soil of Canada's westernmost city-state, Vancouver.

Settling in British Columbia, and this gem of a west-coast city, at the age of twenty-three, was like finding a new set of lungs which I did not know I possessed, but into which I was soon inhaling a whole new type of air- an ethereal air which, unlike the profane atmosphere of the east, I could breathe in through the subtle pores of my broken spirit, and slowly regain consciousness from years of suffocation.

To be sure, Ontario has its many charms, but at that time I was unable to see the roses through the thorns, and I needed to be hit with a monstrous blow of beauty and wonder, the magnitude of which can only be found in the grandiose brilliance of the west coast's mountains, forests, and sea, the likes of which have earned this blessed area of the earth the charmed soubriquet of Lotus-land.

Like a man awoken in an unknown flower garden, in an unknown world, for an unknown reason, at first I could do naught but inhale the intoxicating perfumes of this new life's beauty and splendor. Good god did I breathe. That's all I did. That's all I could do. Nothing more was needed.

I can still revisit the swelling sense of well being which often befell me during those first few years in the vibrant city and land which has never ceased to overwhelm and astonish me. Living in a perpetual state of daze and disbelief, I was seized often enough by an intoxicating sense of awe over what were largely overlooked trifles to the tenured residents of this Valhalla: the megalithic size of a neighbor's verdant hedge, the thickly perfumed air of the early spring blossoming season, the balmy, inviting, animated summer nights on the coast, or the sight of an eagle or heron gliding on wing across a city beach- these types of things were enough to drive me mad with joy, enough to invigorate and sustain me, because they were so unlike the experiences and settings in which I had been reared and to which I had said goodbye, heading off to my new life in a new land with new promise, new adventure, and, to be sure, new trials, upheavals, and agonies.

I had arrived to find myself ensconced within a wholly novel feeling, a new vibe, so to speak, which quickly filtered in through my skin, washing away the other life I had been living- the other life I had been dying- and began the germination and fertilization of a seed I had not imagined I was carrying.

In the beginning there were days in which I would walk around in a state of profound amazement and relief, delirious with thankfulness that I had been led to find and live in such a place. I recall riding across the Burrard Street bridge one evening, heading home after a soiree with some new friends, and all of the sudden, without any effort or expectation, I was as if lifted up by the breastbone and a wave of gratitude washed over me the likes of which I have rarely felt since. It was the type of gratitude that arises out of nowhere, for no specific reason, and goes off in no conscious direction. I have no clue to whom or for what I felt this surge of grateful acceptance, I can only say that it was directed at existence itself, and the explosion of thankfulness had arisen out from somewhere behind my mind, and it grabbed hold of me, and possessed me, and the grace of appreciation swelled and wholly consumed me for a spell; I was grabbed by a hook from the sky, lifted off of the earth for a moment, where I watched from above the glorious gift I'd been given, without purpose or reason, and was let back down to the mundane and the tolerable world. The feeling then eased away slowly, and I rode home with the scent of joy and magnanimity trailing out behind me.

It was the regular experiences of such upliftment that carried me through for a while as a citizen of this western metropolis.

And yet, not many years later, although I was still hopelessly smitten with Vancouver- with its new stage, new sights, feelings, inspirations, friends, and wonders- the exuberance and lightness which I had found would begin to dim and fade. In fact, even in this city of God, the insidious aspect of mankind *en masse* would soon turn foul within me and would drive me away from my habitation and comfort again, forcing me apart from my familiars, out into yet another world altogether- an even mightier and more magical world- a world where I would again experience wonder and gratitude for the privilege of this unimaginable earthly existence of ours. Oh and much more, much, much more. I would discover the true spirit and true earth, all feverishly served up on the wild and untamed coast of British Columbia and Alaska, and my affinity for civilization and its tortured constructs would be finished for good.

I speak of the years of departure; the times when I left my place of welcome, to wander lonely in the void without another- to lift up and stay there, to float on the splendid confusion of disorientation, far above the thorns of context; these are the chapters of life when the soul sets out on an uncharted course, perhaps never again to return- when the spirit finds again that lost fluidity, unbound nor gathered in a name, and the hard parts crumble from the eternal stream gushing free now from within. That is when the spirit relearns its passion dance, and chooses never again to tangle in the game.

*

three

It's what you can't see coming that truly belongs to life. And life, if not a great adventure, is at least a fabulous misadventure.

Most things that happen are much different than they appear, existing beyond the borders of conception and reason. These are the inexplicable, the immense, the evanescent doorways and portholes into the essence; the blinding core of impossible conditions, of realms and layers stacked upon each other, within each other, through and all around each other; the convulsive pandemonium of surprise and imagination; the real and implausible, the recognizable and the nebulous; the presence and absence of the unexpected conglomerations, residues, and idiosyncrasies; the outright exquisiteness and brilliance of the whole trembling edifice, held together by nothing, heading towards nowhere, beyond meaning and purpose, out and in and tossed into a heap of wriggling preposterousnesses all oozing and biting and thrashing about in the calm and tireless ubiquity.

Given this, I was lucky during those first few years in Vancouver- a time when I was still capable of living with others, a time which did not last very long and was followed by many years in which I would either need to be out in the free and open expanse of the wilds, or furtively locked away behind four impenetrable walls in some dingy apartment, alone and in perfect silence except for the ever present cacophony of untamed voices ringing out in grand disharmony within my perplexed cranium- but I was lucky, as I said, in the beginning, when I was still somewhat of a social creature, and not yet burdened with the solitary life, in that I took up neophytic residence with a young man who would help me break a few of the chains which bound and hindered me from expanding the dimensions of my formative self. And he would do that simply by living as an example, right before me, of a way of surviving in the world without being driven mad by it.

I was lucky- or perhaps *blessed* is a more accurate adjective- because prior to arriving in Vancouver, I had been acquainted with mostly beer-guzzling buffoons and thoughtless toadstools, and had not met a single soul who had prioritized the spirit over the world, and so I was on an uncertain path, barely caring for the way I lived, because somewhere deep inside I knew that something was wrong, horribly wrong, and yet I had no idea of another way to exist, and so I had been doing what everyone else did who was caught in a life which didn't belong to them- I drank and partied, chased women, and talked about nothing in particular. Oh, I was already irrevocably immersed in the esoteric and recondite texts of antiquity, but for all the effect these had on me I might as well have been reading fantasy novels, for what had eternal, cosmic truths to do with food, drink, and rent, anyways? I was born of substance and had no idea of how to live without it as my mainstay.

And so my new roommate shifted my paradigm, as it were, for I realized soon enough that he spoke in a language which I had never heard before, and yet one which I understood instantly upon listening to it; a language which came before mankind's superfluous conventions took charge; a language which sang in my ears of another song, another rhythm, another aspect of existence which indeed I could sense beyond the inharmonious pitch of society's discord, but which I had not isolated nor paid proper attention to until it came and laid itself before me in the living form of Glen.

Even to this day Glen has a way of standing in the midst of the tumult, like the eye of the hurricane, and being unaffected by the hysteria and chaos all around. He is a classic adept, with all the equanimity and poise of a master such as Nagarjuna or Dogen, hovering effortlessly above the mire of endless troubles and their repair. It was from his example that I realized no one need commit themselves to a lifetime of toil and struggle simply to exist; one needed merely decide to exist in the magic and beauty of the day, and the universe would take care of its own, for this is an inalienable right of ours- which is, simply ...*to be*. And that means to live without the futility of the daily grind hampering our exaltations.

This was a recognition which dawned upon me slowly over the time Glen and I roomed together, during which period it was a regular occurrence for me to awaken to the insult of the clock, jam down a couple of Tylenol in an attempt to quickly counterbalance the previous night's excesses, gobble down a frantic, unsatisfying breakfast, and speed off on my bike to sell my soul in return for my humble daily keep; while Glen, on the other hand, would arise gently and only when his body was good and rested, would partake of a calm and peaceful breakfast, would go out for an easy stroll along the beaches and parks nearby, would perhaps read some poetry or a spiritual tract, and then he would sit down to the typewriter and pour out his own voice, his own vision, his own understandings, experiences, and delights at the privileged glory of existence. He was a master, I was a slave.

Each evening I would return from work, worn and shell-shocked and a beaten man, driven mad like a whipped beast from the continued onslaught of drudgery and repetition- a yoke I had convinced myself was the necessary addendum to being alive on this earth. And there Glen would be, sitting quietly, perhaps listening to jazz or classical music, enjoying the relaxed cadence of life which comes from living at one's own pace. And I would burst into the apartment, contaminated by the disruptive vibrations of the false round to which I had been willingly shackled, and head straight for the refrigerator and crack a beer and begin anaesthetizing away the disharmony within me and the chorus of harangued and tormented ghouls which I was only able to still, at that time, with enough booze and dope to kill an elephant, pouring down draught after draught so as to forget how wrong it was for me to every morning spit at the sky and cast away the cherished gift of life I had been benevolently vouchsafed just so as to serve my wallet.

The night of drinking, accompanied by the ongoing conversations Glen and I would engage in, would be followed by another disquieting departure, and another day of tedious torture, all the while holding in the back of my mind a vision of my buddy, free and relaxing, because he had forsaken all of it, and had learned to live on little, need little, and do little, and so had beaten the world at its own game and returned himself to his own way of life and the passionate living of it.

This man's living example, during the precarious years of my so called work-ethic development, was incredibly important to me, because my whole life I had heard that one must go to school, do well, graduate with honors, strive to be somebody, and sign on for a tour of duty in the hallowed halls of money and make-believe existence which would not end until the spirit collapsed and the flesh gave it up to the wind. And I certainly was not fit for such a life.

And so Glen's presence was incredibly important for me to witness. And yet it wasn't until I myself broke away- it wasn't until I made the decision to live my own life, regardless of the status quo- that I began to cherish the gift I had been, up until that point, taking horribly for granted and abusing. As such I began to turn the tables and work far less, so as to live more fully, rather than to work hard and not live at all.

I soon recognized with the detached eye of one who has gone a certain distance away from an event in which they were once wholly bemused and ensconced, that the system had grown sick with greed and stupidity, and that it was only from myself, and for myself, that I would begin to nourish the seed within which had been lying dormant and dying and would need some tender care to get it to sprout and thrive, but which would end up growing strong and fecund and would itself choke out the weeds which had been planted in me by the collective confusion of society since day one.

And it was Glen who catalyzed this reaction within me; it was his own personal force which I recognized and which then stirred the tepid stew within me into a fomenting cauldron of intention and drive which would in the end provide the escape-velocity necessary for me to leave the gravity of our culture's torpid conventions behind.

I would not call my life a conversion, merely a version, for there are truths I would not come to understand until after many years ahead of confused digression, false intent, debauchery, idleness, unfaith, and agony.

For me it began as a wild and manic ride of booze and anguish, dope and euphoria, destiny and freedom, psychedelia, mushrooms, madness, humility, and wonder. I would not come to the nothingness that is everything until all the blood had been letted from my putrid corpse, until I had mapped out all the blind alleys within myself, until the heavens had murdered me without pity or concern, until I loved and cursed and followed God, and then was broken from the mold of the manifest, and inhaled back to the Source, like a creature caught in the throat of a Creator who had just begun to breathe.

It was a troubling and euphoric period for me. Life was as bewildering as it was grand. I couldn't get a hold of it, and I couldn't get away. I couldn't get lost because I was always lost. I created it and was created by it. I was caught inside, and trapped outside. I was bored and amazed and worn thin by the background exaltation tapped into the electric din. I tried my best and didn't give a damn either. I piled it up, and let it crumble. It all fell away and went nowhere. It came back but never quite got to me. The mayhem and order blended in and disproved each other. My senses betrayed my mind, my mind betrayed my heart, my heart betrayed my spirit, and my spirit betrayed them all. It was a witch's brew of laughter and tears and the nonsense which excited them both. I never really started nor finished and the path went on without direction, goal, nor demand. My self both dissolved and remained, though I could never see anything but that which obstructed it. The vortex tightened, the way widened, the show of consciousness broke open, permeated, shrank and congealed, and all the while the dream-host existence ran on and on without boundary, property, method, nor time.

Had I known then what I was in for, I would perhaps never have chosen to walk down that tunnel. Or perhaps I would have had no other tunnel to choose. No matter. The best thing to do when caught in a whirlpool is to quit struggling toward the vanishing surface, to give your energy to the vortex, and to dive as deep as possible, waiting until

you hit bottom and are torn away by the river, at which point you can prepare for your return to the surface.
That is when you come out of it. You come out wild and crazy. You come out hard and ambivalent, finished and yet hardly begun. You come out through the threshold of indifference, of care, of suffering, of life, of death, of meaning, of meaninglessness, of noise, and of silence. You come out from nowhere, out from a person you never were, to a person you no longer are. You run free at these moments when what always mattered finally ends, when life breaks stride with the current of its own disbelief. Out and out you come, all the while falling inward. Falling into the self beyond the self, into the centerless happening where nothing and everything occurs. You come out into it all, broken away from the tether of purpose, the chains of need, the bonds of striving, the shackles of the trapped and abandoned. You come out and the wind licks your wounds through the blood of your losses. There is no need to haunt the world ever again, nor find yourself simple comforts or worth. You belong to no one and nothing, not even yourself. Beyond salvation and damnation, nothing can stop nor hold you now. You are free. And it doesn't matter. And that is why you are free.

*

four

I can say now, with absolute honesty, that I did not learn a single worthwhile thing about life and living until I left school. Not one. Not unless you include the brief course I took in typing, and the one-week canoe trip I went on in a highschool outdoor-ed class, which was a singularly life-altering episode because it showed me that what I had been experiencing as a youth and young man, and calling life, had nothing to do with life at all- not compared to the beauty and silence I experienced on that trip into the austere comfort of the northern Ontario lakes, with the lonely call of the loon, and the feel of the breeze on my face as I was falling asleep outside.

I consider it an insult to my existence that I don't even recall seeing a single moon-shadow until I was twenty-two years old- and I know the exact time I saw it because I remember being shocked that I had a shadow at night, and I could not believe the moon was its cause. Not that I hadn't seen shadows at night. Oh no, every porch and every street corner in my neighborhood had a blaring light on it, making certain old Luna never got to sing her song.

That canoe trip was the beginning of the end for me, for it was then that I had begun my romance with the wilds. I had fallen in love with the earth, and it would not be long before I gave myself to that love, left humanity behind, learned to own nothing but what fit into a backpack, to care for nothing but to sit on a remote cliff and stare out to sea, and to wish for nothing but that a few other kindred souls were there beside me.

I set out to the wild lands, to the forests, and the sea, and found myself looking for a way to forget all I had been helplessly bequeathed, and to remember instead all that had been left out.

I had no real understanding of what the word 'ugly' meant until the first time I spent a couple of months in the towering forests of the west coast wilds, and then returned quickly to the land of pavement, square structures, signs, lights, idiotic haircuts, automobiles, cosmetics, and functionless clothing. Never have I forgotten the shock which these unsightly creations betrayed to my virginal sight. How my eye became so weary and sore all of the sudden, just standing on a city street, or sitting in a house, no matter how superlatively decorated. What a wound it became to my very soul to spend day after day immersed in such visual and psychic excrement.

I realized then that the natural glories and miracles which the earth has brought forth cannot help but make mankind's constructions appear like the finger paintings of blind, insecure brats. I wonder if this is why we have been so eager to rid ourselves of the earth's great treasures- the forests and the beasts- because these make us feel so little, so unimpressive, so dumb.

That trip to the true west-coast wilderness had put a black mark on my mind, for I now had a vision of what had existed before electricity, metal, and internal combustion engines. My prize city, Vancouver, had suddenly become a sewer, and I was now swimming in shit and quickly losing the strength to tread water, though tread it I did for many years to come as I slowly learned how to live as a free person in an imprisoned world.

My life on the coast would become a series of comings and goings- a migration of sorts, from the cancerous cosmopolitan clime, to the verdant lands full of sustenance and hope. I went out, time and again, to sift away the ore and try to find the living gold scattered thinly within the limitless dross. My peregrinations most often sprang from the hub of my movements, Vancouver, and widened out, covering from Northern California, up along the west coast of Vancouver Island, to the Queen Charlotte Islands, and into the Alaskan panhandle. It was in these places, where the mighty trees meet the pounding surf, that I held communion with the land and spirits therein, with the unique individuals who willfully populate these remote and untamed places, with God, and, most importantly ...with myself.

Were it not for these stretches of awe-inspiring, deserted, primordial wilderness, untainted nor scarred by the likes of men, I would surely have passed from this earth long ago. Were it not for the sweeping cedars, the awkward croon of the ravens, the peace of the eagle, the untamable spirit of the bear, and the freedom and abundance which is a gift of the sea, I would have gone crazy amongst a society for which I had grown sour early in life, and for which I held little need, little respect, and little expectation.

To wander amongst the great forests of the Pacific Northwest- or what little is left of them- is to live and grow under the glorious canopies of ancient hemlocks, towering Sitka spruces, and gigantic redwoods; it is to have the existences of these titanic organisms implanted within your very being, so that you become like a grafted branch, no longer yourself only, but a part of the land as well. And so to return to civilization is to be like a voyager from a forgotten world, containing the old vision and the new curse for mankind. To blend in and become one with the majesty of nature, is not only to know the peace and beauty of these colossal wonders, but also to become that very peace and beauty itself, and therefore to recognize from a different perspective the horrors of mankind's rapacity. It is to be sucked into the belly of a wonderful whale and then be spat out in Nineveh with no desire to do what you cannot avoid doing.

Which is to say, I had come, over time, to certain essential, troubling realizations, and I could no longer hide the pain from myself, and my pain was the world's pain, and so I could no longer hide the world from itself. And when that happens, let me tell you, the world will take up arms against you, because you did not, or could not, lie its lie, and you now cannot help but expose its worst repressions to itself, and that means you are a monster, or worse ...a man.

And so it came to be a regular pattern of my existence that I would live for a while within the structure, lights, noise, distractions, and trapped souls of civilization, and would fill my pockets with cash enough for my next journey, and then, upon reaching my breaking point, I would realize that to stay there any longer would lead only to despair or the madhouse, and so I would break free again from the troubles, ideas, creations, and pathos of the world, and would wander up the coast somewhere, to sit in the forest or by the sea, and to lick my wounds and weep the whole damned jumble away.

The problem was not that I was inhuman and did not belong, but that I was too human. Too much pain, too much wonder, too much love, loss and sorrow. Too bloody much. In the center of it all I came to be ripped in two by the intimacy and separation I could not explain to others but with a stoic laugh and an accepting sigh.

This period of wandering and isolation did not come about because I had stopped caring for my friends and family. On the contrary, I cared very much, and yet there was a gnawing ache inside of me from which I could not get away, something which spoke in a voice I could barely hear, but which said something like, "If you really cared about them, or about yourself for that matter, you would forget life as it has been presented to you, and get to the bottom of the whole gory mess of it."
   Ah yes, what a mess indeed. I couldn't continue to exist without finding out why life on this marvelous earth had become so disagreeable, because I can tell you I didn't have a single answer, and I could sense that no one else around me did either, regardless of how confidently they walked through their illusionary lives.
   So I left my home and familiars like an Apache scout who sees the coming winter and the barren fields, sees the impending starvation and suffering, and wanders off to other lands in an attempt to find another place where food and shelter are plenty so as to later return for his tribe, that they might survive the long and merciless season.
   And for that I became a lost and hungry man, wandering about in an empty wildland and not even knowing how to get home.
   Yet it was there that I received the insights and inspirations which become possible only from taking a step away from the corporeal panoply and societal encumbrances which consume and debilitate body, mind and soul in the most subtle ways, such that one might not even feel themselves being overwhelmed until all clarity and repose are gone and no memory left of their absence. And that is an irreconcilable absence, which is why it was only at a removed distance that I could begin to understand the true nature of existence and my consecrated part within it.
   And so the grand and virgin cedar forests and wild coast of British Columbia, dotted with softly tinted islands running out forever in the mist of the setting sun, would bring me to a voiceless, lonely rapture and open me up like a vacuum, sucking all of mankind's dross and memory from my core, for it was on this part of the great orb, amongst the magnificent forests, the crashing surf, and the unknowable wildness of it all, that I had become intoxicated with the earth.
   I have never known such uncluttered beauty as exists out there on the coast. It must be how the soft light mingles up from the ocean and onto each successive island, until the sky is reached, and the panorama sits like a shifting water color of gentle hues composed of no color the mind can capture, for it is not a color, it is a feel.

*

five

I would head out into that brilliant and impossible land, losing myself in the intoxicating earth and the natural life, and then come home, over and over again; I would leave and return, repeatedly, always carrying out, and then following back in, the Ariadne's thread of the Self, back to a city changed and become less friendly towards a me who was no longer the same as the one who had set out.

And so it was always hard to find myself again, after my time away from the world- because I returned as something other than what I remembered myself to be; it was as if, because I had chosen to pendulum between opposites- diving into humanity, and then resurfacing, again and again, into the natural world- that I had to quickly learn the art of pragmatic amnesia, or else I would have spent my whole life trying to be what I no longer was; I had to forget what I had been, and be who I had become.

This is the way of perpetual transformation, the way to the eternal liquid life. Which is to say, it is the way ...of Life.

The self which adheres to form or conception dies within its own rotting womb. For the inmost self can neither be captured nor named and therefore needs no permanent residence in the form. The inmost self holds to no image nor finitude, and therefore can ever change and still remain the same. And if you come to live from the inmost self rather than the outer form, you find yourself becoming fluid as the wind, and supple as the sea.

At those times when I would finally break away, leaving the vortex of society, and the identity it encumbered me with, behind, I would know somewhere deep down in the lost requiems of my soul that I had left the world only so as to experience myself again, for I knew I was not whatever I had to become so as to mingle and cavort with others in the world of separation and identity, and I was determined not to know myself as such.

And so the sojourns out into the wilderness, time and time again, to die again and again, leaving behind the self they said I was- to die away until the only thing left was whatever I truly was- were the continuing chapters of my life as a gypsy of the woods. Never have I been able to stay amongst a group of people who have a rigid concept of who they are, but that is the hard reality of learning to thrive in the living flow through the dead stasis of mankind.

I recall being out on Flores Island- one of the outer islands populating Clayoquot Sound, on the west side of Vancouver Island- in the early spring. I recall having been driven out there by a greater will than my own, forcing me out and away, to face the loneliness again, because to not face it meant to lose the beauty, the wonder, the message, the dream, and instead to face only the cold stare of concrete and plaster. And so I thumbed and bussed my way out to Tofino, walked down to the government wharf, jumped on a water-taxi destined for the native town of Ahousat, and from there marched for two hours out to the wild coast. There, alone, I spent the next four days, walking up and down the brilliant expanse of untrammeled, driftwood-laden, wind-whipped beach, with the surf crashing, eagles soaring overhead, and not another soul in sight. No one.

Where was everyone, I wondered? In a place as incredible as this, with a brilliant break in the weather. Why am I the only one out here- one of the most peaceful and beautiful places on earth- where are you my people? my kin? my peers? my fellow wanderers, sisters, brothers, and freedom lovers of any kind, where are you? It was maddening. Everyone else was locked away in comfortable cement mausoleums, under warm duvet blankets, with toast and eggs, coffee and light conversation awaiting them in the morning, and I was out there under the moon, alone, marching up and down that glorious beach, trying to burn the madness of a world gone wrong out of me.

There was a time, apparently in the late sixties and early seventies, during the free-love and wandering hippy movement- an era which I was too tardy out of the womb to take part in, and so, like one who arrived at Woodstock the day after the concert, when everyone else was leaving and bursting with loquacious panegyrics about the incomparable affair, I was left to cuss at the dumb luck of being born in '66- there was a time when hordes of young folk lived on Longbeach, near Tofino, in squatter's huts made out of driftwood. They caught fish, played music, drank wine, made love, and lived with nature, like a long lost band of space-wanderers, finally rendezvousing in a remote area, on a remote planet, and having there a celebration for a good long while so as to get to know each other once again. In fact, this utopic lifestyle went on for almost ten years, until the mob of un-free citizens and their henchmen ran the freedom-lovers off the beach and back onto the pavement.

Seems this is always the way though. No corner of the earth is kept open for a worthwhile, carefree existence. Everything must be surveyed, stamped, ordered, ruled, legislated, registered, and paid for in the fine old feudal way. Not even a madman whose pants are full of piss and whose beard is full of snot is allowed to sip his whiskey when and where he wants, or lie down and rest where he pleases without hassle. The moment someone bucks the system and tries to live without losing their soul, innumerable trespassing signs and fences spring up all around. Every man, woman, and child must be properly dressed, indoctrinated, and carrying identification. No one shall be excluded from doing their part in the ruse. It's a game of cats and mice and the cats make all the rules, and they train the mice to obey them, and then they let the little rodents loose for a good chase and some dinner. I have heard that without real prey around, a cat must stalk something anyway, for this behavior is built into its Mendelian code, on one of the double helixes near the food and fun section. And so you can often see cats fervently stalking stuffed animals, shoes, a dry leaf in the wind, or people's shadows. Which is the way it is with authorities; give someone a uniform and they *must* create rules and enforce them, for that is their job and their job is their identity, and soon it becomes an instinct for them such that if no one is breaking any of their other laws, then they must invent some more. More laws, more limits, more stalking, more game. These precarious effigies of their own shadowy existences, who, in their irascible homage to progress, find no time for the alter dimensions embracing the hemorrhage of time.

I have heard- if you can believe this- of a man in a small town on the coast who is banned from laughing in public. That's right- he is given a fine every time he laughs out loud. It seems the well-groomed and respectable, established town folk couldn't bear to hear a real, spontaneous, raucous, shameless guffaw- for it must have exposed their own repressions too blatantly- so they banded together and had a writ against him enforced. The Nazis. The dimwits. The obtuse, insidious failures to exist as human beings who then turn themselves into jackals. It is to them and their likes, for whom, like the dead, there is neither sin nor rapture, that I turn aside.

But enough of this misanthropic diatribe.

On that specific trip out to Flores it was on day four, alone and walking up and down the desolate, wind-swept beach, in which the bubble finally burst for me. And by that I mean that the haze of society, the clutter of spirits, consciousnesses, and souls mixed within me, and the discord of all my own worldly thinking and ways had at last vanished, and all that remained inside ...was me. I became again a clean and polished vessel staring out from nothing at the deep blue, unvexing sea. I was as if virginal again, and inside of me were my real eyes which had for so long been closed or not allowed yet to see.

I am describing this now, though it wasn't until many years later that I would fully understand why the urge and directive came to me regularly to leave the cosmopolitan refuse heap, to go and be alone for a while in the wilds, and to let the cosmic bowel movement happen through me.

After the cleansing, when finally I was empty of the chaos and confusion I had been carrying, and could again sense my own spirit within, then I could finally feel the self behind my eyes, could rejoin the subtler rhythm, and somewhere in the hidden vestiges of my soul I could remember what it was like when we were a living part of the earth, and of God- the days of yore when life had been beautiful and without separation nor struggle.

These trips of purgation would take anywhere from one day to one month, but no matter how long they took, at what expense, under what effort and duress, no matter how cold, alone, or confused I became, and no matter what I missed while I was away, they were always worth it in the end, and were the only thing which sustained me during those years in which I lived in the chaos of the city. For, after one of these trips, I would head back to Gomorrah, refreshed, renewed, re-inspired, and ready for another assault from the invasive mob.

Upon returning I always had great plans for a world which had no desire for such plans. I felt great understandings for a world which would only forcefully defend its lies. I felt great peace to bring to a world wrecked upon the reef of distraction. Like Lazarus arisen from his own ashes, I came back again and again, hollow and calm, and charged by the source I had re-found within. I had stepped back only so as to surge forward. I had gone under in order to soar. I had lost in order to gain, and had gone away, only so as to return.

Often the Tao of life became obvious to me just at the threshold, at the membrane between the two worlds, just as I was leaving the bush and heading back to town; I could see then, as I crossed over from one reality to the other, how easy it was to flow in harmony with the spirit in all things, if all thought was allowed to dwindle softly into oblivion, and the heart regained its song. How I planned at the end of each trip to return to the world and not be drawn back into the disturbance. How I planned to maintain a profound equilibrium in the ether, and live as if in the dance of the spirit itself, never moving but to the grace of life, never wanting but for the beauty of life, never indulging but for the love of life. Ah, but then the world has its own plans, its own noise, and its own wayward course, and the spirit is at best a silent visitor, wafting around the impervious obstructions rather than hopelessly trying to tear them down.

It is both bitter and beautiful for me now to recount such things, for as I do I wonder and worry about those who are to come after me- those of a similar temperament- what will they do, and where will they go, when all the forests have been rendered to ash, and the seas lie barren, and the land is foul with the garbage of moribund societies? Where will those like myself go to find respite, to hide and breathe, and live, and learn, and be saved as I was saved?

I have no answer, but I suppose that doesn't matter, because I never had an answer for myself. I only went where I had to go in order to survive. And I survived.

*

six

During my second year in Vancouver I had a dream in which I was being held down and helplessly pinned. I had the feeling of being absolutely immobilized by an incredibly strong weight, to the point that it felt as if I was going to be crushed and smothered.

I awoke in a panic and with a dreadful sense of being oppressed, and yet at the end of the dream, just upon awakening, I knew that the oppressor ...was God.

This ambiguity sat quite strange within me. I couldn't figure it out, because God was supposed to be a loving liberator, not an amorphous despot, and yet I could not deny what I had experienced. Nor did I know then what sort of forceful and ruthless chastening this dream actually portended. But over the next eight years or so, I was unavoidably going to find out.

I'm thinking that this visitation, so to speak, may have come about partially as a result of my time with Glen, or perhaps it was due to my own introspection and questioning and an all consuming need to come to peace or freedom somehow, which created a window for God to look in and see a little maggot writhing about with a few books in front of him and a strong desire to grow wings and fly off of the stool. And that might have been enough to set the old curmudgeon after me.

In fact, I realized only after the terrible smelling salts had been administered that in the very desire to be a worthy part of this magical thing called life, I had released an army of angels, spirits, forces, or what have you, upon my limited being and destiny, and from that point onward all I could do was hang on and live it out, for a decision had been made, with or without my consent, I am not sure, but I am sure that life began to take on a glorious and yet arduous twist, because from then on I was never prepared for what was going to be asked of me, nor what was going to be given nor taken away.

I turn away now at times when I see others in the first throes of the ghost's descent, because it is a horrible sight to witness God's initial penetration into a person's well ordered and heavily guarded life, for the games will soon be done away with, the frivolity and entertainments are finished, and all the little hiding places are now ruthlessly exposed in the light.

It is hard for people to accept that their Good God is responsible for a great deal of their pain. Though this is not done in malice, but rather like a parent who watches their child run out into busy traffic time after time, even though the child is told continually not to do it, until finally the parent realizes that if this behavior continues, the child will eventually be hit and killed, and so it is better to take out the whip and the cane and beat them until they'll never do it again rather than let them die because you didn't care enough to hurt them.

When God comes down like this, and infiltrates into the world, and you can see God passed around like a contagious disease into all the lives of all the unsuspecting people you meet who want nothing more than to continue on with their oblivious lives, you can be sure to witness agony, because the entrance of God into one's life comes at a dear price- and that price is one's life, and the price will be paid, and the house set in order, and the goad which accomplishes this through the traumas, and trials, and troubles which come, is as certain and irrevocable as the rising sun.

Perhaps this is why the Prophets are always getting the pillory and the post, because it is they who bring the horrible consciousness of God into the unconscious lives of all others, and this begets the dreadful chastening destined to destroy a person and all they have in order to bring them into the perfection of the light. And the more a person has slept through their life- the more they have denied, repressed, hated, or caused harm- the more excruciating will be their redemption. But it will happen, to be sure. And when it does the poison of unconsciousness will be sucked out of the open wound which has been spilling forth bile onto its brethren, and the sore will be cauterized, and the unsightly scar will be the ticket to heaven.

Having said that, it would be quite a time before the long arm of the law was able to reel me in and subdue me. Oh, I put up one hell of a chase. A true bandit from the fire. I see now that often I was not trying to come to God, I was trying to get away. But I could never get away, for wherever I ran I always carried my cage.

In some ways I am still running, still being pursued, still being caught, bludgeoned, incarcerated, released, and then I'm off again, running wildly away from what I cannot get away from, but running nonetheless, away from the light, into the darkness, where none can find me, except the light, for the darkness is disintegrated by the light, and so I'm spotted again, chased again, caught again, and brought home again like the prodigal son in chains.

Oh, the ways back home are as many as there are exits, and though I have tried to flee so many times, I now look back and see a circuitous spiral leading always back to God, a path on which I ran until exhausted in a direction which I could not avoid taking, although I avoided it all I could.

One of those directions in which I unknowingly ran came as a job, which was bestowed upon me, thankfully I may add, at a time when I both needed a thorough shift in my life, and, more practically, needed to earn some money as well.

I maintain that there are few jobs on this earth worth having, few tasks worth doing, few buildings worth entering, and few options worth seizing. And yet there are hidden designs and forces at work in the fabric of the soul's destiny which guide one, knowingly or not, into situations which, although seemingly commonplace and perhaps counter to one's own will, turn out to be cornerstones on the path which one ends up gratefully taking. The spiral always leads to the center.

Everywhere there is intention and design running invisibly through the world. To look closely into life's sublime patterns is to not need the I Ching nor the stars to tell you why life is bringing to you what it is bringing, for life carries to you what you need or deserve, or what others need or deserve from you, because nothing is arbitrary in life, not in my life anyways.

For myself such a well choreographed and serendipitous event came about, as I said, simply by landing a job in an organization which would become the epicenter of my Vancouver existence, and would provide most of the reasons for my continued coming and going from a society I had long ago forsaken. That job was at a wilderness equipment cooperative which sold outdoor gear for camping, mountaineering, kayaking, and so on; an organization devoted to help people return to the splendor of nature, and therefore to help return them to that long lost aspect of themselves- their true nature.

It was a 'good job'- as the cultural lie goes- but for me this was truly the case, for, among other things, it was one of the only places of employment where I could carry on an itinerant lifestyle and, upon returning to the city, at a moment's notice, sign on for some shifts to earn some green, instead of having to head to the welfare office, employment center, or soup kitchen, in order to get by when I had nothing to get by on.

If you must toil, a non-profit Co-op is as good a place as any to hang your hat. For a cooperative mandate instantly removes all the pernicious tricks, false smiles, and histrionic courtesies which are part and parcel of every purchase and interaction in the world of profit.

This particular Co-op specialized in, as I said, wilderness gear. Specifically hiking and camping supplies, tents, sleeping bags, backpacks, boots, rock-climbing equipment, kayaks, canoes, telemark skis, and cycling gear. It was an adult's toy store, if nothing more. And, to be sure, there was a lot more. For it was under the hallowed roof of this collective that I would find something far greater than a mere livelihood, or a niche for myself outside of the tiresome round of useless toil and fruitless labor so common in our day.

For it was here, beyond my wildest expectations, that I would meet my brothers and sisters on the Tree of Life[1]; here that I would learn the skills necessary to set me free amidst the forest and the sea; here that my soul would grow from the dark unconscious seed it was, into a plant as yet unheard of, and I would begin to see some of the secret ways of the one great being flowing through and all around us, and I would learn to dissolve and merge into this being, and I would come to see and know the world from the center of its happenings, like the *genus loci* of old, whose ubiquitous spirit comes to encompass all and everyone, infiltrates the dreams and psyches of every soul around, quickens all, and vivifies all into the one life of which we are all a part.[2]

Never have I found in a single organization like the Co-op such a varied and eclectic array of black sheep, dark horses, white elephants, renegades, mavericks, outcasts, and free spirits. The building was a continually changing cast of eccentrics, artists, writers, pioneers, explorers, adventurers, political refugees, wanderers, scholars, nature lovers, partiers, drunks, druggies, nymphomaniacs, dancers, alpinists, mountain-bike racers, river-rafting guides, white-water and sea kayaking guides, mountaineering guides- both men and women alike- mystics, angels, craftsmen, bush women, druids, gypsies, hedonists, Christians, Buddhists, Hindus, dykes, inventors, dropouts, outcasts, and all the rest of life's improbable ones, mixing together in a Pandora's box of work and play and every event in between.

It was as if this forum had been constructed specifically for these individuals, iconoclasts, and wayfarers to have a sublime convention of similar spirits, brought together to gather and commune with their brethren, under one roof, once and for all.

I could write volumes on each individual from the Co-op who crossed my path, entered my life, and changed the inner sanctum of my being forever, and barely would I scratch the surface of the lives and destinies of these unique and unheard of individuals who were drawn together for a while to grow, and learn, and heal each other. So many hearts, so many minds, so many diverse fragments of the infinite whole- it is enough to drive me into a stupor at the slightest thought of the wonder and implausibility of the remarkable sea of mankind into which I found myself gleefully bobbing about.

I could speak of a few like Dennis, for example, who was singularly the best athlete I have ever met- balanced inwardly between his male and female parts, and so balanced outwardly in the manifest- who could scale tough, expert rock-climbing crags for a lark on a weekend, could ski extreme descents in steep and wily backcountry territory, could mountain-bike down formidable problems with professional ease, and then back at home could create and construct unique pieces of equipment or gear for any need around, by refitting, redoing, or remodeling the world in any way he saw fit to better. He could take apart any piece of machinery, from diesel engines to welding torches, like a seasoned mechanic. This was a man whom I was once involved with on a one week mortise-and-tenon, timber framing course, in the interior of British Columbia, and within the first five minutes, on the first day, he was already more skilled and confident than the instructor. I kid you not.

Back at home Dennis could cook up an exquisite meal with a palate and dexterity to shame the finest French chefs in the area. Alongside this he'd be pouring out a perfect martini, regaling the crowd with subtle metaphors and artful anecdotes, and then begin a series of drunken parlour tricks which would include wrapping his ankles behind his head and standing on his hands, or crawling like a monkey through a person's legs, then up and over their torso and then back through their legs without ever touching the ground. Or he'd be dropping beer caps from his clenched bum-cheeks into an awaiting cup below, and then uninhibitedly changing out of his clothes into a slinky set of silk lingerie and treating the astonished onlookers to a burlesque routine fit for Soho. I say, freaks as well as faeries worked at the Co-op. Dennis was a true mad genius, a master of the manifest, as I often called him.

Then there was Oscar, a poet, actor, and garrulous metaphysician all rolled into a wiry, pendulous, elf-like frame, and charged with extemporaneous loquacity and thespian showmanship. To listen to his magical and eloquent yarns was to abandon the likes of Dylan Thomas as an antiquated old fuddy-duddy forever. Oscar's words came but as prayer and poetry, or not at all.

He was also a wilderness-survival instructor and a skilled homesteader, and so he was equally at home amongst the cosmopolitan pretense of the city stage, and the raw medium of the temperate jungle. He once saved his dog from being carried off in the hungry jaws of a cougar- which is an act requiring no small amount of courage nor love. A whole man, a real man, a man who shared with me that as a youth he had fled his own existence in a wild chase across the continent of Europe, only to be finally cornered by the Spirit on a beach in the Mediterranean and then, taken by the will of the kenosis, suffered his spirit to descend like a diving falcon through the firmament and land with a thud to fit perfectly into his very flesh. And the word was with us for a while.

Then there was Sylvia, a wise and venerated, mystical Eastern European woman, and an incredible artist and writer who had spent many years living in, exploring, and paddling amongst the wilds. She had been an environmental activist in the visible realm, and in the hidden one she had taken on the torment of separation which plagues all of mankind, had sat with it, endured it, and transformed it, and had emerged out the other side like an ancient wise woman of old, toughened in the fires of the Eleusian mysteries- a wise woman who had come through effort and trial to know that in the end life is not about finding solutions, but of creating solutions; it was this stoic vision of acceptance and strength that you could feel in the august light of her youthful eyes.

So many of them. So many people. It boggles me to consider. The wilderness athletics of the group alone is enough to exasperate me. There were extreme rock-climbers who headed south every autumn and spring to climb in the American desert, or to scale the granite walls of Yosemite; there were professional mountain-bikers of national acclaim, and others who were simply unknown experts, tackling the most arduous and precipitous trails of Vancouver's infamous north shore mountains; there were white-water kayakers running class five rapids, canoeists engaged in season-long expeditions which would impress the voyageurs of old; others who would cross countries on their bicycles, or ski the steepest couloirs from Washington State to Alaska; and there were world-class alpinists ascending peaks in the Andes, Hindu Kush, and Himalayas. The skill and dedication of these people to their chosen activities was rivaled only by the forgotten yogis, locked away in caves and standing on their heads reciting the *Bhagavad-Gita* upside down for decades on end.

I could speak of another quiet and discreet young woman who, without anyone's knowing, wrote more lucid, recondite, perceptive spiritual observations of the sublime and transparent realms than most of the so-called experts publishing their commonplace balderdash these days. She lived- and did not just seem to- half of her life in heaven and half of her life on earth, spent a great deal of time in the bush, and took young people on extended trips into the mountains and down rivers and tried, in her own way, to help them get a glimpse of what she knew but could not explain- which is to say, that ...God *is*, and that is all there is to it.

And there was the shy and brilliant German alpinist, linguist, and family man who spoke no less than six languages fluently, translated ancient Chinese texts of meditation on his own time, climbed the most arduous rock-climbing routes in the area without a word of pride or accomplishment, organized film festivals, and had soft, bewildering eyes that would stare right into you, right through you, and would leave you fighting for breath, for a place to hide, for a way of saying- "yes man, I know, I know, we're all too far apart from each other, we can't get close enough, and if I could vaporize this minute and fall into your eyes and touch your soul within, I would do it, but I can't and we'll have to live with what we've got instead, and that is- loneliness."

I could go on and on, and the list would barely grow shorter. But I'll end with a man who was, in a sense, the epitome of the west coast itself. Jim was one of the rare few, born and bred in the culture and climate of the Pacific Northwest. A true seed from the age of pioneers, mountain men, and adventurers; a great pagan man-hero. Throughout his years he had climbed the highest peaks all over British Columbia and Alaska, had spelunked in many of the caves under the vast land, and was both a recreational and professional diver, scouring the world beneath the sea. There were few places along the coast which he had not walked, climbed, swam, paddled, skied, or crawled upon.

Along with this he had designed his own alternative-energy home, was a beekeeper and researcher, raised chickens, and had a vast organic garden from which came an abundance of delectable fruits, vegetables, herbs, and giant pumpkins. He was an ex-sharpshooter, a demolitions expert, skilled woodworker, tinkerer, fly-fisherman, woodsman, wine and mead maker, and baker. It seemed that he was always doing something and yet never doing anything, for he moved with the ease and equanimity of a Taoist adept.

On top of all of this he owned a quaint log cabin, which he had beautifully refurbished, in the big woods just half an hour from Vancouver. It was here, in that little Valhalla-like enclave of ancient cabins and trees, that he claimed to have communicated with the 'little people' of the forest- the gnomes and faeries who exist as orchids on the profane plane, but are accessible as their true, living selves once a privileged person has fallen through the trap door from our world into theirs.

It was up in Jim's cabin, and its druidic vicinity, that many of us would occasionally congregate *en masse* to electrify the ether with the joy and exuberance of our collective spirits.

Indeed there was little more vivifying at that time in my life than a gathering of like-minded, reckless and restless, unrepressed individuals with bellies full of grog and psychedelic mushrooms, minds full of grass, and a growing hunger amongst the crowd to revisit the land of Pan and wash away the veil of this profane earth.

There is much to be said for those all-out, uninhibited, intense years of debauchery which we enjoyed to their fullest, with as few or as many other willing folks as we could cajole into joining us, or who could cajole us into joining them. To be out in the raw world, hyped and opened up and obliterated from the mundane plane, on a pharmacological cornucopia of narcotics, booze, and hallucinogens, and to throw yourself into that midsummer night's dream, to tear your clothes off and go running uncontrollably through the bush, to stand far off on a hill and bellow out a call of indescribable euphoria and intensity, and to hear it echoed back to you in a chorus of intoxicated and charmed hoots, howls, guffaws, and acclamations, and then to trundle back down to the focus of the crowd, all souls in invisible communion with their extra-selves, and bouncing off of each other's vibes, and to pass a bottle of whiskey around, then a joint, to devour a plate of barbecued salmon, a baked potato, a hash brownie, a chocolate mushroom, and then off again into the twilight zone, without plan or concern, always lost and always found, leaning suddenly against a giant spruce, or yellow cedar, gasping in disbelief, rolling about in the moss in blessed depravity, then sitting down in a circle of jocularity and repose, hearing the ribald laughter of another group somewhere off in the night, stopping to stare into one of your mates eyes for a brief second of siblinghood and contact, and then out and away again, another beer, another hug, or kiss, a wrestling match, more tom-foolery, singing out at the top of your lungs nothing in particular but for the inability to any longer squash the earthquake of delight and gratitude that cannot help bursting forth in your every word, move, and offering. The hallowed madness of it all.[3]

These divine gatherings and the constant influx and outflux of the community of the Co-op would come to allow me to see the subtle aspect of being which permeates all life- the spiritual archetypes, mythos, and cosmic or subterranean relationships which direct and order humanity like a living blue-print behind the scenes; the sublime, intelligent projection, recounting and reworking similar permutations and acts, at different locations around the world, yet always playing the same drama which, over time, runs on towards a further outcome and is only disguised by different stage drops, props, and costumes, while the ancient, formless characters remain the same. For if you look deep and long enough into a dynamic group of people, you will see the building blocks of performers occasionally alter and change, as is the way of the theatre, but the wholeness and combinations of the show must remain the same; and so, on the world's many subtle stages, when one character leaves the play a vacuum is created drawing another, similar type in to fill the void, so as to complete the show.[4]

Thus it was that I stayed on long enough on this one stage in the infinite puppet house of the spirit- long enough to see the changing of the guards, so to speak- one cast replaced by the next, and then the next, and so on, so that I came to understand that what we perceive as separate beings- autonomous of thought and will- are merely invisibly choreographed fragments of a gigantic hologram projected from itself, observing itself, and living within itself, and so there is no separation nor specificity, nor singular identity which can be applied to the apparent particularities of the whole- not, at least, until one of the actors wakes up in the show, abandons their role, and walks off of the stage. But this is an understanding I would not come to realize until much further along in the ridiculous list of characters I had unwittingly chosen to play.

This is a hard point to relate, for it implies that all is reflected in all, that the 'in' *is* the 'out'; it means that no one is only who they are; that the unreal creates the real and the real creates the unreal; that the self is only one because it is many, and the many are infinite only so as to hide the mystery that they are one. It means, as I have seen, that we dream other people's dreams, live other people's lives, and think other people's thoughts; that what we appear to be doing is not really what we are doing, that what we know is not what we think we know, and what we see is the unseeable, somehow come to stasis and held in the transfixed stare of false conclusions.

We are less than we think we are, and more than we could ever imagine. The shapes and forms, abstractions and tangibilities of life are but shadows of shadows leaping about in the heightened confusion of repressed dismay.

All this I realized would be impossible to relate, as it was slowly unfolding before me, impossible to share with my fellows who saw life as the linear and material event which it isn't, and who, I thought, would never imagine nor conceive that we are caught in a crazy, tangled dreamscape of profusion, assimilation, and release, for the conventional mind would have an instantaneous meltdown were it to open-up and allow in even the most limited potentiality and significance of this vision of our beingless existences.

Bread and circuses for the masses indeed, and pizza and television, and popcorn with the movies; the ontological placebos come in the most profane forms and guises while the groaning hordes run from the slightest glimpse of the limitless pleroma interwoven into a matrix of design and undesign, reason and fantasy, magic and mayhem, all spilling out before them in a surfeit of absurd unavoidability.

I expect that the soporific entertainments of society, which numb the subtle vision, must be our unnatural way of keeping the herd grazing on life's provender, while calmly fattening the populace on their way to God's abattoir. I say this because I sense that mankind is obliviously involved in an arrangement which allows the masses to move forward, albeit with sloth and trepidation, without the slightest inclination of where we are headed. An allegorical event from the natural world occurs when Orcas are on the move; for most of the whales in the pod have been discovered to be sleeping while swimming, while the few who remain awake create a continuous projection of sonic waves into the brains of the unconscious others, thus guiding them on their course until it is time to awaken and feed and breed. This sociobiological procedure is only slightly dissimilar to the subconscious movements of mankind, whose collective will is directed by forces which no one is truly aware of, towards a destination none can imagine, for reasons which are not supplied by the architects of the dream.

Such thoughts came slow and sublimely through the staccato and formative years of my tenure at the Co-op; what would begin as a routine job would grow and become a living part of my spirit, and I would witness the magnetism of the entire scope of our community slowly congregate under one roof, and raise the angel of our communion back to the sky.

If I claimed to understand any of this at the outset, or even now as I write this, I would be confusing what I have seen with what I have known. For what I saw I still do not fully comprehend; and that is, I saw, in the years amongst my kith and kin at the wilderness Co-op, that the spirit running beneath and through all things occasionally seeks to rear its head up through the static and dark manifest of the day, to harmonize and recognize and free itself at last, in and through groups of individuals brought together for this very purpose. It had been attempted in Camelot in the middle ages, in Paris early in the 20th century, and in the hippy movement a few decades later- and it was happening on the coast, as far as I could tell, and the heart and fulcrum of its strengthening palpitations was found in the collective soul grown strong in love, sincerity, and grace floating just below the surface in the culture of the Co-op.

Life has always the element of myth buried deep in the catacombs of the wider Self, and if we dig deep enough beneath us we will find our vastness flowing out into everywhere, and our divinity dancing rapturously upon the profane plane.

From such occurrences come the fabulous accounts of spiritual upheavals over the history of mankind's yearnings, from Atlantis and Lemuria, to Sumeria, Easter Island, Machu Pichu, Eleusis, Samothrace, Jerusalem, Medieval Europe and its bandwagon of aching saints, Avalon, the Salem witch hunts, Paris in the 20's, Tibet in the 50's, and the flower children of the 60's, all of which speak of the eternal will of the spirit attempting to overtake- or perhaps confiscate, as it were- the flesh, over and over again, and then to be beaten, pillaged, punished, driven underground, again and again, only to rear its mighty head up in another place, at another time, among another ready people, in another guerrilla assault upon the dark and binding gravity of the mold.

*

seven

Looking back now I see how my patterned routine of exodus and return began on my first extended trip up the coast, riding in a rusty old pickup truck with a most beautiful and severe young blond woman named Sandy, who was a true, incarnate, spirit of the land- as some people are, who get in touch with the earth and assimilate it into their very beings[5].

At that time Sandy was in her early twenties and was already an incredibly capable naturalist who had guided both kayaks and rafts throughout a great portion of the coastal waters and rivers running through British Columbia. She was the one, chosen by the cosmos at that time, to blend her spirit into mine, thus becoming my *anima*,[6] and, as in the way of myth made manifest, she would lead me in the flesh to the Avalon of North America- the misty and mystic Queen Charlotte Islands- where I would, for the first time in my life, experience a genuine understanding of what the word 'wild' really meant. I say this with absolute sincerity, for I had been to a few of the untouched places on earth earlier in life, but never before had I seen the staggering display of Tolkienesque landforms, forests, and people as such exist in the Charlottes. It is a land unlike any other land. A world set apart from the world. A unique, thriving, ecologically astounding archipelago often referred to as the Galapagos of the north.

I have read *The Origin of Species*, and I can assure you that had Darwin voyaged to the bountiful forests of the Queen Charlotte Islands instead of the desert landscapes of the Galapagos, he would have forgotten instantly his *ad hoc* hypothesis based on the spurious mental constructs of survival and mutation, for he would have at once fallen to his knees in awe-struck bewilderment and been forced to accept what every scientist spends their whole life attempting to disprove- their own inexorable stupefaction.

Had *The Beagle* sailed north to the Charlottes instead of southward, students of biology everywhere today would be trained in the poetics of mystery and the art of appreciation, rather than the mechanistic obscurations of statistical analysis, laboratory research, vivisection, and the laughable, fascist confines of the scientific method.

Had Darwin studied the outlandish Puffin, or the irrepressible Pigeon Guillemot, rather than the common Finch, his eyes may have been opened to the incomprehensible living spirit animating all things, instead of arriving at his inert conclusion based on the precise mathematical attrition of obsolete budgie colons.

Darwin's essentially morbid outlook, formed on the barren rocks of the Galapagos, necessarily produced a theory whose main operating factor is death, whereas, had he set his eyes upon the thriving plenitude of nature's finest, he would have instead propounded a vision based on Life, and life's inherently vital mechanisms. For a philosophy based on 'life' belongs innately to a living universe- one which is still expanding, even after eighteen billion years! After all, the *Big Bang* implies a sexual super nova, not a chaste black hole; it implies a life more abundant, not a cosmos based on scarcity and struggle.

Had Darwin not been a biologist, he would certainly have been a mortician.

When I first arrived on the blessed isles, I walked about in a sort of disbelieving stupor that such a magnitude of life actually exists on earth. I have heard tales of visitors to the islands walking into the forests and bursting into tears, because they, like I, could not believe in the beauty and majesty that the earth has brought forth, and which has been eliminated almost everywhere but for a few isolated areas on Vancouver Island and along the coast of British Columbia and Alaska.

To walk into one of these ancient forests is to be transported to another planet. It is to walk through a time warp, and enter Eden before the Fall. To stroll about on thick beds of moss, with ten-foot diameter trees running up to the sky in gothic piety, or to paddle in a kayak or canoe along the deserted shores while watching for sea-lions, Orcas, humpback whales, water foul, raptors, rainbows, and deer dancing on the shore, is to tear at your hair because you finally realize you are on the planet of the apes and you now know what the simians have done to your home.

It was partly for the power and privilege of witnessing and becoming a part of this rare and priceless world that I would return many times after my first trip to this blessed sanctuary. And yet I came back often for the island's equally wild people, including one individual whom I would encounter, on this first trip, in the life, mind, and wilderness refuge of the man who was to become my mythical *mercurius*- a man named Hans.[7]

It is strange indeed when the myths and secrets men read about and think of as fable or allegory begin to occur within your very life. It is strange when one's conventional mind begins to slowly awaken to the underlying drama of spiritual archetypes and mythic journeys in the sea of spirit in which we are eternally swimming, and strange to find that you are a player in a sublime game that the Gods may have even forgotten they were playing.

Such was my unwitting induction into the hidden folds of the universe, as I headed north that rainy afternoon with the young and inspired Sandy, driving up to Prince Rupert, ferrying across the aptly named Hecate Strait to the main town on the islands, and then onto a day-long water taxi, heading to the rustic hamlet where Hans lived- a place which would, over the years, take away and give so many things to me that, for quite a few years, whether I was there or not, I would consider it my home- Rose Bay.

Never had I met another individual so burning with their own nebulous fire as I did in Hans. I doubt that in all the epochs of all the worlds there never has been one such as he, and perhaps there never will again. You would have to merge the idiosyncratic characteristics of Nietzsche, John the Baptist, Daniel Boone, and Beethoven together to come close to the fiery stew of eccentricities this one specimen of mankind enveloped.

Having left his German homeland in his early twenties with the sole intent to become a child of the earth and to "reclaim his rightful heritage", as he put it, he bounced around Canada for a while and finally ended up the last place you'd expect to find a growling, fastidious, Teutonic intellectual- in the uncultured bush, one hundred kilometers by boat or plane from the nearest community.

It was in that remote utopia that he hacked out a life for himself, building two exquisite cabins, a massive organic garden, chicken coop, goat house, and solarium complete with grapes, figs, lemons, and other geographically inexplicable delicacies.

Over and above his carpentry and horticultural skills, he was a top-notch musician, playing every conceivable instrument with assured finesse; from raucous, Appalachian banjo tunes, to self-styled guitar solos, to Celtic recorder riffs, to piano adagios which made the Moonlight Sonata sound like a Russian fighting march.

And there he was, in all the splendor of a crackpot, genius, hermit mystic, mad and fanatic and full of a life- which is as rare on this earth as the dinosaur- as I arrived to my delight and astonishment to find that such a one as he could exist in this world, at this time, in this way. I had stepped out of the twentieth century and right into middle earth, and Gandalf and Treebeard came out to greet me, and the comparatively inexperienced hobbit that I was at the time crossed his furry little toes and prayed that he was not dreaming.

Back then I was still little more than an uncarved block- a young man who had only begun to piece his own world together, had only begun to find his own voice, had only begun to write and believe in himself- which is an essential step towards binding the disparate worlds of essence and form into a functioning whole. Yet Hans and I quickly latched onto each other like two derelict prisoners in a sea of idiots. And there we clung together, grappling through the darkness of words for ways of understanding each other and our common lot, for ways of sharing in each other's visions, for ways of saying- "Yes, brother, yes, it is all crazy and impossible, this life, and no one sees it like we see it, and you see it differently than I, and I differently than you, but damn it, not that differently, and at least we- two out of six billion- at least we know it is all mad and misunderstood and that there are realities running on behind the scene that would freeze the average man cold where he stands were he to get even the slightest glimpse of it."

Poor Hans was like a castaway who had been adrift even longer than I; a voice crying in the wilderness in a language that was no longer spoken, of a reality that had been long forgotten; a lost remnant of a lost race which was suddenly thrown upon the shore of my implausible world- a world in which I had begun to realize was far more tangled, far more psychically polluted, far more afoul with the stench of mankind's sordid history of folly and blindness, and far more enmeshed in the hidden dream of the Gods who had forgotten they were dreaming than I ever could have imagined.

But now I had met one who was calling them to account. One man, alone in the wilderness, raging like an awoken beast with the scent of divine blood on its nose. There was Hans, driven like an exiled Pharaoh, out into the bush, driven by an unknown force, with an unknown need, out into the wilds to vent and curse the heavens, and build himself a life and try to heal the rift he could no longer avoid seeing.

And we took to each other, as I said, like two beings lost in an alien world who had finally found another to whom they could communicate. Albeit we reached out to each other through naught but vulgar grunts, and howls, snorts and scratchings of all varieties, but we knew at least that we were pointing at the same wound, the same darkness, the same hidden and yet ubiquitous sea of bile and oppression which oozed out into the soul and mind of every one on earth whether they were aware of it or not.

Every year from then on I would find my way to the Charlottes, traveling by thumb, or bus, or boat- and usually an odd collection of each of these vehicles- and I would arrive in one of the island towns, fill my backpack with booze and some dope perhaps, and hire another boat or plane to whisk me away from one world and into another. And there Hans and I would sit together, machinating and articulating, from sun up to sun down, day after day, week after week, together like co-researchers, hammering out the secrets and unspoken notions of this mysterious universe, all the while conversing in esoteric yarns, metaphor, parable, and rhyme- arguing, disagreeing, commiserating, debating, propounding, relating, and coming together on occasion to formulate the new thought, the new understandings, and new intentions that would solve the conundrum of existence now and forever.

We'd run the whole gamut of thought from lost religions, to recondite metaphysics, occultism, philosophy, anthropogenesis, and the like. No topic or observation was excluded; no idea was beyond our ken, no possibility too outlandish or remote. The Gods had had their day, had messed things up royally- or so we supposed- and now we sat there, a force of two men, bantering out how to right it all, how to fix this wholly botched experiment and bring it to a rapturous finale.

To be sure, as similarly as we saw the world we also saw it completely opposed. But the flint needs steel to strike it in order to create a spark and bring the fire. And fire is what we needed, and fire is what we got. And that is what kept our cloistered, insular brotherhood burning hotter than the sun.

What to say of Hans' metaphysical outlook? It was an idiosyncratic collage of irrefutable absurdity, acute introspection, and volatile cosmogenesis, all artfully combined and delivered in passionate, thundering filibusters by the intransigent attitude and towering intellect possessed by a man who had followed the call of his spirit fifteen years earlier, had left mankind behind, and had learned another way of seeing.

Among many of his other esoteric observations, the greatest problems besetting not only mankind, but also the heavens themselves, lay, according to Hans, in the foundation of denial and guilt, which were built into the superstructure of the cosmos from day one. He saw how these two stumbling blocks to the freedom and joy of the spirit were brought into existence at the same time as everything else- at the beginning- and that these pathologies were created by the same power as everything else- the Creator; for God was once but an insecure, guilt-ridden misfit, like the rest of us, and so God's imperfections were inexorably woven into the human experience, and thus what we were up against in attempting to solve our inborn dilemmas, was so massive, so ancient, so thickly embedded in our souls and beings that to turn the tables would require no less than a superhuman commitment and intent, because we had inherited the guilts and denials which were imprisoning and destroying us, and now no one could help us but ourselves, but we were so confused and deluded by our own distortions that rare, if at all, was there a person who could see themselves with perfect clarity, and therefore undo the knot of denial and guilt.

Adding to this impregnable obfuscation, Hans saw legions of infirm and warring angels thrown into the discord, an armada of dark seraphim, innumerable formless maleficent forces, mindless Lemurian refugees, and heartless Atlantean survivors. All of these so torn apart and removed from their true existences that they were pitted against each other without really knowing why. Hans saw an intermixed, dysfunctional, endlessly troubled spiritual milieu the likes of which even the most creative fantasy writer would consider well off of the approachable map. And yet he had convincing arguments and observable examples for everything he propounded- that is, if you could turn your mind inside out in order to re-examine life from his cosmological point of view. He was determined, resolute, indefatigable, and had a laser-like vision that I could only avert from its focused gaze with the most dexterous and delicate of jousts and swipes into the rare and almost imperceptible cracks in his conceptual armor.

It was a magical tête-à-tête for me- a young man who had for too long been cooped up in his own head and his own notions without a living sounding board, let alone a loquacious artifact from the astral plane to challenge his visions. It was a dialectic into which I tossed my own skull with burning veracity, and which would test everything I had come to believe in and felt that I knew. And though I hold Hans' exceptional mind, otherworldly philosophy, and unquestionable experience in high esteem, we eventually came to a place where our stimulating disagreements turned into a giant metaphysical chasm that neither of us could cross without throwing away his whole *Weltanschauung*. That is, Hans, no doubt having his own perfectly sound reasons, had recognized that we were all in Hell- a perspective in which I was somewhat in agreement with at the time; but for Hans, oddly enough, it was better to be in Hell than to be in Heaven. And why was that? Because, according to him, there were more 'colorful' characters down here, and Heaven was full of nothing but uptight perfectionists who flew around in boring white gowns listening to the same phlegmatic harp music all the time. In a way he had a point, though it wasn't until a few years later, when I experienced a dream-visit up to the firmament, that I could see he wasn't completely right. And besides that, there was something disagreeable in his conclusion, for, though I agreed that Hell existed on earth- that we were in Hell- I, myself, didn't like it at all, for the real truth was that I believed that we were in Hell only because Hell was in us. And not only that, but Purgatory and Heaven were also within; not the heaven which Hans found so tedious, but the true Heaven, and the true Hell; the immanent realms which are made visible and brought forth into manifestation only so as to reflect our turmoil or peace within. Yes, indeed, I was in Hell, but I had caused my own incarceration, my separation from the One, and I ...I was paying my dues and walking back out.

*

eight

It is only demanding relationships- like the one I had with Hans, in Rose Bay- which have the force necessary to flip one inside-out, and bring about the great transformations needed to move a person through incarnations without having to die. For the shifts of the soul do not come easy, and they will not come when sitting around comfortable coffee tables and talking peacefully of soft and shiny things. You have to find your match in the arena of the spirit. You have to come up against your equal, and dig inside yourself for every last ounce of reserve within, if the two combatants in the verbal and psychic milieu are to both emerge stronger from the duel. You have to lock horns in a bitter and beautiful struggle to test the mettle of everything you've got in you, if you are going to attempt to build your home upon this world of sand. Because you can bet the sea will come and wash away the foundation out from under you, and it's only then that you'll know if what you perceive is real and true, or if all your realities are merely sand castles in the air.

And so I say that Hans was my *mercurius*. And I say that for both mythical and actual reasons- because this world is both mythical and actual. For the drama into which I fell exists on many planes at once, and so the story which I tell exists both in the actuality of our temporal lives, and also in the eternal myth of our spirits as well.

Only internal revelation and sublime communication from the other world will convince an individual of this reality. No one can point to it nor prove it to another. When you walk through the membrane of permanence, into the shifting twilight of the Self, only you, and you alone, are there to bear witness to it happening, for we are each given only that which we are capable of receiving, and so we must therefore learn to be capable.

During my time in Rose Bay, on any given profane day, at about four o'clock in the afternoon the worldly chores which Hans and I had abandoned while transcendentally critiquing the incomprehensible universe would catch up to us, and we'd have a frantic couple of hours tending to the animals, weeding the garden, stealing octopus from eagles or ravens who had cornered the unlucky delicacy in a tidal pool, or we would head out fishing to a nearby shoal where an abundance of black bass, lingcod, snapper, and an assortment of rockfish were available and soon epicurean victims.

One late afternoon while we were out fishing I felt a strong tug on the line which I was hand-jigging, and then a stronger tug, until I was pulled to the side of Hans' zodiac and realized I had caught me a lunker. It was a gargantuan effort to reposition myself and drag whatever leviathan had chanced to nibble upon my lure up from the depths, but eventually up came a mammoth halibut- mammoth to me, though not all that huge as these type of fish go, but a gigantic one and a great struggle to reel in on a hand-line- about one-hundred and fifty pounds. The moment Hans saw the denizen of the deep come near to the surface a burst of approval and delight escaped him and quickly he had his gaff in hand and when I had wrestled the beast nearly to the boat Hans lunged down and hooked it and with the titanic force of which he was surprisingly capable for a pint-sized man, and the supremely skilled fisherman he had become from a decade and a half of foraging on the coast, he hauled the catch into the boat and before it had a chance to thrash-about he had beaten it senseless with a hammer.

It was a victory to be sure, but one that was not long lived. On pulling in the whale, our Ahab had dragged the lure across a main tube of the zodiac, opening up a giant sucking-chest-wound which was emptying that side of the boat in deep exhalations of precious air. With no time to patch the fissure we placed a sodden piece of tape over the gash, held it there by hand as best we could, hooked the foot pump up to the valve, and Hans jumped on the wheel and headed for shore while I pumped feverishly attempting to replace the precious air as quickly as it was leaving. When I was exhausted we switched places and I took over the wheel while Hans pumped away wildly, and then we changed again, and again, and finally Poseidon had also had his chunk of flesh and was appeased with our ridiculous efforts and we made it back to shore, hung the prized halibut up by the tail and lived off of the fresh game for the next many days until the meat was about to turn, whereupon we dried the rest.

Little boats and big fish are a dangerous mix. I recall being up in Alaska, where I was working as a kayak guide one summer, and standing in the museum in Sitka, in absolute awe as I inspected a traditional Aleutian seal-skin, bone, and driftwood kayak (there are no trees on the Aleutians, so the builder's task was further burdened by being dependent on another world's jetsam), and a sealskin dry-suit, and I could hardly imagine an intrepid Inuit hunter out on the tempestuous sea in this precarious contraption, harpoon in hand, waiting bravely for the whale to resurface. Good God, a whale! Taken in this jury-rigged mish-mash of found objects and imponderable rigging. I was set aback, for I realized right then that all true heroism had long ago vanished from our world.

There is not a man alive on this earth today who could take a whale with a harpoon from a kayak. Not one. Compared to the hunters of old, we are all faint-hearted, lily-livered, pitiful excuses for the gender. All the men are gone from earth and only little boys with toy guns and wet dreams remain.

I was satisfied with that thought as I sat eating the hotdog which I had stealthily hunted down at the local supermarket in Sitka, and began recalling the time when I was out on the sea, kayaking on that first visit to the Charlottes with Sandy and our buddy, and impressively experienced paddler, Greg- whom I would consider to be one of the few men left on earth if it weren't the case that none remained- and Greg also hooked into a halibut- which, in a kayak, is a different story altogether than in a zodiac, deflated pontoons aside- and I recall the almost manly and yet idiotic efforts we engaged in to bring the catch aboard, rafting our kayaks up together for stability, and taking turns reeling in the squirming monster. We had decided to land the beast while out at sea, despite Sandy's continuous admonition that we were fools, and the best and only possibility was to paddle to shore, towing the monster along, and then land it while standing on good ol' *terra firma*, where the odds would be more even. Sandy, my *anima* in the flesh, was right of course. And yet I was not ready then to accept the voice of my *anima*, my female side, for I had not the humility necessary to be whole and not just male, nor, I realize now, was I even prepared back then to accept ...the earth.

I see now how symbolic this whole event was, displaying perfectly the polarized state of my soul at that time; I and my male buddy, Greg, a guide, happily tangling with a creature from the depths of the unconscious- a duel in which we were certain to lose, though I could not see it. And there was the one voice of wisdom amongst us- a young, beautiful blond woman, my *anima*, living on the other side of pride, on the **earth**- who was able to see the solution which our bravado precluded us from seeing. No, we were men. We would not paddle to the safety of shore, we would hover above the depths and never accept that a man needed more.

So while I was draped over Greg's kayak and holding the fishing pole and line, he, with his strong and almost manly arms, gaffed the beast and lifted it out of the water, which was a feat in its own right, and the halibut began to put up a fuss like the devil was inside of it or something, and Greg was holding it aloft, somehow, as if in the reverse iron-cross, and his body was gyrating and being whipped about in the sympathetic vibrations of our whale's mania, and I was desperately trying to keep us from capsizing, and the fish flew into a more spectacular tantrum, and Greg continued holding on I don't know how, and neither of us knew at that moment why we had ever attempted such idiocy nor how we were going to get out of the mess, for the fish was now hooked twice, once with the line and once with the gaff, and it was in an insane mass of fury and force and certain to sink us both because we had never considered the voice of reason within or without us, and instead we had tried to be men in a world of spoilt brats, because we had heard about men but never met any, and because we had heard about heroism but never seen any, and damnit someone had to be a man and it was our chance, only we were going to have to die to receive the medal, or so it seemed, until Poseidon stepped in again and pardoned our puerile foolishness and the halibut thrashed its way off of the gaff and snapped the fishing line and in a moment the epileptic fit was over and all was calm.

We were living boys in a world without men, and we had lost our little whale and our chance at heroism, and though all we had left was laughter, boy did we howl. It was the thankful howl of two spineless white guys in kayaks loaded with bread and cheese, salami, crackers, peanut butter, German mustard, pasta, vegetables, and wine. Two anti-heroes on the slow and darkened path to wholeness, who did not have to paddle back to their village as failures, as gelded stallions.

Not us. Luckily enough we had come from the tribe of comfort and plenty, and we had only to paddle back to camp, eat and drink like emperors, forget that we had lost the battle because we had chosen it, and forget that we could have raised up the animal from the depths, from the unconscious, had one of us- namely myself- been humble and strong enough to believe in the woman within and without him, the woman who sought only to make things right by luring him down from the heights of disillusion, from the distance of mind, from the separation of the male spirit, and thus leading him back ...to earth.

*

nine

Soon after that episode I returned to my refuge in the sordid city once again- the blessed Co-op. It would be hard for an outsider to understand the ways in which the waves of spirit moved through the group of us co-workers who were privileged castaways in this isolated sanctuary- a single island in the great sea of Gomorrah. Indeed it was impossible even for most of those who lived and worked right within the medium of our liquid day. But that is the nature of the spirit- you have to see it working to know what it does, you have to give yourself completely to it in order to learn to love what it loves.

Since groups of people always carry a certain vibration with them, you can go from one building to the next, from one home to another, from city to city, or country to country, and each place will have a distinct feel, a distinct consciousness, and a distinct function within the evolution of the whole. As such I believe that, by whatever divine impetus, there was a time at the Co-op when a large number of us had been brought together to exchange aspects of our spirits and souls, and to grow together in ways which we could never have grown alone.

I recall one fabulous autumn, in fact, when it seemed that all the vagrant strands of our colossal plexus had finally merged at the nexus of our common substratum.

I recall how one individual after the next had their own unique, unbridled experience of the godsoul waking up within them, however apparent or obscure. I remember how one buddy of mine lost his mind for a while because he suddenly began to realize that God had, so to speak, held him for months like his own son, during the darkest darkness of his days, and, during this episode of insanity, my buddy spoke a number of prophetic things to me, about my life, which would come true only a few months later; I recall how another person revealed to me his idiosyncratic awakening- when the cosmic sound of OM resonated with such force within and about him that the splendiferous visual mandala which is said to accompany it during such mystic states of apprehension appeared to his bewildered eyes and he knew with the certainty of the inalterable Self the unequivocal realization which he could only describe as simply ...I AM; I recall another brother arriving at my hotel room at three in the morning in a fevered pitch of worry and excitement because a shift had occurred within him, an avalanche, a veil rent asunder, and now a terrifying hole loomed out before him in the ether, and he and I wandered about together all night in the chilling rain, discussing what was beyond our ability to discuss, and a few days later he was a new man, and you could not see the backs of his eyes anymore, for the space within had grown so infinite, and he walked with ease towards me that day and said he had decided to move to Europe because that's where he was supposed to go, which he did; then there was the diaphanous and charmed young woman who, during meditation one day, rose up in her light body into an astral dimension where she mingled with other light beings in a boundaryless energy orgy until she felt the horror of being pulled back away from that freedom, lightness, and love, and back into the clutches and limitations of this gross corpulescence; I recall the fabulous crescendos of the nameless visionaries amongst us, and their unlettered panegyrics of euphoria which would cascade spontaneously off of their desperate tongues; I recall the young women witches suddenly awakening to the art and wisdom of their ancient souls and taking root amongst us; I recall the flow and dance of those days in which our souls mingled into the unseparate song of the one; I recall the nebulous stare of each and every pair of incredulous eyes as it glistened back the rapture and confusion at first glimpsing the vision of the new way; and I recall standing in the middle of it all and wishing it would go on and on, grow stronger and stronger, and the focal point which had been created at, of all places, our workplace, would become the critical mass required for the spirit to finally leap up from within all peoples across the earth, surround this weary globe, and devour the forces which bind us whole.

Ah but the spirit has its own agenda, and ours is not to question, but only to find where the wave is climbing to its crest and to ride it until it smacks the shore.

I was on the wave, and I was riding in a kaleidoscopic medium that I was only beginning to be able to see.

It was beautiful, and terrible, dark and light, sublime and ridiculous. Angels were blossoming everywhere in the land around me, the underground stream was swelling and the firmament was falling, the Spirit breached in breathless ardor, and God was returning once again as the Father and Mother of all who were free within. It was the end of the millennium, and I was back at our center. The hub was finally repaired. All that remained was to be decent, humble, and true, and through God and faith we would learn again how to fly.

About this time another episode in those tempestuous years was also playing itself out; it was a time when myself and three other energetic, unencumbered, inspired souls- an ex-minister, a musician, and a woman film maker- would come together and receive such a charge off of each other's vibrations that an evening together would grow in force from a few social drinks to a climax that you'd think would tear the roof off, and because it didn't, we tried to make it happen anyways. And so began an era of our separate and intimate lives commingling together, in which we would set the world aside for a day, or perhaps a weekend, so as to simply blend, and bond, and enjoy one another, and occasionally to tangle with the mighty mystic spore- the magic mushroom of mythic legend.

It was during these intimate soiree's, that our certain select core of individuals- our essential quaternity- would gather together at the house of Mick, the musician, on the shore of Howe Sound, to drink, smoke, ingest the soma, and unearth the glory and fury bound up so tightly within all of us that you had to smash yourself over the head with a mountain of intoxicants so as to set the beast loose and let it roam free for a while.

If you take such strides, be sure that the tsunamis and whirlwinds, the willywogs, will-o-the-wisps, specters, poltergeists, and gremlins will come bashing at your door, the fog will set in, the lights will go out, the heavy breath of a forgotten foe will resonate behind you, Mara will rear up her ugly head, the Gods will confuse you, the tricksters will dance about your stumbling form, and the only thing you can do is do nothing but let the maelstrom clammer on until it runs itself dry or devours you and moves on to its next host.

We were raising up our own angel, and we were doing it our own way, on our own time, sitting on Mick's patio overlooking the sea and watching the storms come in, and passing a bottle of hooch around, then going for a walk and losing each other, then reconnecting and sharing the universe which had befallen us in the meantime, and back to the patio to hear some music, or to sit in silent awe at the hidden majesty of the spirit-world writhing in delight before us.

It was during these events that, in the silent, wordless mixing of close friends, I would come to sense how our spirits merged into each other, blended, and communicated in ways far beyond normal understandings; how, intoxicated or not, the body is but the nucleus of our much greater self, which sublimely extends out from each of us in less dense and invisible forms, and which converges, intermingles, exchanges, and stays together for extended periods, within other people's greater self, just as waves come together, combining oscillations, and then flow apart, each still separate and yet now modified from before their intermixing.

It is these subtle bodies of ours which are the hardest to get to know, and yet the ones which have the most effect on others, and on the world around us. It is the subtle body which can sense another truly, feel what they are carrying inside- regardless of what they are saying-

and become elevated by their love and integrity, or contaminated by their hate and confusion.

This was the beginning of my understanding of how there is no separation in life, that we are all connected, and that a person's love or hate does not end inside their heads, in their thoughts, but is sent out into the world to ameliorate or exacerbate the plight of all those fortunate or unfortunate enough to be in its way.

Sometimes the nicest people have the most violent demons inside of them. Sometimes an angry man is a saint. You can't tell until you mix inside of them, for the spirit behind the flesh is oft like a wolf in sheep's clothing, and rarely like a prince within a frog. You take others on often without choice, and so your *I* gets jumbled and grafted with other *I*'s, and then what you are is not what you've always been.

These are matters of the spirit which I would experience but would not come to grasp and make my own until I had left the world of drugs and psychic crutches behind, and had, with a determined leap, walked into the truth and stillness of the self with nothing but my own peace to guide me.

The mushroom had offered me the evanescent visions of an eternal place, but it could not take me there. Yet there were solo trips which I would take, ingesting the spore, and then opening up to the cosmic radiations, in which I would see the fabric of spirit behind the veil of matter and mind, and would receive many insights that were incredibly profound but which, in retrospect, were perhaps imbibed too early in my spiritual growth, and therefore, in a way, simply stunted the natural process which would have come about more smoothly anyway; I was like a youth taking a glance at a Playboy magazine, and upon seeing the full show, so to speak, destroying himself with a desire which need not have been there and would have been more rapturously fulfilled had it lay dormant until finally aroused at the time of his actual deflowering; I was no longer spiritually innocent, though neither was I mature, and that, if nothing more, merely added to the growing pains I was already being over-trodden and consumed with.

Still in all, the four of us had great times together, offering a rare episode of communal friendship the likes of which I had never encountered before, and may never again, along the solitary trail of wandering I have accepted as a large part of my self-chosen life. And yet I remain close to those dear ones and a few others who walked right inside of me back then, during our dance upon the same page of life for a while.

In fact, a year later Mick decided to join me out on Flores Island, after I had been out there alone for a few days, relinquishing my contact with the empire, and disgorging my soul as per usual. He came out and brought with him his guitar and sang sweet melodies to me for three days straight while I sat back in the sun, watching the sundog covenants emerge overhead, and soaking up his tunes in the rapture of the wilds. Nights we'd spend chomping down mouthfuls of limpets in garlic, gooseneck barnacles and fried onions, and an assortment of other epicurean delights, all washed down with litres of red wine and followed by the bliss of brotherhood and song.

It was a splendid treat to have a comrade finally out on the coast with me, walking my favorite beaches, exploring the hidden alcoves and intertidal islands which had, over the years, grown to be my friends as well, and so it felt as if I was introducing them to Mick and enjoying the meeting of these two.

It was a heartwarming few days- the kind which almost brought me to tears at its closure- so much so that a couple of years later Mick and I planned a sequel to that trip, but unfortunately when the time came around he was unable to attend.

So what? So I'd be out there alone again, nothing new in that, I thought. I decided to go anyway and had only a short, two-week, biological contract to fulfill before leaving. I was to serve as a pack-mule and secretary for a few guys climbing old-growth trees on the coast, looking for the working nests of endangered Marbled Murrelets, so that the environmental community could use these finds as a reason to lobby the forestry industry for the preservation of those enormous and diminishing trees. We didn't find any nests, but it was a fruitful stint of employment anyway, meeting some genuinely good lads, and providing me not only with essential funds but also with the ontological data necessary to confirm another secret pattern in the universe which I was slowly awakening to, and that is, simply: a void must be filled.

What happened is that on this contract prior to my Flores trip, a young fellow from Australia was working as another of the slaves along with me; a young man who looked uncannily like Mick and played guitar brilliantly as well.

Well what do you know but after our work was finished I gave this Australian bloke directions out to the secret beach I usually camped upon- though he said he doubted if he'd make it there- and after I had been camped out there for a few days he did show up and suddenly I was on the beach Mick and I had planned to have our reunion on, listening to his look-a-like play guitar and eating limpets, and gooseneck barnacles, and drinking wine and wondering how much of this came about because a thought planted in the ether must come to fruition.

To be sure, the recognition that we are integral elements to the creation of the cosmos was becoming clearer to me. This was simply one more piece of evidence in the case I was building in my mind- the case which suggests that the drama requires certain characters at certain times for the fulfillment of its mysterious agenda, and if one character happens to leave the stage, a similar one is pulled into the vacuum.

I have seen this occurrence now time and time again. It is as if God is creating the same stew in many different parts of the earth, and each spice must be included in each separate batch, according to God's taste at the time, and the spices are the sublime archetypes carried in the spirits of subtly similar individuals.

Everywhere on earth this is attempting to happen, and a similar cast of characters is operating on different stages, in different costumes, with different scripts, and yet with one consistent intention- to complete the show.

Thus I found that there were patterns of spiritual archetypes running as threads through my life; individuals playing certain roles, in certain aspects, at certain times of my existence, and when one went off in a different direction from mine, another of their strain stepped in- another person carrying the same spirit, who was there to replace their predecessor, perhaps years or even decades later, but sooner or later the whole must be sealed again and all the missing parts must appear. These parts are the *types* of the arche*types* from which we draw out our completeness; the separate rooms by which we build and come to live in our own illustrious castles.

*

ten

Unfortunately I wasn't living in any external castles yet. Not even close. And after a few years of hopping from one cockroach-ridden bachelor's suite to the next, then moving into my van for a while, then selling it and buying a little Honda Civic and living out of it- which, frankly, is much more comfortable than it sounds, for the front seats in a Civic lay way down and one can get a very pleasant night's sleep, and not suffer too much exertion during the night if one has to urinate, because, while lying down in the front seat of such a vehicle, one need only roll to the side, crack the door ajar slightly, and let the stream run out onto the road without ever opening one's eyes, which is at least one advantage over sleeping on a king-sized bed in a carpeted palace.

Finally, however, I parted with the Civic as well, because I was intentionally paring down my material goods so as to have nothing except what would fit into a backpack, just in case I felt the need to up and quit the world in an instant, which could have come any time, and I wanted to have everything in order so as not to leave a trail behind.

I then began a period of taking up residence on any friend's couch who would have me, though this proved to be the least amicable of all situations to my furtive soul. Not that I was ungrateful for the places I was benevolently offered to stay. The problems were far more irrevocable and subtle than that. For nothing was more annoying to me than the chronic hum of an apartment's refrigerator, which I could hear from a great distance, even if I was sleeping in the living room and the fridge was in the kitchen. Often I would have to do at a friend's home what I had done so often in my own apartments, which was to unplug the whining beast at night and replug it in the morning, hoping that my host's succulent lamb chops would make it through the night without harm. And if it wasn't the refrigerator driving me insane, it was an electric wall-clock, ticking ever so patiently and agonizingly along. There must be some masochistic strain in our culture's attitude which provides these subtle, well-disguised Chinese-water-tortures everywhere you go. But I couldn't endure it and so the clock would have to come down and I'd put it in a drawer, or another room, or outside, and try to remember to put it back up on the wall in the morning, so as not to disturb the ambience.

  It was for these reasons, and because I could not bear any longer living in another person's reality- which was unavoidable while living on their couch, in the middle of their illusion- that I began fantasizing that there had to be some system set up for vagrants like myself, some gentleman's home or temporary residence which allowed a person to come and go as they pleased, and not be bound by the overburdening restrictions of rent or leases, nor to suffer the fate of living within another person's psychic bric-a-brac.

  To be sure, Vancouver and its environs was already culturally centuries ahead of Toronto and the east, from where I had originally fled, and where the slumlords make you sign a full year lease, and the employers will only take you on at forty hours per week, and fifty weeks per year, and nothing less, or not at all. The bloody insanity of it all. These poltroons had sold out long ago and were intent on making sure that everyone else got caught in the same dreary march to death as them. They had lost their lives to the dollar and the locked door and if you wanted either of these you had to lose your life as well. And that was something I could not stomach. Take your idiotic ways, and your leases, and contracts, and take your two weeks of holiday a year, and your wavers and conventions and give me back my life.

  Thankfully the culture of the coast was at least a little more civil than this; here one could find acceptable seasonal work, allowing for six to eight months off per year if you knew how to handle your sheckles. And here one could have an apartment with no more investment than a two-month rental agreement, so as to have a roof over your head at night that didn't bind you for an entire year. But even two months is an outrageous impossibility when you're following your dreams, which I was, and which, on any given night might say- "OK bud, time to get up and out of here and move on, onto another task, in another place, for reasons you'll never know until you get there." There is no option when you live like this- you have to leave, instantly. And I left so often, on the turn of a dime, so to speak, that to return meant to return to an infrastructure that was becoming less and less welcoming, and less and less functional for my needs. Indeed the foxes have their lair, and the birds have their nest, but the free and reckless wanderer has no place in which to take his rest. Not, that is, until he discovers the Ivanhoe Hotel.

Ah, the Ivanhoe. No place like it on earth, not this earth anyway. The rooms of this down-and-out, wayfarer, and drunk's hotel were the cheapest in the city, and had become a sanctuary of sorts for all those who belonged nowhere else, and who had been chased to its front door by the invisible dogs barking at their heals. And the bar down below was no different. Walking into it was like entering the alien bar in *Star Wars*. Every being imaginable was there. It was a mirror for the confused and erratic, cosmic convention of lost and alien souls which populate the subconscious frontier. It was here that I would first experience the throbbing pulse of the world's underbelly- the thick Tartarian ooze of men and women, all vibrating in tune with the lesser frequency of the fallen realm, and weaned on the succulent lymph of the poisonous Kali herself; all detached and spinning wildly to and fro in the depths of the descending plane of living apparitions and unascending souls, where the minions of dark angels and their grey carnival of false delights invoked the ghoulish laughter of Hell and its ineffective respites.

It was a bar unlike any other bar, a place where all were welcome because- as Hans pointed out to me on one of his infrequent visits to Vancouver, while sitting in the Ivanhoe one evening amongst the multitude of mutants- "Everyone is welcome in Hell."

And yet it was not the Hell of eternal damnation, it was a chosen hell for most. A Hell, in fact, in which those people found their peace and acceptance, away from the other Hell, which existed everywhere else. The Ivanhoe was an oasis- absent of the real and living water perhaps- but an oasis with its own inexhaustible well of draft and rift-rafts nonetheless.

Every manner of individual would happen in at one time or another. It was a culture of captives who had lost all thought of escape or emancipation and had learned to sing and play and fight in a world which was an imperfect, despairing, disastrous world, a blissless world of exile and hopelessness, but a world after all, and, more importantly, it was *their* world. And boy would they ever whirl up a hoot and a holler and a celebration of the unavoidable Armageddon being perversely drawn out in the collective menagerie of those purgatorial homecomings brought about every day and night under the surface of a sea which none of them knew they were drowning in.

The mutant enclave from the Arnold Schwarzenegger film *Total Recall*, would be as good a visual as I could paint from this scene.

Gathered together were bums and charlatans, hippies and crack-heads, retirees, natives, travellers, businessmen, students, dropouts, homeless beggars, mystics, whores, laymen, soldiers, vagabonds, pushers, and renegades, all and everyone, no one left out, no one denied, no one judged because all were judged, no one condemned because all were condemned. A crowd of thieves dangling from their crosses and not a messiah in sight to be traded for them.

I'd often slide quietly in, sit down at a table by a window, order a beer, take out my notepad, and let the madness begin. Hardly had I written a single line when a man named Mustaf- a huge, powerful, constantly drunken Muslim man- would approach me, grab hold of my hand with his iron grip, sink to his knees, and wail out- "I know who I am, I know who I am. I am nothing!" And an authentic tear would trickle down his cheek, and he'd begin his melancholic soliloquy on his duty and reverence for all life, and how he had never wanted to kill any man, but had to, for his country and his soul, and his thick lips would suck on the ever-present cigarette dangling from his mouth, and he'd declare his oath to God and move on.

And then another pilgrim would arrive at my doorstep. This time it would be a homeless Italian barber who lived in a warehouse, begged for beer and cigarettes, and claimed to have a house in Rome with three-thousand bottles of wine in the basement. And his toothless yarns would begin and he'd sip his beer and tell me of his fishing exploits, his economic ruin, and his favourite places in Chinatown to get a two-dollar meal.

Then he'd be gone and a young junky would come along, a fellow who had been a great musician until his whole family was killed and he took to the needle and bottle to escape what he could not escape. And he would sit down and patronize me and pretend to befriend me and then try to coax a few bucks out of me for another drink- which I gave to him at first but then I realized I was only adding to his and everyone else's dumb luck by paying for another round of misery and I learned what might be the most valuable lesson I was to receive in that bar in all the days and nights I sat there- to say no.

I learned how to squash a vexing spirit from invading, cajoling or guilting me out of myself. And that is no small thing. And for me it took a bar full of ever-invasive, determined and skilled individuals so that I might learn to see some of the ways in which others can climb inside your skin; it took this antagonizing throng of separated selves to create the fluid obstacle-course necessary in which my spirit learned to surf, to glide, and to fly free.

"No" became my battle cry and my banner- one which I would have to learn to deploy in the future, in many different places, under many different circumstances again, as the vexations of separated spirits became all to obvious and affronting to my softening shell.

Sitting there, learning how to drive away those who would steal my peace was quite an effort. Men and women of all types would come and sit or filter past, hawking their stolen goods, or their art, clothing, sausages, cheese, dope, cigarettes, or booze. It was a constant train of reprobates and street merchants, attempting to get rid of their disreputable wares. One spectre would leave and another arrive. Another story, another pint of beer, another woe-begotten song about their dance through the dark and disorienting doom they were not aware of creating for themselves.

One such middle-aged native woman who was always in the pub wearing a drunken smile sat down beside me one evening while I was having a thick and juicy metaphysical conversation with a good buddy, and I could see she was slightly intrigued as well as befuddled, and so she tried to wheedle her way in with her limited tools of ribaldry and sensuality, and we kept on talking, trying not to obviously dismiss her, but finally her digressive invasions became painfully annoying and I turned to her and coldly inquired, "What are you doing here, in the bar, you're always here, what are you doing?" She was set aback but quickly tried to counterbalance my thrust, rebutting with a coy smile, "I'm not hurting anyone", to which I quickly rejoined, "No one but yourself", at which point she burst into tears and bothered us no more.

And yet, to be sure, there was laughter as well at the Ivanhoe- uproarious, uninhibited, end-of-the-world laughter. And there was care, and joy, and pleasantness also, all a part of this burgeoning Pandora's box of disconsolate humanity.

I once saw a woman attain to a level of ecstasy which only the most purified spiritual supplicant could normally accomplish after decades of mortification and discipline, and she was only a drunk and a junky. But she made it to the stars, to that type of ecstasy which can only come about in Hell- the type of release which rockets you up into the distant sky, only so as to let you tumble down even further. But it is that twinkling instant of escape, when everything vanishes but the dream, which keeps the pendulum ever swinging.

I saw her stumbling slowly along the bar, and then she suddenly stopped in her tracks just as what must have been an old, nostalgic rock tune for her came wailing over the stereo, and it was as if she was held there in suspended animation as the tune grew and soared through her, and at the moment of the elevated chorus her head went back, genuflecting in exultation, her arms went limp beside her, and she was as if lifted off of the ground for a millisecond of Hell's ecstasy, an ecstasy caused by the remembrance of a time when life spoke of beautiful and awesome things before the collapse of reality; an ecstasy which was always available, always pretending to be worth the plunge which followed, always beckoning to be known. The ecstasy of Hell. Always waiting there, offering another fix, another moment of forgetting, another tranquillizer or upper to white-wash over the shit, before the deluge of remembrance came and blew it all away.

These are the false redemptions that lift your mind up and shroud your heart but take your spirit nowhere and weaken your already bleeding soul; I know of these phantom pilgrimages into delusion and its hopeless possession, where at every turn in the carnival of lights and attractions the spirit reaches out for life and receives only a picture of life, and in the peril of its anguish and confusion imagines that the image is the thing, for with the heart gone the mind can tell no difference, and so the image is what is sought after from then on, for the real is unattainable, or worse- almost impossible to attain. The fact that it lies at a great distance makes it all the more woeful than if it were gone for good. Like a lost love somewhere far across the ocean, on a different continent, which wrecks you nightly instead of having died to let you grieve and then go on.

It is a horrid difference between the artificial and the real; as if a glass wall separates the soul from its source; as if a person reaches out for what can be seen, but cannot be touched, and in that woeful distance they get only visitor's rights to see themselves, because they come nearer and nearer, only to not come near enough.

I know now of a hell where the living spirit dies in the tomb of misdeeds and misunderstandings. For the living spirit alone is what connects us to the whole, and to each other, for it is life, and everything else is hollow, separate, and dead.

The ecstasies of hell, always displaying their hollow temptations with a devil's smile and the charm of medusa before she strikes. For there is no true ecstasy based on need, because ecstasy is the absence of need, and is a fulfilment beyond need, and therefore cannot be arrived at through need.

It was a game of shadows and their many disguises at the Ivanhoe, a dance of laughter without joy, friendship without brotherhood, and beauty without beatitude.

Yet there were other types of folks there as well; many decent, thoughtful, serious folks who were not there to destroy themselves but only to sip a beer and watch the goings-on.

I fell into a conversation with a balding, fifty-year old, slightly built man one evening and found that he had been a bare-foot, wandering, Buddhist monk in India for ten years, begging for his daily rice, meditating, and following as best he could the eight-fold path of the dharma. We had a few drinks together and then went back to his low-income housing flat, where a giant, five hundred pound brass

Buddha sat surveying his sacred domicile. Along with the icon, he had a wall full of sacred texts, all in Sanskrit, which he had mastered during his time in the east. He gave me a pocket-sized version of Seng Ts'an's *Poem on Trust in the Heart*, which I had read already and adored, and so it was a lovely gift and synchronicity at the same time.

This man was a gentle soul who had unfortunately lost most of his western vigour during his decade of surrender and alms-seeking, and therefore was having a tough go of it back in North America, where to be a sannyasin meant to live without an historical structure based on sadhus, monks, and holy men wandering around and bequeathing blessings onto all those who tossed rupees into their begging bowls. No, to be a sannyasin in North America meant to be an unwelcome, misunderstood, and guilty traitor to the rule of 'money made is money paid', and you don't get nothing just by asking, you must work for it, because no one is going to believe that their karma is lessened by giving you donuts so that you can pray instead of toil.

On most nights at the pub anything could happen, and usually did. On one of these evenings I hooked up with two middle-aged dudes who came into the bar every so often for a chat and a pint. Jim was a softened veteran of the hard life. I say softened because he had lived out his fight with the world and with others, had won some battles and lost some, and had come through it as a very genuine, mellow, streetwise ex-tough guy, who had, out of benevolence that night, brought his neurotic artist friend, Stanley, to the Ivanhoe to get him out of the lonely hiding spot he called home. Stanley was impressively uncomfortable; a man with no walls and no armour around him; a mouse who was therefore incapable of defending himself from the judgements and willpower of others. And, more importantly, he was unable to recognize that he was terrified because what he sought to defend ...was a lie. A truly pitiful creature, though immensely lucid, like all true neurotics, due to the absence of protection between him and all else.

So Jim and Stanley and I ended up putting a few pints into our bellies at the Ivanhoe and then we walked a couple of blocks down the street to another bar to listen to some live music, and Jim and I got on quite well, digging deeper into each other's life, as Stanley sat fidgeting about like a mouse who had escaped his cage and then realized he was soon to get stepped upon for such a disobedient act.

Jim and I went on though, talking about what real men would talk about if there were real men to talk about real life, and I suppose I had shared some of the pieces of my own turmoil and distress with him, because after a while he turned to me with the wizened look of a true street sage- one who had gone the distance and knew that the only answer is to tough it out- and he looked at me and offered a piece of news about life which I could not apprehend from my perspective at that time, and which didn't really change anything for me, but in retrospect I can now sort of see what he was pointing at. What he said was simply: "It gets easier." That was it, and he turned to sip his beer, and I knew that he believed it because he had been through the ringer and had come out, perhaps not in the same shape as when he had first entered, but he came out nonetheless, and he spoke to me as one who had already climbed over the wall I was now desperately clinging onto.

In the next couple of years I was to meet a number of younger folks who were going through what I had been going through at that time, and this little piece of advice might have also suited our conversations well, had I ever chosen to plagiarize it, which I didn't.

But anyway, that bit of blue-collar pedagoguery finished, we toasted off a few more pints and then went outside to say our goodbyes. It was then, as I was walking away from my new chums, that I finally got an appreciation of how open Stanley really was to the cosmic precipitations.

I must relate here a note that this night came during the time in my life which I would call 'the emergence of the shadow'. I don't know what the Jungian analysts would say of this, but to me it appeared that over the course of a few months certain characters and occurrences were showing up in my outward life, signifying submerged pieces of my inner being which I had been slowly, arduously, raising to the surface.

Thus, as I was walking down the block away from the two of them, I heard Stanley yell out to me "Hey, what's that behind you?" And I turned to look but didn't see anything, and thought perhaps that he was off in his own little crumbling kingdom again, and I kept walking. Then he yelled again, "It's your shadow." And as I kept moving I looked back and, sure enough, I was just passing under a streetlight and my shadow was behind me. But then in a millisecond I had crossed under the light and it was gone. That's when Stanley yelled out again, "Now it's in front of you." Which it now was. And so my shadow had gone from behind me to in front of me, from the unconscious into the conscious, and Stanley had heralded the movement which I had been examining but had not known for certain if its absolute translation had occurred from the dark into the light, so to speak. And so another message, pertinent to the stage of my internal course came flying at me out of the ether, this time from the puppetted mouth of one who was so transparent and willess that God apparently could make him speak whatever he wanted, and did.

Say what you will, but the messages come from anywhere, at anytime, you only have to know who's sending them to you. The wheel keeps spinning and the patterns keep changing, but the weaver stays at his loom and never asks why you must walk with dirty feet upon his carpets. Imponderable, disastrous, ridiculous, and grand, this life, full of fable and foolery, purpose and plan. The substratum moves and goes nowhere. The outside gnaws away at the inside which created it. The inside feeds upon the outside until it's done. Whatever was there, becomes here. Those who were they, become we. And the wingless phoenixes look to the sky and assume without flight they're not free.

*

eleven

I was free, and so I fled back to the Charlottes once again, back to the land of inexplicable wonders, magical vortices, and natural abundance. Back also to the land of elves, gnomes, silkies, trolls, gremlins, and smurfs. I say this because it was here that I would meet all these mythical species hidden in the disguises of the craziest litany of seekers, bush folk, renegades, musicians, anarchists, occultists, hippies, angels, demons, tree-huggers, and an implausible assortment of other fringe types who had found their way to the outer edge of the known world, and there paraded their sublime beings on the diaphanous veil of the corpulent flesh. Which is another way of saying that my frequent sojourns to the luminescent isles were regularly peopled by a plethora of colorful locals, drifters, and eccentrics; individuals who, for one reason or another, had seen fit to step aside from the stampeding herd of manic degenerates- from civilization, that is- and venture out into the isolated and forgotten reaches where the malaise of the mob had not yet fully infiltrated.

One such self-exiled woman springs instantly to mind: a fifty-five year old American lady who had changed her name to River Eagle, had dropped out as far as one can drop out of convention, had lived the last ten years or so without a proper home, building squatter's shacks out of whatever materials were available wherever she ended up- which, previously, had been the American San Juan islands and their vicinity- and had made her way up and down the coast by trading her labor, finding odd jobs, and selling the most delightful, authentic rosaries I had ever seen, let alone smelled. As a matter of fact, before I had met her, I thought a rosary was a string of fake gem-stones strung along a cord which tired old dowagers somehow found solace in fondling after everything else worth living for had died or deserted them. River set me straight on that presumption. She had disinterred the historic art of rosary making- boiling up a large vat of fresh rose petals in a viscous, glutinous mixture of wax and oil, and then rolling this concoction into little balls the size of marbles, setting them to cool, and then stringing them into a genuine rosary, fit to lei the pope with, which smelled deliciously like newly opened roses for an inexplicably long time.

This was her main craft and venerable vocation. And yet she was an incurable gatherer, tinkerer, and artist in almost any medium available; and on the Charlottes that largely meant nature's ever-present offal.

To stroll around and watch her gathering sundry stones, shells, sticks and boughs, wild hops, berries, reeds, and flowers, and to see nothing but an armful of compost of it, and then to view, a few hours later, the outcome of her free inspirations and imaginings, blending these disparate items into an incredibly unique work of art and beauty was to witness a lost way of being- a way in which the earth and humanity melded together from different directions and out of which the spirit was made visible. She was a Renaissance sculptor carving out the essence of existence in the wilds of the twentieth century, an animated sprite come to life on the living canvas of Bosch's Garden of Earthly Delights.

In her early years River had done many things in many different places around the world. She had lived in Europe for a while, had been a surrealist painter, an actress in New York, a seeker of the mystical arts all over the globe, and had spent time studying the esoteric likes of Gurdgieff and his inverted universe. And then one day it seems she just sort of floated away from it all without even trying, and began her new life of mendicant homelessness, gathering, wandering, and living in a way that had become her own. She would even smoke dope in a way I had never seen anyone do it before, or since- carving out a thin tunnel through the center of an apple, and then, at one end, creating a little bowl to put some marijuana in, then smoking it through the tunnel, and passing it around, and when it was finished she'd claim the pipe and consume the apple. Then she'd be off again, meandering on her easeful way, taking facile observation of this or that, then turning away, taking hold of something else, and letting go of another. I understand now why she had changed her name to a most fitting label- River Eagle; because she had learned to flow on her own course with life, to not obstruct the gifts of the Giver, and to take and cherish and modify the beauty she alone could see with her subtle, artist's keen vision.

She was a delightful breath of fresh air which I inhaled insatiably during the few days we spent together; a stray flower floating about in the wind and loving life for its own sake, without needing everything else that most of us need without loving any of it at all.

Another time on the islands I was to meet two memorable fellows, each named Grant, each a recluse and dropout from society, each a brilliant and capable person in many ways, one of them living on the north island, one on the south island, one an ex-Freemason of the twenty-eighth degree, the other an ex-Templar who had, by then, given up the dangerous ways of magic and all the karmic pitfalls incantation unavoidably contains. Two Grants, each one a glowing ball of fire in his own right, and yet in the small circle of crazy misfits who inhabited the islands, neither of them, to my knowledge, had ever heard of the other.

Grant number one, a huge, imposing, long-bearded, beer guzzling, red head, lived on a ramshackle houseboat, and moved about in the little bays which populate the east side of the south island. He had been immersed in the culture of the occult before his self-imposed exile, and considered Aleister Crowley to have been the voice of truth and keeper of the Law. But nowadays Grant was simply staying away from it all, brewing his own grog, chasing down the occasional bush hussy, making flint knives the old Indian way, and making enemies the old fashioned way- by looking out for no one but himself- which was perhaps his greatest talent while waiting for the day when his pride would call him back into the dark and imperfect ways of gesticulation and sorcery.

The other Grant- a wiry framed, scowling, long-haired son of the islands, had, as a young man, fathered a handful of children with two native Haida women, and then had set off on his own around the world to discover the secrets calling and waiting for him. I suppose he must have found some because he certainly carried one of the most burning, passionate minds I have ever come upon.

I met up with him a few years after his return to the islands, when he had come across on the ferry with only a few bucks in his pocket, and had lived from that point onward largely off the land- or so he said. He had a wise and penetrating distaste for all authority and stomped around in knee-high moccasins claiming to be able to speak with the animals, specifically a few of the rare 'warrior bears', as he called them, who unanimously considered most humans to be absolute idiots and wastrels.

As I said, this Grant had a blazing fire inside of him which he regularly aimed at anyone in uniform, or anyone claiming even the smallest power or authority over the island- his island. He was incredibly entertaining to listen to as he brandished his recalcitrant, truculent, voluble sword against all that stank of prestige and politics- the cloaks of assumed position draped over the infantile minds of those who parade themselves as leaders.

He had an eye from which no corruption nor deceit could escape, and he suffered the inevitable blackballing by the authorities, which comes to any jester who turns his keen wit and acumen against the King.

It was from him that I heard about another man, one whom had been perhaps the most notorious resident to ever inhabit the islands- Jerry the Bear man.

Grant had lived with Jerry for a year and a half, had been a good friend, and had quite a story to tell about this iconoclastic comrade of his.

Seems Jerry was a different sort of man altogether, which is to say, he was a *gentle*man. Apparently he had always been set apart from the average bloke on the streets. As an adult he had gone off and spent eight years in meditation in one of the remote valleys on the island, and when he emerged from his hermitage the animals had grown to trust and love him and followed him back to town. It was there, at his house overlooking the town, that all sorts of beasts would gather, hang about, and play as if they had returned to the Garden of Eden and no one had ever heard of the Fall.

Grant showed me pictures of crows doing antics on his porch, dear grazing in the backyard, raccoons sauntering about as if they were card-carrying citizens of the state, and, of course, bears- all living within Jerry's home. The bears were the most astonishing. Coming and going as they pleased, eating breakfast at his kitchen table- sitting up, holding cornbread like proper Victorian ladies- and sleeping on his couch.

Grant told me that though the bears were absolutely wild, they accepted anyone whom Jerry accepted- which was everyone- and had never shown any sign of fear or hostility.

The Queen Charlotte Islands are home to the largest black bears in the world, so we're not talking here about any scrawny, goat-sized Himalayan dancing bears- we're talking about the big boys.

At one point there were as many as six bears coming and going as adopted members of Jerry's household, and never a problem, never an attack, never any aggression of any type. And yet this was too much for the authorities to assimilate into their neolithic heads. No one should be allowed to love and harbor such unpredictable and terrifying beasts. It was unheard of. And the uncreative, imprisoned, confounded consciousness of the cops could, in the end, no longer tolerate such a preposterous, unprecedented, and potentially dangerous event. And so one day the thick skulled gendarmes entered Jerry's house while he was away and gunned down all the bears that were peacefully hanging about in what they had come to know as their home.

And that was too much for Jerry. The story goes that, soon after the genocide, Jerry set his house ablaze to release the massacred spirits of the bears, and a rainbow could be seen coming out of the inferno. A few days later Jerry's vehicle was found on a logging road off in the hills, destroyed as well by fire, and with a mess of what were assumed to be Jerry's bones amongst the ashes. To the authorities it was an obvious suicide, but Grant claimed Jerry was a different kind of man than that, and though the murders of his friends had been horribly grievous to him, he was still alive somewhere, and had simply gone away to where he would not have to endure the violence, brutality, and stupidity of humankind ever again.

*

twelve

Back I went again to humankind, back again to Vancouver, to the land of karma and cage, fornication and foolery, benedictions and balderdash. By this time in my life I was often drunk, and aloft, and writhing about in a stupor of myth and mayhem, surrounded on all sides, my bullets quickly dwindling, and still holed up in the last Monastery of Capitulation on earth- the Ivanhoe Hotel.

In the few years that I came to inhabit the Hotel, I often found myself locked away in my cell in that moribund cloister, as I had done in my apartments years earlier, though now my room was amidst a condemned fraternity of other men, most of whom were twice my age- in wearied appearance if not in years- most of whom who had fallen away from life, who were unemployed, divorced or never married, drunks and junkies, oddballs, idlers, morons, and thieves, and also a large number who simply had no desire for the troubles of respectability and success required in the showboat world; such outward ostentations were superfluous divergences for which they had no need and yet which the world still proceeded to hold up to them as mirrors of condemnation and judgment everyday.

It was a domesticated pack of lone wolves in the Hotel, all seeking shelter from the unendurable rain, all under the same sorrowful roof, in rooms stained with a hundred years of blood, semen, urine, wine, and tears. A prideless pack of ugly ducklings, runts, scapegoats, hobbled stallions, and flightless eagles cursed to the ignominy of the crumbling perch.

All that most of these men wanted- and all they got, for that matter- was a cold beer before noon, a cigarette every hour, a hot meal at night, and the deathly silence of the halls and rooms of this outcast's priory, in which each in his own solitude could slowly, methodically recount, contemplate, and admit to the broken steps which they had chosen and which had led to their troubled and valueless lives.

The whole place was like a living morgue, where the undead cadavers moved about in sloth and melancholy, haunting their own rooms with a sentence placed upon them by no one but themselves.

Thus the many rooms I came to inhabit over the next few years became my inner-city castle and keep. It was within the protected confines of these cells that, locked away in the inner altar of the soul, the images and tribulations within me would ferment up and boil over, spilling out onto page after page as manic notes, taken like an incarcerated secretary receiving dictation from a verbose and brutal master. In short, I was becoming a writer, which is a simple way of saying- all hope was lost.

I say this because I was not born blessed with an affinity for the artist's finesse in life, but rather for its rough and wild side, and so instead of effortlessly penning artful sentences, eloquently delineating the subtler aspects of life, I had to learn to write as one with only a battleaxe for a quill, and his own blood for the ink.

As such, in the ominous bloodletting now underway, notebook after notebook was soon filled with the flotsam crashing onto the shores of my consciousness- a detritus which was more than likely exhumed, in part, because of the innumerable texts and treatises I was omnivorously devouring at the time, for I consumed anything and everything to fuel the fire: mystical Christianity, Buddhism, Hinduism, Taoism, Zen, abstract secularism, literary exegesis, poetry, psychoanalysis, philosophy, alchemy, esotericism, and all the rest of the extant tomes to be found by the perplexed and uncomfortable mind. I would devour one book and instantly be ravenous for another. Nothing could fill the void nor satisfy my hunger. As soon as I came to one realization- or what I erroneously thought at the time was a realization- I was instantly ready for another. The movement had to keep going, to wherever, and however, it didn't matter, as long as it didn't stop. I had forsaken the world, and it was only in between the covers of books where I sought comfort, company and inspiration, and the delirious effulgence's awaiting therein.

I was so easily transported into exalted contemplation during those days, insatiably attempting to gobble down the entire breadth of numinous writings from the past. It seemed that whatever I picked up at the library, or bought, or was loaned from a friend, inevitably contained precise and timely import into the current riddle I was facing inwardly. And if not, at least the book spawned another, deeper, more all-encompassing riddle which would swallow up its predecessor, as if saying- "Look here, you're not a bloody mystery, you're nothing but a puzzle waiting to be solved. Stand aside, for I come as a true enigma." And generally it was. As such I can honestly say, in all those years of reading and research, that instead of getting closer to understanding, I fell farther and farther away from it. And what a glorious and unexpected delight this turned out to be.

Early in the week I'd put on a large batch of homemade beer, wine, or port, buy a small supply of dope, and cook up a huge pot of curry, or chilli, or some such muck that would stick to the ribcage, and would last me the week, so that I could get on with the rest of it. Whatever that rest of it was.

I'd lock the door to my phrontistery, close the curtains, sit down, and begin the incessant reading, writing, drinking, smoking, thinking, eating, sleeping, wondering, going nuts, entering into euphoria, then meaninglessness, then bliss, on and on, as these multifarious aspects of my now wholly self-contained existence filled one singularly consecrated purpose- to figure things out. For months and then years on end I, in my own very imperfect way, chased down the disorienting conglomeration of antiquated, conceptual tunnels to which we are both the heirs and prisoners.

It was as if I was engaged in an internal inquisition, in which I was both prosecutor and defendant, where I sought and exposed the renegade phantoms, mute wise men, cowards, shadows, heroes, madmen, rebels, harlots, hags, and cherubim which populated my subconscious. I was unearthing myself with nothing but a pen to gouge out and excavate my insides, but I was doing it. Word by word, sentence-by-sentence, notebook-by-notebook, the endless array of thoughts and images came streaming out of me to expose the hobgoblins and therefore liberate them onto the page.

There is nothing so painfully delightful as being seized and overtaken by an art form when attempting to cleanse, divulge, and purify one's chaotic insides. Oh, perhaps art is merely a crude, and obsolete method, one which a little prayer and some sound humility might not accomplish in a tenth the time, and yet perhaps not, for when you get right down to the cesspool of the soul you find that you're dealing not only with your own imponderable universe, but with the entirety of history and humanity, perhaps even the interminable cosmos itself, and so to take the irreversible plunge within is not so simple after all.

The only person I saw during this time was a brilliant, lachrymose woman about my age who had recently lost the last member of her family, and therefore was floating unanchored, as far off of the earth as I was and not binding me in any way to the ground. We were quite a pair, a regular couple of disembodied phantoms with barely enough flesh between us to make a baloney sandwich. We were so far away from life that we could only meet in the unproblematic stratosphere where touching and sensuality have no jurisdiction. It was a purgatorial dimension up to which we effortlessly arose and commingled; an abstractedness from existence which felt not unlike a careless Nirvana compared to the complications of life we had both, in our own ways, fallen away from.

We would rejoice in a passionate, grace-filled, fleshless and platonic communion over a few joints and some wine and allow ourselves to forget all that had come before and all that was to follow, for there was little more either of us cared for, or could accommodate, than that.

Oh, to be sure, life was no torture chamber, and there was always a bevy of young strumpets flitting about in my wayward existence. The Vancouver area, in fact, is a romantic fool's playground- what with the surfeit of idyllic hot springs, out-of-the-way cabins, choice little valleys and alpine meadows, and the earth's ever-present sex scent to get the juices flowing. For the lonely hound there were always enough uninhibited, bright, and talented wood nymphs roaming about who were often more than pleased to tangle in the pleasures of the flesh just for the freedom and joy of it.

The city seemed to attract these fresh, adventurous, west-coast vixens who just loved to coax you down to the sea with their clothes off, splash about, and then share a bed under the starry sky.

And to be sure, there is nothing like coupling with a most willing, sensual, free-spirited woman, on the wild coast, under the greatest cedars the earth has ever produced, amongst all the glory of mother nature's finest. The two go hand in hand. For in the heart of every woman, just as in every man, is the unquenchable love of being naked with the earth.

The Gods tossed us out of Eden, but they couldn't toss Eden out of us. It's as simple as that. At the center of every human being is the desire- the need- to be unclothed and frolicking, untamed through the untamed wilds with desire and passion in their souls.

This understanding was well hidden from me in the puritanical denials of the east where I grew up. But not on the coast. It must be the salt air that loosens up the loins and sets us free to enjoy the more rudimentary pleasures.

I remember driving out to Bamfield, on the west coast of Vancouver Island, with three young women one summer, then hiking out along Barkley Sound until we arrived at the beach where we planned to camp. I had not even time to put my pack down before not one of them had a stitch of clothing left on and they were suddenly splashing and swimming about and then taking photos of each other and I was watching the whole innocent burlesque show in disbelief.

It was a similar experience the first time I went with a couple of buddies and a car load of women to one of the many geothermal pools which dot the coast, and I was joyously astounded to see how they, like we, couldn't wait to get to the tubs, strip down, and prance about in natural glee.

I must have been cornered as a youngster by a demented Calvinist or something, because I had no clue that this kind of thing went on. But soon enough I had assimilated this delight into my working reality, and it was a solid fact that if you took a bottle of wine and one or more of the hussies out into the wilderness, all of the sudden you were Krishna with the gopis and the pastures were limitless.

To take your lover from behind, doggy-style, on a big, flat rock overlooking the sea, is to inscribe the Kamasutra on the trade winds, and send your liberating incontinence across the entire frigid land.

I was gaining some notoriety with my colleagues at work who saw my occasional parleyances into the vulvic playground, which caused them to gossip a little flame into a wildfire of licentiousness. Little did they know that I spent most of my time alone, staring off away from the fleshy forum and its contextual limitations. Little did they know how nothing in my seemingly free-spirited and bountiful life had sufficed to quench even a fragment of the eructating miasma welling up within me. Little did they know that I was riding on a conveyor belt through a chasm whose walls were a thousand feet high, and within which, as I was going along, I would come irregularly upon one of these delightful female companions for a brief encounter, only to find that they were not on the same conveyor belt as myself, and I couldn't get off of mine, though I tried desperately often enough. And so the tryst or friendship would soon become a memory full of longing and loss as I watched one after the other drift away and out of sight while I turned another bend in my unassailable canyon.

This observation I wouldn't fully understand until I was living in that loveless dorm, and had fallen so far away that I couldn't even remember from where. And so there was nothing to do but dig my heels in and take the labour on, for there was no other option, because to not take it on meant to freeze in front of the monsters, and then be devoured and shot back out like a disfigured piece of excrement.

I was in the pit of lions, and there was no denying it nor was there escape. The only thing to do was to forget everything else, take up arms, and learn to survive down there, inside myself; learn to sit deathly quiet and listen as the mongrels roamed about, and then learn to leap out and bludgeon them before they could attack or fight. I had to enter the eternal night of the self with my senses heightened and guns blazing. The creatures and bugbears were waiting for their game, and to avoid their cunning I had to go after them and meet them in their own lair. I had to become a hunter, then a cave man, then a Neanderthal, a Homo erectus, Homo habilus, a prosimian, a dog, then a bear, and then the lion itself. I had to go all the way back, back into the dark and unknown, back to where it all began, if I was to make it through the dungeon of the underself.

I am certain that the Bardos[8] which we encounter during life are as weird and fantastic as those after death.

As the ground-water tide within suddenly surged up, breaking the surface, and the rigid life of pattern and habit began to sink and dissolve below the surface, I had to learn to breathe with another set of lungs, and to look out through another set of eyes, beneath this thick, primordial soup waiting to engulf and ensnare me. To survive the descent I had to learn to stand and face the darkness, and to become not only the hunter, but the prey as well. I had to forget the eagle nature of my highest self, and become a common gull, an ignoble scavenger, if I was to survive the dereliction of the soul, and the chaos of the night. I had to become low, and stay low, so as not to be shot out of the sky, skinned, stuffed, stuck upon a wall, and forgotten.

There are caverns and caves of lost and unknown universes within us. There are inexplicable domains, unheard of beasts, incomprehensible, infinite labyrinths, and armies of bandits, forces, and fiends. To dive within yourself with reckless abandon is to enter a netherworld divorced of logic, rules, succor, and comfort.

The chthonic realm took me in, spun me around, twisted itself about, contorted and confused me, spat me back out and hauled me back again; it let me think that I knew where I was, who I was, and what I was, and then it inverted everything, converted everything, crammed the cosmos through a meat grinder, changed the pattern and the context, distorted the form, brought me to peace in its prison, and when I thought it was all over and I had escaped, it exposed the endless chains and walls around me, laughing at me, torturing me, feeding upon me, and making me wish I had never looked in, nor entered, nor awoken in the inescapable, phantasmagoric, underworld within.

And yet it was there I had to go to conquer the anarchic forces which possessed and controlled me from below. It was into this abyss of fantasy and non-meaning which I had to plunge without hope or promise of a way back. And I could neither grieve nor petition, but had to stay down there and fight until all of the dragons had fled or been slain. And that, it seemed, was a greater task than building a hundred pyramids with a butter knife, or flying to the moon on a kite.

The distance became infinite before I knew what was happening. I was swept down the river and out to sea without saying goodbye, nor taking care of my things, nor grabbing onto a life preserver. At first I swam against the unbeatable current, then capitulatively treaded water for a brief period until I was utterly exhausted, and that was when I was forced into the survival position-head down in the depths as long as I could bear it, and then up for a quick breath and a peak around at the unrelenting ocean, all the while being taken farther out, and losing all hope of ever being found, and my head would have to go down again, holding my breath under the surface of life until I would almost explode, then up for a second and back down before I sank, trying desperately to live beyond my ability to live.

I existed for a great duration like a gypsy of the mind; within the infinite, boundlessness of being did I wander aimlessly from one inhospitable region to the next, never finding my home without nor within me. For the limitless Self is a strange, atopic land, at times indifferent to our changing whereabouts.

I sought myself so far within that I held no sincere hope of ever returning.

Like a camel did I drink insatiably of life before leaving, but I went too far; on the desert journey of becoming I had consumed a vast portion of my rations in order to get away, but I could see no welcoming oasis. I ran blindly, without direction, and charged recklessly into lostness.

Nothing, nothing, nothing, so much of nothing. To walk and walk, down the empty streets inside oneself, past empty houses, amongst empty people, while nothing matters except to keep walking, because to stop means to succumb to the madness, futility, boredom, fear, weakness, or shame.

I became accustomed to the loss of everything, to dying in life, as they say, and to having no function, no responsibility, no place, nor role in life. This was the loam upon which the seed of my spirit had sprouted and taken root. There was no turning back, I had already come to that dreadful conclusion. I was outside of life, a foreigner to all that is.

I had come fully undone; whatever had mattered no longer mattered. It was a time when I was allowed neither God nor the world; a time when I was on the outside completely, and a place from which it seemed I could not get back.

But if I pursued what the world considered impossible, if I desired what the world proclaimed could not be had, if I required what mankind could not offer, and demanded that which no one could give, it was because I knew one thing, and it was that I had to go for it with everything I had.

I had to take my failures, doubts, and discouragements, and either cut them loose or carry them on my back up the hill.

To walk away was easy. But where then to go? God knows? Just away. I had left no marking by which to find my way back, for I was never returning. I had to forge ahead without thought of right or wrong. If it was God's need to strike me dead for some unavoidable error, so be it. That was God's need. I had to move forward. The further I went, the further I had to go. I had to look ahead without any memory or regret.

I saw clearly then that the point of no return *is* the starting point; if you can go back ...you have not yet begun.

It was one of those events which went on for so long that I forgot to think that it may ever come to an end; I forgot the possibility that something or someone might come along to scoop me up and take me to shore- and so I came to live only in the reality of the survival mode, forgetting that peace may exist because I forgot that I was not at peace, forgetting that suffering may be lessened because I forgot that I was suffering, and the days and nights came and went without a change because this, I thought, was what life is, and this was all it is, and so I looked for no land ahead, did not wave at passing boats, nor did I think to beg for relief from God, because there was only myself and the endless deep which held me until I was beyond holding, and from which I came up for a breath only to quickly return to the depths.

At these times I beheld consciousness in the grip of the hallucination which invented it. I fought like a Titan wrestling with his own powerless shadow. I drank up an ocean, and pissed out a world. The planets swarmed to knock me down. The winds howled to defeat me. The moon cast thunder down upon me. The sun went dark. But I kept on going, moving on, or something, to somewhere. I was walking through the Self. I was going. Didn't know where. No one came with me. Still I kept going. On and on I say. I kept going on, on and on. Lonely as the wind, strong as the tree which withstands it. I kept going and going, on.

It seemed as if from the outset I was set adrift and my whole life was a journey back home, a home which did not exist because ...I was supposed to be adrift. And it was this alienship to all being which was in fact my true birthright, my inheritance, my blessed freedom from all that dies. And the momentous movements out and away were the caustic baths of purification, the baptisms by fire, the parched and deserted lands the spirit is left to eternally roam.

I had to go on ...because I could only go on; because once you have gone a certain distance, even if it be digression (or perhaps especially if it be digression) you cannot return from such remoteness, you cannot find your way back, ever; you have scurried about in the labyrinth's dark expanse an irreconcilable distance. Once you are away, you just keep going.

While everyone else had been carving out a niche for themselves in this life, I was filling mine in. While everyone else sought to be found, I inherently sought lostness; and by this I inexorably betrayed the continuity of the manifest, and fell in amongst the chaotic, foreign beyond. The sun set, the moon rose, and the night became my homeland.

I became a refugee from being- I came to exist on the periphery of everything ...that is.

It was a fine, horrid enterprise that branched and widened, flooding out into my dreams.

In the vestiges of that engulfing miasma, dizzy in the peaceless calm, I flailed against life in a merriment of fears, and shivered around the lost fire.

I sang though I was mute, jumped though I was lame, and loved though my heart was hard as Hades'.

Cold in the stupor of reason, life bled listlessly from my soul.

Hardened in the chaos, I listened without hearing, touched without feeling, and changed without becoming myself.

Softened in the realm between victory and defeat, the Great Play consumed the player, but all that remained was the spent, broken shells of yesterday's home.

And yet exiled from the continuum, I performed intangible duties, healed secret ills, and reckoned with imperfect eyes.

Oh yes, here and there I grasped and held onto things, to thoughts, and to lies. Later or soon I was forced to let go.

When predicament ensconced the days, oblivion forsook them.

Resignation became my fountain and my thirst, while misery tangled about in the lyre.

Fear crept in through the fissures of my nothingness. Sadness purged it out. A hollow conduit of incompleteness was all that remained. Through this the Source oozed rapture and healing into my unclosable wounds.

It was never enough. The distance itself was damnation. I was alone, absolutely alone, and only the pit of my troubled guts had the honest strength left to grieve it. There you have it.

Still it was all a miracle, of that there is no dispute.

How I saw it is all that can be said, not what it was I saw.

Aglow and wandering, free of context and meaning, writhing unkempt in the dark, terminal madness of becoming, it was the decadent insomnia of consciousness that held me gripped and staring. I was an unclosable Eye, casting about hither and yon, hunting frantically for a mirror to find itself within. To look, to see, to comprehend.

New Eden, old crime.

*

thirteen

This was how I found myself, years down the road- somehow alone and distant from everyone I had been close to and I couldn't even try to swim back to them because when I entered into the survival position I did it because I was thoroughly exhausted, and it was the last resort, the last act of which I was capable, and nothing was left in me to attempt another option.

I was alone in the subconscious and conscious alike, listening to a voice I alone could hear, following a star I alone could see, and chomping on a bit I alone could bite into.

It was a path which I chose without knowing what was coming, which was impossible. I only came to a fork in the road, made my decision, and never looked back. There was no point in this. I had to keep my eyes straight ahead, my ears cocked, alert and prepared for anything which might come at me. But I was never alert nor prepared when something did come, and usually I was knocked flat on my back and held down to the ground and gnawed upon by the hyenas of the mind until they had had their fill and let me back up to lick my wounds and debrief myself on the terrible lesson.

Oh there were inwardly magical times as well. Often there was nothing more delightful, in fact, than sitting down in the afternoon, having finished typing into the computer the notes I had taken the night before- one of the only disciplined acts I maintained in my runaway life, but one which I took seriously, and rarely made excuses to avoid- and after eating lunch and having put what few tasks I allowed to invade my researches in order, I'd uncork a bottle of homemade hooch, light up a cigarette, and sit back, relaxing into the aimless mental space which would be the open window allowing the inspirations to blow in, lift me out of myself, out of context, and out of the ideas which bind and constrict the work, and then do my best to pen a sentence or two describing what I could hardly describe, and then I'd fall back into the space and the oblivion, openly awaiting another dispensation.

I was a willing and excitable, cheap-as-they-come harlot; a regular whore of the Muses during those years. The little morsels they'd fling down to me sent me fluttering about inside and hankering for more of those the crystalline moments in which everything would stop without ceasing, and the non-movement which exists prior to being would flood in and couple with the ebbing movement of life, as the substance and shadow converged in an orgiastic, contiguous array.

Were a sentence to emerge out of the clatter and clang, and end up on the page in some agreeable, unique, or odd manner, I'd have a fit of satisfaction and exuberance, and then I'd ease back into the space, and wait for the next installment.

There I would sit. Alone. Silent. Waiting. Willing. And in that space I would also occasionally come upon the place where words could neither come nor go- the place where all ideas ended, where the mind gave up, and where the full complexity, marvelous absurdity, and stupefying profundity of existence would descend upon and consume me, and I would be held there, gripped in the claws of mystery again, a thankful and delighted victim, never wanting to be released and given back to the vulgar and profane world of concept and false light.

Ah, how the paradoxes of life exist to deny and also fulfill us, as I found while hovering in suspended animation all those years. What I found is that the self behind the self cares little to be assuaged, or entertained, or encumbered by the exigencies of participating in the manifest; I found that there is a livingness which is made obvious only when the subject falls ambivalently away from the object, and behind that screen of boredom the witness, which refuses to be enticed into, or amused by, the passing artifice, becomes obvious. And so the ego must abate and lay down like a beast of burden confined to its squalid little pen, and the self behind the self must become the focus of consciousness if the wheel of samsara is to be ground to an effortless halt.

In a way one must be tired of life in order to find Life, for the never ending round of creation and destruction is only stopped when the vehicle runs out of gas. And so the stimulations and distractions of modern life only come to create a riot of digression in which the captivated soul flits about like a pinball, hither and thither, and never comes to settle in the ambitionless lethargy of the unbothered and purposeless self behind the self.

It is only through this lack of outreaching, lack of attainment, and lack of care that the undamned flood of gyrating, antecedent energy pours into the awaiting absence of the impoverished, open being; it is through this living, womb-like abyss that the universe spins itself out, funneling into its own spacious accelerator, mixing, swirling, fermenting, and exploding out of both ends of the antipodal cylinder. And so it is through the positionless, directionless, unaspiring host that the influx and outflux intermingle and give balance to each other, while the acolyte of apathy hangs precariously between the two worlds, hovering at the estuary of being and non-being, where only those who have evolved in both the salt and the sulphur can survive. Here the creator and created dissolve from their differences, pattern is shifted, form mutates, and the infinite essence betrays its hidden laughing volition. And this is the shift which turns the soul toward home.

When you have learned to endure this reality, that is when you fall in step- you stop walking in the maelstrom of the mind's apologies, you spit for the last time on the ground, halt short in your tracks, forget the reason you were moving, forget where you were headed, why you were going there, where you are now, and who you are. The earthquake of your life ends softly, and you realize nothing of what you were is you. The mad movements are merely over, the interference has cleared, and the blessed congress of perverse redemption forces you out of the storm. The clouds blow away. The birds begin to sing again. The children come out to play. But nothing really changes. The clarity of your absence negates nothing. You still sleep, and wash, and hope, and wait like before. And yet ...and yet, something has changed. Everything has changed. And that war is over.

    It was from that estranged position of absent presence I was chronically basking in while living in the desperate melancholy of the loveless Ivanhoe, that I had an experience which would provide a clear and indisputable sense of a form of love which would make relationship love- although blessed, and beautiful, and one of the most precious gifts we have in life- seem like a surrogate revelation given to us before we are capable of being bequeathed our fullest reward.

    What happened was a far stranger event than I had ever imagined. I was in my room, sitting alone on a decrepit mattress, in that sorrow-soaked building, listening to the mad shouts and grunts of patrons entering and exiting the bar below, and at some point during the evening I must have totally switched off, that is about all I can say- I left, and in walked God's love, filling an absence I did not even know I had. It was as if there existed a tunnel running through me all of the sudden; in fact, there was no me, only the tunnel, and the incredible, healing, accepting, connecting, and redemptive flow of divine love was rushing through me and emanating out onto earth, and I knew without a doubt- in the unquestionable clarity of such a blessing- that this was a miracle that could heal the agony of loneliness and separation which was so prevalent in the substratum of every human life.

    There was an immense feeling of ease and tranquility accompanying this love, and I saw that if I could continue allowing this to happen through me, I could then walk through the world casting the grace of God's love wherever I pointed my hollow attention. All the while this was happening I was doing nothing, it was just happening, and I couldn't understand how; I had no idea of the way in which it came about, nor how to prolong it. It was beyond my reason, and filling the room, and I was mentally trying to understand the process- how was I, who had never felt such transcendental power from this type of divine union, and who, without choice, had become an empty channel through which this love was now pouring into my vacant room- how was this benediction possible, and how was I to further its happening?

    The love went on for quite a while, and I contemplated and received it, and my brain could make no headway as to what I was doing, or what I had to do, to allow this love to wash through me perpetually. And then, as the wonderful feeling of the invasion of God's love was fading out, an answer came to me about how it would come again, if ever it did- an answer which made no logical sense but which I knew was *the* answer- the only way in which it was possible for me to become an empty conduit of divine love; and that answer, which spoke unequivocally to me back then, was simply: "Be yourself!"

Ah, but of course, it suddenly made sense. All I had to do was deny nothing, repress nothing, be ashamed of nothing, and the clog in the conduit would be washed away and nothing would remain to block the flow.

Looking back I get the sense that I was being given a lesson at this time- a brief experience of what I was not at that period of my formative existence capable of fully attaining, but what was certainly a goal worth striving towards.

I see now that Divine Love was visited unto me back then, at a time when I felt as far away from it as ever I have been. It was as if I had to get to the furthest end of the anode in order for the cathode to discharge its load and force me back into equilibrium.

And now all that was required of me was to actualize the divine fiat- to be *myself*. Ah but what a task this would turn out to be.

*

fourteen

As a young man my mother told me that a mother's job was to give her children "roots and wings", which I suppose it is, although, unfortunately, as hard as she tried, for the most part I had neither roots nor wings, but was more like a dandelion seed blown about in the air, and so I flew, but not by my own power, and was part of the earth, but rarely grounded.

My father once declared "We are spirits having a human experience, rather than humans having a spiritual one", which is true, although, again, I was often neither spirit nor human, but only an amorphous mass of energy and form, unable to live in the world, and unable to escape beyond it.

My mother's second husband, however, said perhaps the most pertinent thing of all to me when I was young; after he had finished expounding about one of the world's scientific understandings, he turned to me and confessed, "But we really don't know anything. We don't know anything at all."

It was this Socratic disclosure which was perhaps a prophecy describing my awaiting confrontation with conceptual lostness, or mystic ignorance, as it were. And by that I mean that during the years to follow, of struggle and disorientation, while attempting to 'be myself', another psychological valve eventually broke within me, and this new rupture became a massive turning point, because it shattered my novice reality and sent me out into the same old world, but as if I had never truly seen it before.

This event I have called, in retrospect, my hallowed unawakening. It was an experience that has colored the rest of my days ever since, for better or worse, of that I am not certain. It came upon me one evening in Vancouver, as I was strolling leisurely home from a friend's house, after a night of revelry and merriment. I had fallen into that controlled and somnambulistic gait which comes upon an individual traversing the same path which they have walked back and forth many times before, and therefore they can drift off onto auto-pilot, as it were, and let their legs alone ferry them home.

And so I was ambling along, most likely deeply invested in one or more of the many questions that chronically plagued me at the time- the whys? and whats? and so ons of our existence- questions for which no one has of yet provided any reasonable answers. And I suppose that I had chased these fantastic conundrums down to the furthest reaches of which I was capable of attaining at the time, and from which, like a fool, I had expected to return to the surface with a proper answer and so be done with the business of thinking then and there, and then get on with the rest of my awaiting life. Boy was I in for a turn of events, for the exact opposite of my expectations happened; which is to say, at the height of my questioning I was suddenly and inexorably struck dumb with the very fact of existence itself, and, more specifically- *my* existence. What I mean is that I came to an abrupt halt in my peripatetic speculations, my mouth slid helplessly open, I clenched at my forehead and froze- I had become immobilized by the implausibility ...of being, and, more specifically- of my being. And yet this barely describes the state of mystic exasperation into which I had fallen.

I was in the mystery, and ...*I* was the Mystery. Finally I had forgotten everything. Everything. Nothing but a blank, brilliant slate remained. Even that nebulous, impossible word 'God'- even that- I forgot what it means, and, more importantly ...what it does not mean.

Everything came unglued. Everything melted away from probability, imaginability, and conceivability. It was as if my own *I* had suddenly seen the unlikelihood, absurdity, and inexplicability of being such a thing as *I*- of a self who, moments before, knew what a self was, and was nicely contained in names and ideas and the soft numbness of little understandings. But now that very self was the disbelieving center of its own incredulity. That self, which had been nonchalantly pondering over the hidden secrets of existence- that self was suddenly struck and amazed and shocked and stupefied by ...itself; as if the whole universe had inverted, and only mystery remained, and at the core of that mystery stood an *I* which did not know what *I* was, and was now so utterly flabbergasted that all the walls of meaning came shattering down and there was nothing this *I* could do to recreate, or define itself because what was this *I* and what could or would it do if it knew what it was. I was back again at the center, and the *I* alone was there; only the *I*, peering in and astonished that it *existed*, finally uncovered, finally cast back upon itself with no foundation to support it, rapt and stupefied, wondering and gasping for a way out but there was no way out and the awe turned into exaltation and something fell away from me at that moment which has never again re-grown. And thank God for that I say.

As I stood there in the middle of the night, holding my forehead, I slowly regained some of my faculties and walked on further, but then the whole mad show came tumbling down again, and again I stopped without intending and grabbed at my head and my mouth drew open, and again I was caught at the center of the fabulous miracle of self. The surging wonder and questioning went on and on right to the hub of the wheel, so to speak, stopping all and everything in its tracks. This happened a number of times and my life was inextricably altered forever.

Oh, nothing was solved in the maelstrom of my new, immanent ignorance, but, let me tell you, life became a mystery again.

The marvelous magnitude of being had suddenly swelled ferociously up and consumed me whole. Nothing was left which was able to obstruct it; no walls, no thought, no intention, no me. There was neither curse nor praise, but only a transparent, sober nothingness. I was the dumbest man alive. *I was free.*

I have often said that in that single instant of absolute wonder- when suddenly I forgot everything I had been told from day one- I lost my life completely. That is, I lost my life, yes, but not Life; I lost only the blind, heartless wombat I had been made into by others, and by my own spiritless cowardice and sloth.

But after it all came together, or perhaps fell apart, in that one irrevocable, passionate invasion- I was emancipated of all thought, and when it was over I was as if embalmed in a viscous mix of incapacity and exaltation. I was baptized in disbelief.

As if caught in a blessed vacuum of incomprehension, I had fallen helplessly into the infinite mystery where even God did not know himself. I was cleansed in a deluge of hallowed disremembrance, and had the stupor of Noah after the flood; the world was swept pure and clean of taint. Every last speck of the man I was, or had been, was no longer; every idea of truth, every reason, want and torture- everything was done. I was done. But that's what death is anyways- you begin again. What's gone is gone.

I finally recovered enough of my senses to return to the functional delirium of facts and figures, and as such I made my way home that evening. And I slept that night like a new man who didn't know what it meant to be new, nor what it meant to be a man, nor what it meant to *be*, and when I awoke the next morning all I could think of was returning to the splendid magnitude of that wonder.

I now return as often as possible to that zone of unbound grandeur, to the foundation of this exasperating, inexplicable world. Sometimes I can forget entirely where I was, where I am, where I am headed, and forget everything that has gone before me, everyone I have ever met, and even myself. I forget it all and float off into the reverie of the untethered spirit, with neither anchor nor meaning to hold me to the ground.

And yet I have never fully returned to the height of that initial insurrection. I have never since that evening been allotted the power of that staggering vision of the immanent mystery which we are. To be sure, at quiet times, when I am oblivious and empty and have settled back into the source of my soul, I can still walk part of the way back down that blessed tunnel; I can, for brief moments, re-experience the benediction of that bewildering night when divine ignorance swept me clean of all that was and is and gave me wings to forge on through the densely knotted morass of mankind's misconceptions, but I have never come undone like I came undone that night. I suppose that this is the way it must be, for were I to have continued in that state of rapture and idiocy and not come out of it, I would surely be locked up in a loony-bin and eating baby food through a straw. I say this without exaggeration; for the human life, the way we live it, cannot sustain these types of ecstasies for any great duration; not, that is, until we are done with our work on this tepid and sluggardly plane, and have returned again to the liquid fire and bounty of our ethereal homes, which is a dream I carry with me- that when I am done with the labors of this life I may be privileged and capable enough to fall away from all of it again and to return without ending to the living core of the eternal, implausible, wonderful, mysterious self.

Until then, however, I have no reasonable explanation why life is the way it is. I know only that in that inaugural, tempestuous night of absolute astonishment- when suddenly I could not believe that I existed- I know that this event was God's first conscious glimpse of being incarnated as ...me. Who? Me? Who is this me? How could this be? What is this that I am? I do not know and yet I know it was God struggling to believe within me.

Writing all this down reminds me of a dream I had when I was eight years old in which I fell out of a boat into the water and the Devil grabbed my foot and pulled me under so as to capture me. But as I was descending I suddenly transformed into a little infant, and the Devil looked at me, and because I was only a child, he had to release me.

I suppose that my later experience of profound wonder and of childlike innocence of mind, as it were, some twenty years further on, was the fulfillment of that dream, for I was made free from being held captive in the manifest the moment I became ignorant and did not understand what this life is about, why it is, or what I am which is *it*.

I have related these events quite a few times to others, in an effort to share the effect of these experiences upon me. But then I wonder, why am I trying to convince others of the profound lostness of incomprehension that is so debilitating within me? Am I suggesting that one ought to willingly learn how to not know? Should I seek to condemn others to these outlandish confines I must exist within simply to experience myself? Do I seek simply to establish a city-state of wonder, inside an oligarchy of despotic facts? What is to be accomplished by confronting such debilitating unfathomableness? Have I, because of its mildly euphoric qualities, forever banished myself into my own polished stupidity? What is the use if I am merely claiming, vehemently, to not know what is not knowable? Have I been hyperventilating petty truisms? Flatulating ontologies? Have I sought only to parade the mind's inadequacies? Am I merely claiming all others truant from the gymnasium of contemplation? Am I but a weak man flagrantly bragging about having found the strength to bear weakness? Or am I the only fool who sees through unmystery into mystery? Have I legitimately witnessed the unimaginable event of being? Or have I been deceived by the intensity of a false experience? Was I simply soaring over a great abyss and mistaking it for height? Am I but a dwindling salmon, instinctually bursting with its own continuance, yet tragically fighting its way up the wrong river? Must one simply be cured of the mind? A spider extricated from its own binding web? And do I attempt to continue not-knowing because of such pleasant, profound absorption? Have I set myself adrift on the dubious raft of doubt so as to escape an inhospitable certitude? Have I simply exaggerated my confusion by assuming a possibility of clarity? Have I improvised a certainty out of everything that I am claiming to doubt? Have I embraced nothing from this world except the disorienting effects of my own confusion? Has the ability to enter into a perspective which cannot conceive itself become my way of avoiding knowing, however erroneous? Am I more comfortable being thoroughly baffled than being wrong? Has not-knowing become my latest justification for the anguish associated with interpretation? Why is it that I struggle towards the intense lucidity of nescience? Have I invented my own ignorance to cloud over an unbearable event- being? Do I merely hope to consecrate these unavoidable misunderstandings into a more practical, soothing obliviousness? Have I concluded it all unfathomable, rather than it being quite fathomable, and I am simply unable to fathom it? Has the incredible impact of not knowing deceived me into abandoning myself to it and it alone, and then never seeking a possible knowing? Has ignorance become my latest defense, absolving me from confronting unavoidable perspectives? Have I been deliberately confusing myself, intentionally focusing upon what I am definitely not capable of perceiving, so that I would not have to acknowledge what I can see? Is non-understanding an honest outcome of contemplation, or merely a defendable subterfuge- a hideout from the known? Should one cease to be astounded by the astounding? Should one go further than astoundedness? Should one even lose lostness? Does wonderment itself eventually stand in the way, and it too must be cast aside? Is rapture the wet nurse of a growing temerity? Has awe become my latest addiction? Have I been forever trying to feel at home in this world, most recently within the foreignness of incomprehension? Must I abort everything; capitulate into total, irredeemable possibility? And ...and will that be faith?

*

fifteen

Soon after that thorough cognitive emancipation I was back again in the torment of context, back in the created torrent and foam of urbanity. I was on the diastole of my ventricular cycle- living in the city so as to gather some dollars, as they say, and return again to the bush.

Now, however, I was certainly done with the Ivanhoe and all the ills and glories which came with it, for, along with all the other infirmities of the city, I was also helplessly stricken with unrelenting insomnia, which I had endured for much of my time in the urbane blender but which had reached its peak in the stale air of that loveless mortuary, and which had left me, at the end of my last stay, often walking about in a wearied delirium.

Many people offered their amateur advice on how to get rid of the sleeplessness- none of which I took, because I don't take other people's advice, which is a policy of mine that I cannot remember ever breaking since I recognized its necessity- though in the back of my flustered mind I knew my sleeplessness had nothing to do with the drinking, improper eating habits, or lack of exercise; it had to do explicitly with the false light and false noise of the city. I had become too open and sensitive towards these poisonous intrusions to find rest within their artificial spheres. The tireless internal combustion engine and glowing streetlights became hated enemies of mine. Nowhere could I find peace from the ongoing hum and drone of man's imbecilic rushing about here, there, and everywhere. And the offensive light, oozing into every crevice of even a well-curtained room, would pour in and never let me into the deep tranquility so necessary for body and soul alike. I know this now, because the instant I returned to the wilderness, with its gentle, hushed sounds, lack of obstreperous tintinnabulations, and dark nights- no matter what Luna was up to at the time- I would sleep in dead calm from the moment I closed my eyes until Sol began to peak his head above the horizon. And this without ever changing a single habit: I drank no less, ate no differently, and exercised no more.

This made me wonder if most of the cures and medicines available today are not simply synthetic counterbalances to allow people to continue living unnatural lives, in unnatural settings.

Unfortunately I was now in the unnatural city, and wondering where I would turn to find rest and dream when all options had been exhausted?

Ah, but another simple question merely preceded another simple answer- one which came to me as I was looking towards the north shore mountains from the pit of the tangled and tortured east-side of the city, and I suddenly realized how much wilderness lay just beyond Vancouver itself. I had lived clandestinely in the forest while I was working in Alaska, surely it was possible to find a place to hide somewhere in the vast expanse of woods near the city; a little piece of flat ground to build a small shanty and live like one who exists in two worlds for a while again.

I was no Jerry the Bear man, but I had fallen in love with the earth with such intensity that men and their ways came to take on ever darker and darker shades to me. My eyes came to need the gnarled and inexplicable trunks of ancient cedars, my feet the soft and unpredictable step of futon-thick moss underneath, my ears the play of the wind and the songs of the birds, and my lungs the crisp moist tickle of the west coast air. How soothing the true wilderness was to my soul compared to the riot of mankind's ubiquitous pandemonium and all the noise which came with it.

And so I stepped onto a city bus that day, headed out of town, and got off at the last stop on the line- as far as the public transit would take me. Off I went with sledge and saw, rope and tarp, ardor and victory, and thundered up the nearest trail a short way, then turned off of it, through the bush, up a ridge, over a rise, and onto a small level area where, instantly, I knew I had found my home- a place to be near and not near the city, in and not in the wilderness, alone and not alone, a part of the world and yet apart from the world. It was quiet, beautiful, soothing and ...free.

And so I hacked out a little area near a bluff overlooking Howe Sound and the Georgia Strait, built a small pole-frame, hung a tarp over it, built a bed out of some twine and six-foot cut branches, created a stone and mud fireplace, hauled up a sleeping bag, some candles, and a water jug, and within half a day I had a hidden hut with a million dollar view, no rent, and, more importantly ...no noise.

This little hermitage would come to serve me well over the next few years as I came and went from the city. It became my Thoreau's cabin, nicely tucked away from society, convention, money, and all the ills these are kin to.

When people eventually heard about this and about my regular pilgrimages out into the bush alone, occasionally a friend or acquaintance would offer their admiration that I had developed the skills necessary to be so self-sufficient, and then they would go on to generally bemoan their own incompetence which kept them from such liberties. This type of comment I would quickly rebut, declaring that the only skill necessary to survive in the wilderness alone was the ability to endure oneself, everything else one could learn in a minute, for wilderness living required nothing more than a tent or tarp, sleeping bag, lighter, compass, and a bag of granola and raisins. Because to be in the wilderness meant to *be* in the wilderness. There was no need to go on an extended hike or paddling trip; the shortest distance required to get away from the hubbub was all that was necessary, it was far too simple.

I reckon this observation of mine- that the only talent one needs to be in the wilderness is the ability to be alone- and that means lonely- is why a certain well known wilderness school ends each of its courses with a three-day solo session, in which each person must not only apply the practical skills they have acquired during the course, but must also be wholly *alone*, which is a different type of aloneness altogether, out in the bush, instead of in the city where, devoid of company, one still has books, radio, television, newspapers and all the rest of the cosmopolitan clutter which never allows one to fall back into the abyss within themselves.

It was that abyss I would enter, up in my hut, sitting alone, watching the glorious sunsets over the strait, sipping port or whiskey, occasionally lighting up the pot-pipe, and wondering, as I always wondered, where everyone else was; wondering why the million and a half other souls down there in the city were content to sweat their lives away only so as to own or rent a crumbling piece of the tormented ant's nest? Where were the others- and there must have been others- who also had been driven like spiritual lepers from the herd? Was I the last man alive from a lost tribe destined to wander unbelonging amongst the children of men? Forever banished, forever outside, forever longing for a world in which our spirits mingled in a singular dance? Where was my tribe, my people, my peerage? Where were the ones who, like myself, belonged to another life altogether?

I was determined never to be harnessed, nor blend-in, nor lose myself in the traps of mankind's errors. I would only dissolve, and live, and become whole in the remaining untouched wilds of our sick and agonizing earth.

I had no home, no responsibility, no bills, no future. I lived in the cold and rainy forest, ate beans and bread, drank cheap wine, made love to wise and beautiful women, learned my own lessons from my own heart, and spoke with God occasionally. I would not trade that period of my life for the whole world.

Despite the love and spirit at the Co-op, I had no real desire to work at all. I was chronically well below the poverty line, and yet I always lived well, traveled many places, drank my share of hooch, and ate plenty of good food. Which makes me wonder if the poverty-line should actually be called the distraction-line, for when you fall below it you have not the disposable income necessary to disguise your true lostness and confusion, and therefore when you fall below it you truly are poor, because you are faced with nothing but yourself, and when you face yourself long enough you begin to see that you are impoverished inwardly as well, and then you're done for.

I say that back then I was effervescent, insouciant, and unknown as the hard and calculating establishment set in to divert and impede me. I say that I was mad and driven to the center as the sides wound to bind me further. I say I was wild and wounded but strong and indefatigable as the whole collapsed inexorably in upon me, and yet I leapt up, dissolved into myself before I was doomed, and the All fell right through itself. Then the winds shifted, the spirits rose, and I flew off without a thought, a regret, or a failure.

I had realized what it means to be a master- to be the master of one's self rather than a slave to the manifest. And that means to live on one's own terms, and to never bend nor be tricked by fear, guilt, or false ambition. It means holding your own chosen course in the sea of mankind's effluvium and disordered consciousness. It means not so much of finding out who you are, but in choosing who you are, and then in being that completely, without a doubt, a worry, or a shudder.

To live purposelessly on this earth for a while is a true stunt and a valuable asset to the rounding off of one's character. To step out on the limb where meaning can't follow, where the world sheds it's linear veneer, and the self sheds all definition, is to walk on thin ice over a bottomless ocean. But at times there is nothing like it. Once you get a taste and a liking for it there is little in life to compare.

The world's grey and banal ways become hideous intrusions into the electrifying and vertiginous heights one can soar up to when the mind is finally addled and the new eyes opened.

To exist in that simple state of disorientation, to desire it, and to need it, is to detest the world of action, purpose, and reason, for these add nothing to the glorious endowment but only obstruct the joy of the glide.

I wanted only to continue not belonging, not understanding, not trying, nor seeking; I wanted to learn to hover in the full-blown magic of life and to fall away without caring. I wanted to desist without conviction, to melt into the mystery laughing and aghast and to be done with mankind's useless games forever.

Oh indeed, the gentle rhythm of the spirit is all but wholly extinguished in these days of unnatural lives and vain actions, and I cared for none of it. Think of what it is to be natural, and you will understand how far astray mankind has gone. Nothing but clothing, clocks, fences, signs, pavement, television, telephones, engines, school, weapons, banks, business, bureaucracy, politics, borders, rules, passports, paper, condoms, surgery, pills, walls, wire, forks, knives, cans, haircuts, makeup, shoes, sports, shovels, stores, diplomas, titles, careers, money, rent, hospitals, hotels, holidays, furniture, wheels, churches, names, dams, factories, fools, failures, fanatics, and so on. The whole mess of it one great, terrible lie. A pandemonium of pernicious delusion. All of it. Everything we have created we have done at our own peril. We have walked away from the beauty, and joy, and the miracle of living. We have made heaven into hell. And there is no way most people will change until God lines them up and puts a bullet through the back of their heads. And who can wait for that? The only option left is to steal as much of heaven back as possible; to work little, need little, spend little, to live and dance and hold your brothers and sisters in your arms with one eye pointed to heaven and one eye keeping a watch on mankind, and never to deny your heart its inmost yearning.

It is the spiritless fears of society which have led to our current destruction. That is why we live in little boxes which block out the light and silence the wind. That is why we live with blind eyes that can hardly see, and with hearts that barely feel. That is what they have done to us.

And though it is easy to accuse the world of the contorted conditions of the day- for certainly therein lies no innocence, and I will never forget the perpetual atrocities committed by mankind which succeed only to further lead the individual away from their true self- in the end it was not the world which bound me into the prison of the false life, but my own trespasses therein, and eventually I recognized that it is up to each of us to stay or to leave, forgive or hate, to doubt or to believe, and until a person comes humbly to that arduous understanding, all their little games of emancipation will merely build more solid walls.

Oh, but how strenuous it is to live free in a world which honors the hard parts; to be on your own, completely and only dependent upon yourself, where no institution, nor church, nor school knows or is inclined to empathize or assist you. To live as a spirit is to be outcast and dishonored among men, because to live as such means you must break their rules, scorn their taboos, and destroy the lie they've come to believe in, for they know not yet that God is insane, and that all who run with God must be mad as well. God exists beyond reason, beyond meaning, beyond right or wrong, even beyond hope. To be with God means you are done for; you are now vermin, now a fool, now a traitor, now an eyesore, now a useless and incapable, worthless specimen of mankind. That is what it takes, that is what God requires. The only question remaining is- are you up for it?

To live as a spirit is to feel and follow the true pulse of the true heart of the true life and to live from that core and that core alone. It is to ascend to the level of the living dream, to enter the portal of sublimity, to exist on the diaphanous plane of passion and piety. To live on this tired earth as a spirit is to enter the stream and get lost in the current, it is to ride the wave that never crashes, and to slip through the walls of false being, false meaning, false worth. But you must live it. You cannot read about it, talk about it, or understand it. The only thing to do is to let go of the world and grab hold of the sky. To embrace the wild fecundity of the soft reality. To banish all fear, expectation, comfort, and worry. To find your essence, grow your essence, be your essence. To live as a spirit is to never set down, to never alight, to never get caught. It is to give way to the Juggernaut of mankind, but to not give yourself away. It is to look to the birds for example, to the trees for love, and to the great soul for communion. To live as a spirit in this spiritless world is to enter a realm which no one else belongs in nor understands; it is to break the veil and dance along the membrane; it is to punch a hole in the heavens and send a flood of life down through yourself to a world of disbelief and anguish. It is to relearn a way of being which will mesmerize and horrify your fellows, and in which you find a new set of ups and downs, losses and victories, sorrows and joys to which the world is wholly blind. To live on this earth as a spirit is to become a spirit, and that means- if you are strong and sedulous enough to maintain it- to break the chain of causality, leap off the wheel, and to leave this hardened world for good.

I had tried long enough to devour our ancient, dyspeptic ambrosia, our emetic soma, and our indigestible manna. But I had come with an insatiable hunger which the world could not satisfy. I was hungry for Life, and I began to eat and never have I stopped.

Perhaps two years into this way of life I was to have a dream in which Death came for me, and in the dream I expected that this was the end, that I was done for, but then suddenly I grew strong and sure, and turned upon Death, and in a furious attack I slew the Death which had come for me, and it was done. And I awoke and knew I had conquered the great foe of this world, that I had chosen and become Life, and that Death had no power over me any more.

And so I say, the hero of today must go beyond heroism, because heroism requires a victim who needs rescuing, but Life requires no victim. And so the real hero saves nothing and no one but lets each and everyone rise and crumble of their own accord and volition.

The hero today is simply the one who finds that part of life which is not a tragedy- which is to say, the hero finds *Life*- and then lives life for its own sake, no matter the direction nor meanness of the day.

To live life is to bring your death back to Life, and then to bring Life back to mankind- back to this mummified race, caught in an endless cycle of delusion and imagination. To live life is to take Life down into the lair of Death, and to dance upon the tombstones.

To live life is to tune into the music of the spheres, to open up and give your whole soul to it so that it will get inside and move you. And when it seeps in and grabs you- grabs you like a wave in a waterless ocean- then you must dance like hell, and never stop dancing. You must rise to the rhythm and song, touch the earth beneath you, kick off your shoes and forget. You must hold your curses, and pocket your blame, because, Spirit, you're only here to dance.

*

sixteen

It was from my humble hermitage that I would engage in attack-and-retreat missions into the center of the cosmopolitan cyclone. These sorties were largely necessary due to my primary addiction- writing and research- which was not easily carried out in the bush, for I regularly required new books, a reference library, and also electricity and a computer plugged into it for my daily inputting and editing of the disgorged muck I had scribbled down the day before.

I was lucky enough to find a couple of drop-in centers for street folk- of which there are aplenty in this maritime city- each with computer facilities available for all the aspiring down-and-out poets who populate the dark district and its muses. And so I'd saunter down from my hill in the morning, leap on a bus into town, grab a bite to eat, and then jump on the keys and start hammering.

After a couple of hours of typing and editing, however, I'd be bug-eyed and ready to disengage from the screen. And this was the moment when the main problem of street life would become uncomfortably obvious to me: where to go to get some peace and quiet when you have nowhere to go to get it.

Of course, back up to my shack is the obvious thought. But if I had plans in the city later that day and the weather was foul there were only a couple of indoor options available- the pub, the library, or a church. Lord knows that the pub was most often my venue of choice, but when I needed real peace, and real quiet, neither the most deserted bar nor even the isolated catacombs of the library would do. So off to church I went.

In Vancouver there are a handful of quiet, large old stone churches in the inner city, and I'd make my way into one of them, find an out-of-the-way pew, sit down, cross my hands, close my eyes, and let the calm wash away the belligerence of the streets and the unavoidable visual pollution which is everywhere and so destructive to the innocent eye.

On one of these occasions, when I was seeking refuge from the outer torrent and sitting peacefully in a church, recovering my inner poise, all of the sudden the lunch crowd came hustling in, a priest arrived at the pulpit, and a Mass began.

Just my luck, trying to duck out of the ever-present hubbub and I couldn't get away from it, even in God's own house. I was just about to split, expecting the whole affair to be mentally excruciating, and make my way instead to the library or a bar, when it dawned on me that I had never witnessed a Mass before, and why not stick it out and see what all the excitement's about. So I sat back down and didn't get up again, despite the regular up and down robotics of the sinners all around me, and surprisingly I even entered back into the calm which had just been stolen from me moments earlier.

It was in this calm that I began recognizing an aura-type glow emanating from the top of a table behind the priest. I had seen auras before, but never one coming from an inanimate object. This caught my interest, though I questioned whether I was seeing just a beam of light refracted through one of the many stained-glass windows nearby.

Well I kept watching and the priest droned on with the Mass and I continued to struggle to make out what the object with the aura was. It seemed, from that distance, to perhaps be an urn, which I concluded was a likely object in a church, and there was no reason why a person's cremated ashes didn't emanate an aura after the bonfire. I had been contented with this erroneous conclusion for only a short while, however, when people began filing up the aisles for communion, and the sexton grabbed the object- which was no urn after all- and placed it in front of the priest. Then I saw that it was in fact the chalice holding the communion wafers, and the aura was all around it.

Well, that was certainly something unique, and it was enough proof for me to instantly decide that whatever kind of Ritz Cracker they had in that cup was soon going to be in my belly. And so up I got from my pew, strolled down the aisle, kneeled down, and received my first communion.

Then I got up, left the church, and headed for the pub.

I would come to tell this story of the chalice with the aura a number of times over the next many months to some of my disbelieving friends, most of whom looked at me askance, as if they suspected that the last chugging synapse in my overwrought cranium had finally stopped firing and now I was truly coocoo. However, I maintained the authenticity of my vision- as I always did, regarding every odd or peculiar event I witnessed or experienced, despite the predictable onslaught of doubt and chastisement from the earthbound rabble- and perhaps two years later I was informed, by my *soror*[9] no less, that Carl Jung had written, in his essay on the Mass, that the vessel for communion wafers, blessed by the proper individual, can in fact contain the body of Christ as a reality.

I was vindicated again. And not only that, I had consumed the world's most energized biscuit- the body- into me, and had washed it down a few heretical minutes later with the city's cheapest beer- the blood. And who wouldn't shout out a hosanna and raise a cheer to that?

So street life had its fortunate side at times. But if the days are tough to endure for the homeless, the nights are even harder. And if, instead of returning to my hut, I had to find a place in which to lie down within the city limits, which occasionally I had to do- if I was working at the time and had an early shift and no bus was running from my hill at that time, or if I had been out carousing too late and had missed the last run home- I'd have to seek slumber elsewhere.

At one point, for about a two-week period, I stayed in a Catholic Men's Mission downtown, at a time when I was so broke that even bus fare to my shack was an economic burden. And so I was given a bed and some meal tickets for a while and it was a tolerable enough set-up, filled mostly with downtrodden and fringe types, some of whom were seemingly just out of prison, and others on their way in. I did, however, meet one unique fellow who slept on the bunk beside me for a while. He was staying there for a different reason than most; he said that he had been living in the east up until a month earlier and then one night he felt a powerful pressure and force in his stomach area- which, as he's describing this, I'm thinking it's a *hara* awakening for sure- and then scenes of mountains and the ocean flashed before his eyes and he suddenly knew, with an inexplicable certainty, that he had to go west. So he dropped everything and took off with the little money he had, and there he was.

He was a good connection for me, for it was nice to meet another soul who was in the state I was in- that is, penniless and living on charity- and not because he had rejected life, but because he had affirmed the spirit. I expect that he was supposed to meet me as well. In fact, I can say that many times over the years I have ended up in places I never would have expected, only to meet someone who had ended up there as well, without intent or expectation either, and I came to understand that things like this were sublimely directed so that meetings like this one at the Mission could occur, and so myself and the other could exchange thoughts and connect our spirits through the eyes, and then part without ever being apart again.

Occasionally I'd have a dream of a person before meeting them, and in the dream there might be intimations regarding the reason behind, or nature of our time together. For the Body, like Osiris, was scattered all over the earth, and I, like Isis, was laboriously finding and rebuilding it.

When the last dawn breaks overhead, I will herald the day and kiss this plane farewell. When the last sun sets I will raise a cheer and toast to our redemption. When the glory-bell gongs for the final hour, I will go down on my knees and thank the one who knew me. When the divine dream is done, I will awaken and claim my own. When the last wound has healed I will throw away my sutures and take up my lyre. When the last foe is felled I will toss away my sword and return to my song. When the final child is born, I will fight with death no more. When all the angels have again their wings, I will fly in merriment amongst their flock. When the light comes down from the sky to take us up, I will go home.

But, back then, it was to the homeless streets I returned. There were many times when benevolent friends had given me the key to their apartment or sailboat, to house-sit while they were away on a trip- which happened often enough amongst the group of outdoor fanatics I was enmeshed with- but if that option had run dry, I would sometimes head down to the beach to find a place to crash.

As such, one evening I was out late and wandered down to a beach where I had slept before, expecting to lay down behind a log and drift off into dream, but there was unfortunately a party full of young degenerates going on, and they looked as if they were going to be there for a while, so I cleared out and went to find another spot. That night the hidden powers must have been toying with me though, because everywhere I went somebody showed up to disturb me, or the lights were too blaringly bright, or the traffic was still too loud, until finally I found a small parkette tucked away from the night crowd and noises, and lay down ready for slumber. As I was about to doze off, however, I heard an odd hissing noise and the sound of rain, but the sky was clear and I was wondering what was up, and then I realized that the park's sprinkler system had just come on- a sprinkler system in a rainforest, what a joke; I knew instantly that it was there simply to chase away any would-be idlers and layabouts like myself, a thought which irked me and made me want to see Sodom sink to hell- but I had no time for such justice as I had to quickly gather up my sleeping bag and backpack and dart away just as the shower came down right where I had been laying. The nitwits. The insolent jerks who hide away in their overpriced sepulchres and plot continually on how to wreck life for those who are still living.

Anyways, now it was about four o'clock in the morning and I hadn't slept yet and I had to work early, so I decided, in a bewildered state of desperation, that the roof of the building in which I was employed was the best option for me to catch a few precious winks without hassle, for then I could just wake up and be where I needed to be anyway.

So I got up on the roof, and was slowly losing the need to be comfortable on my new cement bed, and I had just caught the first little glimpse of the welcoming netherworld, when a flashlight was suddenly beaming in my face, and the security guard for the Co-op, my Co-op, was all a fluster and he'd already called the cops to come and carry off the threatening drifter. So I had to come fully awake and explain to the plastic policeman that I was an employee, and explain why I was up there, show him my company card, and finally he radioed the comptroller and called off the flatfeet. Then he left me alone to watch the sun come up and then I trundled downstairs to work without a second of sleep that night. But that's life on the streets.

You've got to live it to understand it. You learn quickly what it's like to exist in the feral domain of one who owns nothing in a world where everything is owned; where fences and rules exist without limit, and you end up walking around in an inhospitable labyrinth in which you must keep moving, because to stop is against the rules, and so you keep going, past the shops and buildings and houses, through the corridors of the maze of private ownership and the well-policed commons, around and around you go, with nowhere to lie down, or sleep, only the chronic goad of signs, laws, walls, and roads. A dog's life indeed; a third world, haunted, homeless, beaten and kicked mongrel's life.

Urban society is designed solely around making it so uncomfortable to be poor that one is driven to succumb to the pointless and soul destroying activity of passionless work in order for each individual to simply have enough roubles in their pocket to rent a little cage and hide away from everyone else who is hiding away in their own little cages.

*

seventeen

We were born to be naked, and dancing, and kissing each other. We were born to be changeless and changing, mortal and immortal, formed and yet free. We were born to be the stillness inside the fabulous change.

The self is a perpetual baptism, wherein one moves, and moves, and never stops moving; it is the relentless, uncatchable, spectacular, dynamic of the soul that demands to be free.

We each belong to the energy of the moment. In the wildness beyond anarchy, where the individual, rampant from the mean, will accept no compromise, no help, no advice, no method, no limit- that is the point where the spirit breaks free of its mold, flies beyond itself, and dwells in the infinite expanse of the unimaginable, untethered new. To soar where no archetype can follow, that is to be new, and to be true.

Anyone who breaks free of the imposed structure, who lives life for life itself, with no worry or expectation of reward or praise, develops their own individual force, unknown to the greater part of mankind. We all have it, but most of us give it away to convention, or cowardice.

We were not born to follow others, to learn what they say we should learn, to go where others wander, nor to deny the smallest part of our own force for comfort or acceptance.

We are not alive to toil, to lie, to impress people, or to suffer. We are alive to be life- to be the great mystery endlessly awakening to itself. We are all God becoming infinitely godlike. And each of us must live it through. Alone.

God sits in a different seat in each person's auditorium. If we rely on anyone but ourselves, we are doomed; every time we deny the reality that we alone can come upon, we deny reality. And so it is the harsh but essential cosmic law that one who has no acceptance of their own vision ...shall see nothing.

Ah, to be sure, before you can blend into the One, you must stand out conspicuously, as that precarious, uncamouflaged happening so visibly bent, blotched, or broken. For in order to be chosen, you must first become a choice.

And so, within the suffocating alienship of society, we must begin the long and forgotten route through strangeness towards home; we are our own gates, our own judges, our own redeemers, and redeemed.

Indeed each of us is alone to hack out our own cramped, ponderous tunnel, towards or away from God knows what, for no imaginable reason.

The way piles up in fragments behind us, and as endless walls ahead, while we flail and flail and perhaps find nothing but the hollow ring of movement through the moldless form of unknowable truth. So be it. The bearings may be on the outside, but the compass lies within.

A spiritual anarchy of biblical proportions is now thoroughly under way. Each person must sedulously mine their own dark, mysterious life.

I came to accept that to get back to myself I could not depend on another. I could not care about what I had, what I didn't have, what I had been, what I might be, where I was going, or when I would get there. I could not care. I could only try to live completely, without imagining what that meant.

There were many times when tempting options would emerge before me and attempt to divert my way- small or trifling amusements of one sort or another, suggested under the pretext of one reason or another, offering the benefit or pleasure of one desire or another. And though I often stopped to look around and see what all the commotion was about, perhaps even striking up a short conversation or taking part for a brief spell, sooner than later I had to be on my way. Thanks, but no thanks- this became my unspoken motto. Enjoy your reality, have your laughs, and comforts, and distractions. I must keep going, keep flowing, keep moving on to where I don't know but if I stop here and enjoy the delay I'll end here, barren, confused, and out of steam for the next hill.

Just as a person falls over when they stop completely on a bicycle, I had to keep moving, keep going forward, keep pushing towards what comes and goes and flows on forever. I had to learn to be my own current, to cascade over and past all that had stopped moving and was clogging or jamming the river's way. I had to recognize and feel the stasis and fear people allow inside of them and in which the spirit condenses, solidifies, and moves no further.

I had to keep losing myself in order to find another me, keep letting life change and include me in that newness. I had to die over and over again so that ...I could live.

And now I count my grey hairs as one for each time I denied life and blocked the flow through fear, sorrow, preconception, or sloth. These are badges I wear not proudly, but am glad for their reminder of the perilous halts I put in my own way. For it was only after I had realized that all I had been taught was merely a perilous mishmash of rubbish and lies, that the teachers and leaders had misled me unavoidably, and the masters and madmen had delivered to me their flightless swan songs, so that I was on my own again, as I had been so often before- it was then, in the stillness of my heart, that I began again to listen.

I had dreamed alone, thought alone, and walked alone, and I was through with the others. Better to cast my own light into my own darkness, I thought, for then I'd be certain of what I couldn't see. And because I couldn't see, I stood dead still and ...I listened.

I listened, because all the pointless words and actions had gone right through me, and nothing remained but the inviolable hollow. I listened to the hollow of my own being, because that was the only place left which had not been desecrated. I listened, and in that eternal void alone did I hear the echo of my own Great Dream.

Oh, it is a wild and crazy untraveled road we're on. You find your way, you lose your way, you find another, and lose that one, and then another, and they keep coming and going and you keep stumbling along imagining you're going someplace, though the Self never goes anywhere, but only the form and identity find and lose themselves in the flux and flare of the ephemeral.

I say these things not out of any presumption of expertise- there are no experts in the world- but because I have never found a description or inference regarding the experiences which I have had, and so I bring forth my own fruit, and my Promethean sin is complete, and I am released and at peace with my own conscience for having spoken about what I did see.

Through all the reading I had done regarding the many differing philosophies, spiritual accomplishments, and unique realities others have experienced, all of which inspired me to tear down the walls confining me and pursue greater truths, in the end I was thrown back upon myself and had to abandon all I had learned and heard about from others.

I see now that this is an essential step- to understand and accept that no matter what anyone else has experienced, or perceives as reality, that we are each born unto this earth to discover our own beliefs, our own truths, and to live out our own lives. And that these truths and realities may differ immensely from one person to another is a hard piece of news for the mind to accept, but I had to accept it in order to believe in my own vision. I had to become an individual.

To be an individual means to exist without pride nor shame, nor yardstick between yourself and all others, but instead to live out your own life, without a thought that it might be different, or wrong, or right, because that is who you are, and there is no option, decision, nor guise. In this way does a person arrive at eternity, having been born out from under the great sea of undifferentiated souls.

If I had only blended in with the world, only operated within the confines of convention, I would have offered no increase to the dimensions of the whole. But that I extended myself out, the whole had to grow with me, since everything is a reflection of everything else.

I found that to be a part of the whole I had to also, paradoxically, be apart from the whole. For there is no symphony without separate instruments, no harmony without distinct notes, and no whole without separate parts. And this, my friend, is what is called ...the way of sin.

To sin, to be single, to dare to believe in your own vision, and to give God the greatest gift imaginable- something new, something unique, something called ...you. To honour the splendour of being by furthering creation with what has not yet ever been- your self. To dance your own dance, and sing your own song in the middle of the writhing and maddening *prima materia*.

I say there are possibilities for the modern individual which never existed before in the history of any peoples, or, if they did, these possibilities were found and exercised only by the rare few who were driven by some inward daemon to lift themselves out of context and convention and set themselves adrift above the congealing, slothful evolution of the rest of the world; but the modern individual may more easily rip through the snares which previously held history to the ground; the modern individual has the privileged chance to re-write the rules, to cast the nets of presumption and the bars of tradition aside and to face him or herself, as he or she is, alone, in the cold, naked reality of the unbound self. The modern individual, more than any before, has all the tools necessary to forsake the world and its spiritless ways, and to listen once and for all to the only voice in the cosmos which matters- his or her own.

Oh, there are plenty of excuses which the least creative person can dream up who has not the gusto nor desire to free themselves from the fold. There is a cornucopia of ways to lie away the duty of the self, and to quietly rejoin the legion of lemmings on their march to the sea. But the fact remains that anyone who truly wants to heave it all overboard and start again can do it in the twinkling of an eye.

To do this, not just outwardly, but at the absolute inner essence of all that you are, is to turn yourself upside-down, let your pockets empty themselves of all you have ever been or wanted to be, and then stand back up and walk on without a clue of who you are or where you're going. And that takes a type of courage which no one applauds, and no movie actor portrays, and no women sing songs of praise and worship about. But it is the only type of courage which will invigorate and grow the mercurial aspect of the soul; it is the only type of courage which will serve the light-body within; it is the only type of courage which matters in the end when all human roads lead to dead ends.

Such individualism is a stage of preparation, where the soul is tried and tempered, made whole, and utilized in the microcosmic realm before its final turning away from the profane world completely and its ascension into the conscious redemption of heavenly union.

And so our greatest service may be the act of spiritual violence, of disobedient novelty, which rends the fabric and sets us apart from the rest of humanity for a while, until the whole has shifted- as it must- and reassimilated our new reality into its necessarily new position. Thus we have helped evolve the universe. This is why the word 'eccentric' means: to come close to the center.

And so, I say, in the act of choosing myself, I chose God, and thus unseparated the division between us. The moment I accepted myself, I accepted the God within myself. And in that liberating, destructive instant everything joined sublimely together to become the One and Living Spirit, and my God fell from otherness into me and ...I was saved.

I ask not that you sanction what I have said. I'm not asking you to agree. I'm not expecting you to understand. I have only my own life, and my own answers. A man must stand up for the vision inside of him, especially if he is the only one who has seen it.

What is real for me must be real for me alone, or what am I calling me? I have no reason, no need, no desire to embrace another person's reality, for mine is much more real for me than any other's ever could be.

The fact that no one else corroborates my reality guarantees that it is true. *Each man, his own messiah.*

*

PART 2

In, and Of

"*Each spark descended into this world- indeed a profound descent and a state of true exile- to be clothed in a body and vital soul ...so as to join and unite them with the Light.*"
                              Rabbi Schneur Zalman of Liady

"*Man as he now is has ceased to be the All. But when he ceases to be a separate individual, he raises himself again and permeates the universe.*"
                              Plotinus

"*Be- and at the same time know the condition of not-being, the infinite ground of your deep vibration, that you may fully fulfill it this single time.*"
                              Rainer Maria Rilke

one

I had become epistemologically emancipated earlier on, during my experience of irrevocable wonder and the absolute mystery upon which our existence is founded, and yet that event was the disintegration of only one of the walls separating who I wasn't from who I truly was, for the false ego still remained somehow, and continued to inflate, confuse, and degrade me.

It is all well and good and necessary to seek and become an individual, but it is an outright travesty to then define oneself within the limitations of such an existence. And by that I mean that the cultivation of individuality is an essential aspect of perfecting the whole, but it must never be confused with the whole, or the part will become a limiting factor and not an uplifting one.

Ah, the mighty ego, the arrogating hubris, the inimical pride; these tenacious lampreys ride along beside their victim, parasitically sucking out the energy of the host. The untethered ego will betray the spirit and imprison it in the context of the world, because the ego wants to be imprisoned there, for that is where it receives affirmation, which is the only thing the ego wants. Pride will run the spirit around and around as the donkey chases after the carrot, and the only way this will change is if you ask for the spankings which correct it.

I asked, and that meant I was in for it.

The ego is a wise and cunning sleuth, always creeping in and messing up a good thing, and so the overself, when called in to correct it, must take on the roll of the punishing parent and grief giver, if the wild child is to be reeled in.

One such spanking came to me in Alaska, when I had taken ten days or so off of work so as to ferry northward and meet up with a young Parisian tart whom I had been lucky enough to trade caresses in the wilderness with some weeks earlier in Sitka. We rendezvoused again a brief while later up in Haines, gathered together some food and supplies, and hiked half a day down the coast to the end of a peninsula, arriving at a wonderful bit of paradise called, interestingly enough, Seduction Point.

There we stayed for a number of days, cooing and whinnying, drinking red wine, and watching humpback whales feed and play in the bay. On or about the third day I, the great white hunter, thought it would be both delicious and impressive to my European mistress if I was to gather some sustenance from the land for our dinner, and so I went down into the inter-tidal zone and plundered a handful of baby blue mussels from the rocks, knowing full well the whole time that during the summer months there is a coast-wide red-tide alert, and that it's best to stick to an austere diet of brie, patē, olives, and French loaf.

But an oaf is an oaf and the great white hunter scoffed at the ridiculous warning, cooked up the bounty, and polished the entire plate off, while the unimpressed maiden chose, as it were, to decline the knight's offering and stick to her vegetarian fare.

So it goes that sometime in the middle of the night I awoke and my hands, feet, and face were as numb as if a troupe of maleficent dentists had snuck down to our camp and injected me all over with heaping doses of Novocain. Only it wasn't Novocain, it was PSP- paralytic shellfish poisoning. Not such a good thing to have happen to you when you're a five hour hike from the nearest town, a hike which could only be done at low tide and I had no idea when that was, and so I lay there totally deflated and not so full of gusto and heroism anymore- just a wiry white-man who'd found a way to humiliate himself while falling to his doom.

Paralytic shellfish poisoning kills you by eventually paralyzing your whole body, including your lungs, and therefore suffocating you, and there were areas of the Alaskan panhandle which were renowned for the numbers of natives who had suffered this horrible fate. Place names like Poison Cove came to mind as I lay there wondering how much further the process of immobilization would go.

Well, as I said, the ego gets knocked down if we invite the flagellator- whom I had invited, sometime back, when I was full of oomph and piety- and I was shrunk down to my appropriate size that night with a little bit of distress and worry, but after my humbling was complete the flogging was called off and I didn't die nor suffer too grievously, and most of the toxin left my body within forty-eight hours. I recall one finger remaining completely numb for a couple of weeks after that episode as a gentle reminder of my infantility.

Things of this nature occurred often and in many different ways to me whenever my puny ego started thinking it was in possession of its own universe and had full boasting privileges. These little spankings were there to subdue any swelling sense of power within me, always pointing back at me and saying- "Look here you little worm, quit pretending you're so big, so competent, you can't even control your own pitiful life."

Oh, but how many times would I have to come to that same broken place within myself, so as to learn the same lesson, over and over again. Too many times. Or maybe only as many as I needed, until I got it right. But then, even when I eventually did get it right, and was finally through that test, another challenge suddenly reared up and stood right in front of me.

Thus I was confronted regularly with seeming contradictions; which is to say that a liberating experience, high-point, or staggering realization, which I assumed would carry me through the rest of life on a silvery cloud of bliss, was often soon followed by another descent, trial, and further struggle. But it seems to me that this is the way it goes in life. You pass one exam and you walk out the door and into another room, where another challenge lies waiting. Hercules had his twelve labors, each of which was distinct and unavoidable, and so it is with all of us. There is no single realization or experience which is the key to our fulfillment. The locks are many and the keys are many and to get through one door and to think you are free is to be blind to the new walls around you.

When one battle is over another naturally begins. And to be sure the assault does come. For just when I'd think I was in the clear, and the peace of fulfilment was oozing out of the ether from the purposeless great Self into the core of my absence, the ever enduring ego would return again, like athlete's foot, halitosis, or dandelions, ever ready to spring up and blemish the fallow ground of my godsoul, and then the patient tutor within me would turn his numinous pedagoguery to red-alert, and again calmly beat the fight and fever out of me, for the crucifixion of the ego must take place over and over again, until the re-ascent to the godself is complete.

I was slowly getting the picture, however, and learning how to stay low, so low that there were times when I would finally rid myself of my possessor, and would sink down beneath all pride and ownership, and would fall right into the lap of the master of ceremonies.

It was a parade of events like these which eventually brought about even a greater, more humbling fulfillment. This was, in fact, the experience of *my*self- the true self who had felt God's love back in the Ivanhoe.

This came about in the healing of the greater part of my personal pride and neurosis, which had seized hold of me as a young man- a young man who had built up an image of himself based upon what others had told him he was, but not what he really was, and therefore a young man who had grown up defending a mask he didn't know he was wearing but only knew the trauma of being identified improperly and who did not have the consciousness nor strength to correct the rampant error- so the neurosis had taken root and had created many an uncomfortable moment in my life and I had grown to believe it was something which must simply be endured, like chronic back pain, while one continued to shoulder the burdens of their imperfect existence.

The truth, however, would make itself clear to me one rainy autumn day as I was wandering through the forest, back in the recuperative lap of the Charlottes, with the horde of inextinguishable monkeys still on my back and howling in delight at their impenetrable hold upon my flimsy countenance.

On this trip I had been for weeks on end wrapped up in a tight ball inside, trying to figure out how to come to grips with myself, with life in the world, so as to make my peace, be myself, and get on with it. And so, as with all internal processes, the ugly sore would have to come to the surface and discharge its noxious puss eventually, as long as I was sedulous enough in my introverted gaze.

What happened this time came decidedly and unexpectedly, out of left-field as it were, because I had thought, for some unknown reason, that the issue- of how to be myself- would be sorted out by my finally having a clear vision of who I was, and fully accepting it, and then marching back into the world with a new found confidence and aplomb the likes of which would be instantly recognized and revered by all those who had known me as the skulking worm I had occasionally been in the past. Oddly enough, however, the exact opposite happened. And lucky I was for that.

What I mean is that instead of recognizing the exact somebody who had been living hidden and scared within me for the last many years, I recognized instead that ...I was nobody; I saw without a hint of doubt that I was not the identity or personality which I had been confused into believing I was- which was a somebody whom I had defended and acted as if it was me. I was not that personality. As a matter of fact, I was not a personality at all; not a unique, discernible package stuffed inside a figure of clay and then forced to justify itself to all the other clay figures who peered out through squirrelly eyes and into each other with judgement and condemnation. There was no such thing. I was the nobody self in the body of no one. It was unbelievably freeing. The walls which had never really existed, except in the distorted imagination of my mind, evaporated away and the self which was nobody within me leapt about like a bird who had just flown from its cage, for I, who had always been bound and determined to stay and defend myself at all costs ...I became nothing. No thing. And when that happens let me tell you- you're in for one hell of a ride.

My whole life I had forgotten to just be nothing and nobody but beingness itself. And it was only the journey out to the raw and notionless church of the spirit which healed me back to Being. And a wave of peace and understanding washed over me, for I could see what I had lost by my struggles in the world, and, more importantly, in myself. And I could see that I had been lifted out again, out to regain myself, my nobodiness, my soul, my me. My journey had been fortuitous; that specific war going on inside of me was over. The fight had ended, and it had ended because ...I had no fight left, no struggle, no panic, no thoughts. I had surrendered without trying. Nothing was left, and yet the whole realm of *being* remained. Not my being, although somehow I was still a part of it, because I hadn't gone anywhere, I had only worn myself out shadowboxing alone or sparring with God, and when I had no strength left in me, the effort to defend or attack was over, the battle turned into a game, the gladiator's sword into a fencing stick, the opponents became an audience, and there I was in the middle of a circus ring and waiting for the next stuffed lion to be let out of its cage.

In the hollow reaches of no thought, where the form is released from the will of the Law ...I stopped. Everything else continued. Only I stopped. I did not become, I unbecame.

Perhaps it is symbolic that I was horizontal when I hit this ground state of being; I lay there sensing existence all around me- an existence I had somehow, for some reason, been opposed to, or it had been opposed to me, but now it was over, I was finished, and that same existence suddenly took on an unaffecting, benign quality which I had never expected. I lay there in a state of immense tranquility, as if the seven demons within me had just been exorcised, and all that remained was the almost dead and yet living, emaciated carcass of the host. As if someone had come along to finally unlock the cage I was in, but I continued to sit there, because now the cage did not hold me, now it was nothing but a harmless object of interest which I had no reason to be in a panic to leave. And so I lay there, and the existence which had tortured and racked me, and which I had struggled to avoid, or take part in, or modify, or destroy, was still there, the exact same existence, only I had stopped struggling, had stopped completely, and in that total lack I was emancipated from the chains I had bound about myself. I was free because there was nothing left to bind.

Never had I understood what the word which I had read perhaps ten thousand times in my life- and attempted to accomplish but never succeeded- meant: *surrender*. And now I knew why I had not accomplished it, because surrender cannot be accomplished, because surrender is the absence of the struggle to accomplish anything; it is the end of all trying or attempting to conquer or understand life.

I had finally gone still inside the limitless reaches of meaning and mystery, where the atom consumes the universe, and the self devours the whole.

It's a bloody crazy mess to relate, but things change instantly when you're finished with life and yet living. Let me tell you, as I became emptied of the last vestige of recognition, purpose, or need- suddenly I ...I ceased without ending, and remained while still going on. I don't know how to say it better. It cannot be said. It's, like I said- it's crazy.

When the world you have loved, and lived, and laughed in, eventually crumbles helplessly about you- as it is certain to do with all of us sooner or later- and you stand humbly in the harmony of your song's last note, and the light's last flicker- it may happen that you will flinch for an anxious moment as if to right it all again, but if you're quick enough (and at times I was quick, and ruthless, and wild from the passion of my spiritual dismemberment, and wholly determined, if nothing more, to find and be myself, and only myself, through to the bloody bitter end) ...you let it go.

For it is in that moment- as the chastening reaches its cold zenith, and the degradation its dark nadir- when it all comes down, when you've lost everything you ever had- the hopes, promises, truths, pleasures, and words are all gone- and you're alone somewhere in the darkness- dead and yet living- and none of your life makes any sense, none of it, because all of your caring has only led to loss, that is when, as I said, the best thing to do is ...to let it go.

In the wash and fire of the spirit's healing, in the sacrificial disembowelment of the mind, in the fiery assumption of the grosser self, when you know you're done for, because the Word itself hovers hopelessly above the willess flesh- when the shit has hit the fan, so to speak, you let it go.

I let it go. I let go. And that was the finish and start of me.

I had been trying to accomplish what I could not accomplish, but which was accomplished the instant I stopped trying.

It had to become hopeless for me, without a light at the end of the tunnel, nor a happy ending around the bend. Everything had to crumble and be thoroughly destroyed. I had to be wiped out completely before the battle was done.

As truth faltered, as the lies melted from my self's fluidity, and the soul shed its worn out old mind, I was undone, absolutely disassembled. Let me tell you, I did not attain, I unattained. What else can be said? I had come apart at the seams in the midst of life, and walked about in tatters, tripping over them until I was nude.

To stand in the center of it all- without a thought, direction, or meaning, is to fall into the still point of living, and to live beyond the hollow of life.

It did not matter at that point anyway, because there was by then no such me to stop me now. There was no such me; there was only the great complexity, and the not-me not navigating within it.

I had dug myself all the way towards the center of life's tune, found nothing, then dug beyond to the other side. The other side, yes, but not 'other', since by then there was no center, only a tunnel ...no me. Which is to say, I disappeared in the act of trying to find myself.

Ah, to perish, to truly perish, to die while being lives on; to deplete oneself of all intent, understanding, and fear; to eviscerate the soul, to shed oneself, and to not be what remains in the ruins.

I saw then that when finally a person becomes nobody, they become a hole through which the universe can enter and become whole. It matters little whether the cup is half-full or half-empty, you drink it. The point of interiorization becomes the point of exteriorization, so they are the same.

All the things I thought and tried, convincing myself that they were necessary, only to find out that nothing was necessary but this: to cease trying to *be something*, and to dissolve into Being. For only the everlasting non-being can dissipate as such without ceasing, for it alone is the self not trapped in the form.

In those northern, coastal wild lands, where the sea and sky beat the hell out of my memory, and the birds called me by a name I had long forgotten, where the beasts and trees flipped me inside out, and the self that remained was no longer mine, I had learned to become nobody; the little man inside of me had been dragged out of the house, whipped and lynched by the delivering mob, and all that remained was a corpse now living and never again to die. I had entered the infinity of nothingness. And that made me everybody. I had become but an empty stage upon which God did everything and everyone was what was done.

When I became nobody everything inside me was gone, and the identityless nobody self within me was emancipated beyond the structure of people and things. It is hard to relate what happens when whatever you thought you were is totally cast away and all that remains is a presence behind your eyes looking out at the world. But it occurs, to be sure. To continually die into the abyss of impersonhood; to dissolve and not vanish- this is the sublime expanse of essence, anchored to the coagulated form.

At the moment I ceased struggling, and ceased needing the world to supply me with love or comfort, I began creating my own world, and my immanent universe was born. I had surrendered and become nothing, and yet that nothing was everything and was wholly alive, wholly a part of life- a fleshy, warm, wondrous, and yet insubstantial thing. That is when I began to build again the structure of the self, and to raise my own golden city to the sky.

*

two

I consider a certain friend of mine to be a fully realized master of the type of ancient surrender about which I was just speaking.

He is a brilliant, caustic, invective critic named Rick, who poses as a professional astrophysicist during the day, but at night and on weekends he removes his ivory-tower spectacles and returns to the glossy gazed outlook of one who couldn't care less about anything, and wouldn't budge an inch were the whole show to either vanish away before him, or keep chugging along on its merry and despairing way. It's all one and the same to him or any other person who has learned that there is no difference, and so has become freed by indifference.

I suppose this noble acquiescence came about for Rick from all those years of investigating and contemplating the bewildering expanse of the nebulae, the magnitude of which must have placed mankind's comparatively minuscule concerns and accomplishments into their proper station in his mind. When you're dealing in angstroms and light-years, the relative dimensions of humanity's efforts and ways tend quickly to fall between the cracks.

One time when I was visiting him at a telescope, on an observing run, this awful and emancipating reality came plummeting home to me, and, in a way, put me also in my proper place. It was when Rick pointed out a tiny speck of light on the enlarged observing screen used by professional astronomers to magnify the telescope's image- a speck of light that was so infinitesimal it had to be amplified thousands of times for the human eye to even perceive its presence. And yet, as Rick nonchalantly pointed out to me, this was not a single star, but a cluster of over a million stars. That staggered me. That disintegrated me.

I have always loved the belittling feeling of lying on my back and staring up into the night sky, attempting to envision the enormity of the cosmos, but rarely have I felt the full-blown awareness of its imponderable immensity as profoundly as that evening when Rick pointed out that singular, trivial speck- one amongst trillions, one which I could not have even seen with my own eye on the blackest of nights. And it was only a tiny cluster- a mere million stars or so. And there I was, sitting on earth- a little satellite chunk of limestone with a few buckets of water sloshing about on it, which was imperfectly orbiting a small to medium sized star, one star, which we had decided to isolate from all others and call it a sun, our sun. In that moment I became a speck of dust.

No wonder then that life for Rick had become but a trifle at best avoided- an unfortunate bagatelle, which could hardly be tolerated by one who had long ago assimilated this humbling reality into his head.

I say Rick is arguably the most intellectually capable, and cognitively incomparable person I have ever met. A walking supercomputer who can ingest, digest, and regurgitate a limitless amount of data and information about all and everything, and then instantly flash on his mental screensaver which in bold italics declares- *"Who Cares!"*

I recall my personal astonishment and respect for the level of passionless attainment he had arrived at when one day, years earlier, he and I were out and about together, walking around town for no better reason than we were in town and we were walking about, and suddenly a thought came to me of something we could do, some action we could undertake or partake in to enliven the day and bring us some stimulation or other. And so I turned to Rick and presented my inspired option, expecting that he would appreciatively accept the possibility of engaging in life in some way or other. Boy was I in for a teaching. Upon hearing my puerile solicitation, Rick turned to me and, with the surrendered ambivalence of only the most advanced adept, he looked within me but for a brief, disconcerned instant, and then rhetorically remarked, "Why not?"

Two simple words, but let me tell you it was not your average "Why not?" It was a "Why not?" that came from nowhere and went nowhere; a "Why not?" that resounded out of a mind vacant of expectation of succor or release; a "Why not?" that was without hope, and yet beyond the childishness of hope; a "Why not?" that can only come from one who knows that all is lost and nothing ever was ours to be lost; a "Why not?" owned by no one, presented to nobody; a weather-beaten wanderer's "Why not?" which comes from the stolidity of enduring endless days and nights in the over-conscious perception of life's failings and limitations; a "Why not?" that came from one who had arrived at the lucid and immoveable acceptance that there is no solution, no way out, no solace or reprieve, no grand hurrah! waiting up ahead; it was a "Why not?" that implied no "Why?" for it was obvious that whatever must be done would be done *because* it didn't matter whether we did it or not; a "Why not?" so profoundly at peace and unconcerned that I was set aback and shaken to realize that compared to him ...I still cared. And yet I cared in the wrong way, for, compared to Rick, I was like a little puppy, agog in the world, sucking pathetically away upon the dry tit of the dead bitch who had recently spawned me, and wagging my tail in expectant glee. And Rick was my stoic elder sibling, come out of the desiccated womb just moments before me and yet years ahead in reality- light years- and he stood aside, gazing off into the distance, and waiting for me to come to the painful and necessary recognition that the milk of life wasn't gushing out, and that we were in for a great duration of waiting and hunger.

Back then I was still a somebody attempting to placate the gnawing hollow within me, but Rick had come to know that no earthly food could fill the pangs of absence we were destined to live and grow with, and in the end to learn to thrive upon.

I suppose that it was the presence of his acquiescent psychic atmosphere and aura which would, a while after that day, provide a most startling revelation for me- one which would come to modify the entire structure of my outlook on life and its inexplicable occurrence.

It was a springtime venture which found Rick and I escaping the cosmopolitan sewer for a few days and driving out to the southwest coast of Vancouver Island, where another acquaintance of mine had constructed a wonderful little squatter's cabin by the sea, complete with solarium, bunk beds, and wood stove. This little hide-away was a remarkable feat of energy in its own right- it was a structure which had required no less than one hundred arduous trips upon the half-mile of precipitous embankment along a hidden path leading to his building site, down which the fellow who had constructed the hut had carried all the materials and tools necessary to complete this splendid little chalet on government land along the coast.

Anyway, the owner was away for a while, and so Rick and I made our way down to the hut and settled in for a few days of beer and gooseneck barnacles, wine and philosophizing, idleness and the ingestion of some of mother nature's psychedelia- the magic mushroom; a combination of which would send me out into the ether on the mind of God, and bring God back home as me.

I say this with absolute candor and humility. I say that it was under the bewildering influence of the intoxicants, and perhaps the proximity of Rick's previously mentioned psychic predisposition, that I found myself one night sitting back with my eyes closed and witnessing what I could never truly describe but what I can best suggest as the dynamic, uncreated, convulsing, primordial energy of the universe; the fiery, orgiastic rippling cauldron of molten *prima materia*, cascading about within me, and then pouring out into the world as form[10]; and it was upon opening my eyes that I recognized what I had never conceived as plausible- that I was carrying within myself this living, undulating, cosmic clay which I was projecting out and thus manufacturing the world; which is to say, I knew then that ...I was God, and that we are all God, effortlessly producing a world yet without a clue of how we are doing it. I was making everything that night. The whole thing. That is, *I* was making the world, but not the I who the world thought I was, not even the nobody who I was, but the *I* which lives before the me in all of us; the original self, casting out the glowing, red, swirling energy of creation, out of the core, out of the mind of God, out into the realm of form, figure, and content.

And let me tell you I was laughing. I was laughing a laugh I had never laughed before in my life. I was laughing God's laugh- the God-laugh which has never known care, nor worry, nor entrapment; the God-laugh which sprays out the universe from the immanent, infinite, incomprehensible bliss of formless consciousness; the great, emancipating God-laugh of hilarious nonexpectation, disbelief, and ambitionless wonder at the impossibility and unavoidable realization that I, God, was creating the miracle of creation.

I had come to exist in the non-existent space. An infinite bridge across a finite chasm. A flame within an inferno. A drop inside the storm.

I was in the storm. I was the storm. And everything else sped up and catapulted through the living stasis of my soul. It was an exhilarating, innocent act of creation; I gave ground in the hollow of my wonder and the world grew through that infinite hole. The unworldly, horrible stillness in which I basked seemed impossibly to produce the song of everything else. How is that possible I haven't a clue. Not one.

I can only presume that the whole shmeer about becoming what you are, or what you could be- but as yet you never have been- eventually comes right back to where it started- to you. But when it gets there- and let me tell you it gets there, with all the fire and brimstone of your day- there is no 'you' left to conceive of it. Because, instead, you conceive it, immaculately conceive it.

That night the prisoner and the warden had changed places. Good and Evil fused into one. And God leapt up for joy inside of me.

The primitive understandings which had so embalmed me all my terrible and fabulous life instantly vaporized away, and the Creator's eyes ...looked through me. The pulsing, primal, fluid medium flowed out of me, I did not know what I was making, nor how I was doing it, but to be sure it was me.

When finally you encounter the Great Soul, you will not hesitate to call it *I*. You are the source of all things. All of it. Like the root-stock of a great underground rhizome, when you stick your head finally out of the ether, whoever is around you ...is you.

That night the hut and the intoxicants had provided a vision of our most true, inward nature for me. And though the experience wore off, the underlying belief in our divinity and creatorship remained with me, and was to be confirmed in many much more sober ways in the years to come; in future years, I was to experience the infinite vastness within, out of which the motion-picture of life is projected; through the great, vast, dark space, the light shines onto a blue-screen within us, and that image is what we assume is the 'out'. Yet there is no out, there is only the Self, God, I, spinning out the universe from the measureless dark space concealed behind the blinding white light.

That evening had provided a unique shamanic experience, yet the mushroom is but a window, it is not a way in; it lets you see the manifold realm of spirit, but won't let you enter. Its effect is like winning the opportunity to be Mayor for a day; you may sit in the mayor's chair, eat lunch with the secretaries, attend a board meeting, and cut a ribbon or two, but you're not really the mayor, could never run the celestial city, and you wouldn't stand a chance of getting voted into power. The only thing you get out of the experience is a newfound desire to become a Mayor. And that road is long and hard if you choose to take it.

After that trip with Rick the profound implausibility of our integral creatorship would occasionally congeal in my disordered thoughts, and the true gist of what I had come to see would make everything, including myself, take on a different appearance, a new and awkward slant, and with a sort of incredulous acceptance I'd look around at everything and softly declare- "So this is God."

To this day, however, years after that initiatory experience, I still do not understand how it is that this could be, but I know, for many other reasons now, that it is- that we are all God making this absurd, awful, agonizing, and perverse world, and somehow, somewhere deep inside, we are enjoying it with the delight of a child with a magic wand, and we are laughing a laugh that will never end, nor understand, nor care that the joy will go on and on and on.

When the creator wakes up as the created, it is astonishing. When the created wakes up as the creator, it is unbelievable, for God cannot believe that he or she could be the person that they are. And not only that, even if God could believe it God cannot understand it. And that is a hard thing for God to accept.

The closer you get to truth, the less it makes sense, for truth is created and not absolute, and therefore when you get to truth you have to go past it, to the absolute, which is beyond all reason and measure. If a single truth existed other than God the world would come to an end, for that truth would have harnessed the unapproachable absolute which emanates its formlessness without being capturable, and so to trap it in a truth would be like putting wind in a jar and then closing the lid. No more wind. So what we condense down and imprison with our systematized, conceptual effronteries simply creates a windless world of closed jars and everybody pointing at their own hermetically sealed insults and calling these reality.

But now God had unfolded before me, and I before God. The all had become nothing, the nothing had become the all. As I faded away, God remained. As God left, I returned. The God which broke me, also built me up. Through rack and ruin the ship I have sailed glides from unknown sea to unknown sea, is sunk and raised up within each ocean, the wind blows, the shore fades, and ...I accept.

*

three

I had now realized I was God while still I was not yet a man; to be God was easy- there was no sorrow, no effort, no confusion, no care, no duress- but to be a man was a much harder, much more heroic task, for that meant I, the creator, had to accept all that I had created, whether I remembered doing it, comprehended it, or not. Because of this I couldn't really *be* God until I had really become a man, which was my ticket into the true heaven, and one for which I would have to walk the whole way on my own and mature in the crucible of experience and assimilation. And walking the whole way meant to become so small from the gigantic effort, so hollow, so supple, and absent that, in the end, I, a man, could walk through the doorless god-membrane like a ghost through a brick wall. Which is to say, I couldn't cross over into creatorness until I had become my creation. And no drug, nor mushroom, nor meditation, nor shortcut could help me do that. For though the windows of heaven be polished clean from time to time, so that any by-passer can look within and view the delights therein, there is an intransigent gatekeeper standing on guard, and no one is getting in until they've been given the key to the invisible door.

Soon after that experience, and the defragmentary healing into nobodiness which had occurred on the Charlottes, I would return again to Vancouver, and for the first time in my life, I was to stand amongst my colleagues and mates as if I was looking out through a hollow tube into a display of animated wax figures, each imagining that they were a thing inside a body which they called ...me. And I knew they were only trapped inside the form which they were not, but to get out would mean having to relinquish their 'me'- it would mean having to become nobody, and I assumed few, if any, were up for the humiliating mortifications required to undo their somebodiness delusions into the purity of the great absence.

And so, as in each of my previous descents into the steaming pit of stool, it wasn't long after my return this time that the empty, peaceful, defenceless nobody I had won- even more spectacularly this time around- began to accumulate the taint of separation all over again, and to take on the ghastly garment of identity- of creation separated from the creator.

To come back as a nobody to a city of somebodies is a difficult, if not impossible, task. I have heard of established yogis and saints who have the matured presence of nobodiness within them which cannot be moved nor destroyed by the assault of the separated somebodies, but I was not one of them, and I had to accept this limitation.

In returning to the metropolis I could feel the pyramid of my macrosoul shrink and be compressed as I encroached upon the city limits, bombarding my emptiness as soon as I re-entered the world of pavement, pollution, square corners, and signs. I could feel my soul shriveling, my vision narrowing, my breath growing shorter, and my heart slowly pumping less and less blood to my over-stimulated head.

The openness I had attained meant that my shields were all gone- that anyone's repressions or dark energy could enter at will and deposit their fetid load. I had become like a karmic garbage-dump which could only get so big, and so, as I said, had to be incinerated every so often so as to return me to the purity of emptiness.

And the only way for me to do that was to leave it all behind and find a way to purge it out. And so the wilderness became my sanctuary and sanatorium, for there is no stillness in the city- it is not intended for such. The city is where one goes to accomplish great things and become somebody. The city is no place for a nobody, and if you go there as a nobody you soon become a somebody unless you sit in your bedroom with your door locked, your eyes closed, and your ears plugged, and, frankly, what's the use of being in the city if you're gonna live like that. So I found myself launched in the gurgling stream of humanity again, back in a body, and an identity, and answering to a name that made me into a person, who existed on earth, and had desires, and needs, and hopes, and dreams, and friends, and foes, and in an instant the emptiness was gone and I couldn't imagine where it went, nor could I even remember it at all because as soon as I was full to the brim the amnesia set in and I'd forget what it felt like to be free.

And yet I could never forget, because there was a part of me which would not let me, the part of me that remained out on the coast, that never came back with me, and therefore would gnaw away at my broken spirit until I realized I had been caught again with my nose to the grindstone, cramped within the walls and rules and laws of the concentration camp again, and the lightness of my being had been turned into a knotted bolus of indigestible compost, and another war inside of me had to come to an end. Or I had to come to an end.

Life in the city was beginning to feel nothing like Life at all. As such, back at my own primordial, fenceless hide-away on the hill, one night, on one of my solo ventures, so to speak, I had another of my most profound experiences, which would corroborate my subtle sense that something was wholly amiss with life as I knew it; a feeling which had been smouldering within me, and the flame of which would suddenly be blown into an all consuming inferno of undelight.

The horrible episode of which I speak came about the evening after a day in which I had stumbled upon the Apocryphal account of what had happened to Adam and Eve after their exile; what happened to creation after the creator was forgotten. I say this with absolute, undogmatic, unorthodox candour; I say that this one book is perhaps the most important, and heart-wrenching books so thoughtlessly- or perhaps strategically- excluded from the Old Testament by its ancient, God-fearing editors. This short work is the unexpurgated exposition of the horrors and troubles which transpired in the hearts, minds, and lives, of our- symbolic or real, as you will- historic ancestors.

I sat there reading it in the library, astounded, aghast, empathetic, disturbed, and distraught, for there it all was, finally, in unabashed black and white, an almost exact description of what I had known and felt all along and which the world of the lie had chosen to effectively deny and bury; there it was- the great division, the exile from unity, the confusion, the agony, the contrition, petition, and ...the irreversible sentence. Out went the Old Adam and Eve, out from the fabulous union and love of the Godhead, out into the guile and distortion of manifestation, into the struggle and loss, and, most disastrously- the separation. There it was, what I had known and felt but could not relate to anyone who did not feel it as well- which was nobody around me- and that is: a separation had occurred which was calamitous to our spirits, and which we now longed to correct, somewhere deep inside, and though the despair had, over the centuries, been pragmatically repressed, each of us darkly remembered that intimacy and warm union with each other and the heavens which we had enjoyed once, and we remembered also the sentence and the separation which would bring about a life of toil, loneliness, and death.

I knew that somewhere long ago that horrible chasm had indeed occurred- a division of what was not intended to be divided. To remember the Fall is to remember when we could fly. To taste freedom just makes unfreedom that much more punishing. Life is an odd requiem for anyone who has the remembrance of heaven, however subtle or obscure. Why we lose ourselves at every moment to the lie, and do not flow in laughing rhythm to the eternal tune cascading through all of life and all of time is not a mystery to me anymore. I have seen clearly what the brotherhood of men have wasted in their useless, spiritless, and abject pursuits. I have seen how ninety-nine percent of life is but a tragic interruption from the moments of ecstasy and freedom which are our birthrights, our privilege, our true life.

And the sentence was irreversible, the covenant could not be broken, not yet anyways- not until God took on the same bitter medicine which had been handed out and finally descended back into the separation which each one of us endured; not until the God within each one of us descended out of the garden and into the mire, so as to return that part of ourselves we had so long ago abandoned back to the peace of the One. But perhaps I am looking ahead too far.

Oh, there will be many who read what I say and see it as nothing but pure bombast, poppycock, and fairy-tale. That is no concern of mine. Until an individual comes to see, feel, and know the separation of the Self, for themselves, that person will continue to live life and assume that misery and loneliness are a necessary quality of the show. The problem for me was that somewhere, barely below the surface, I remembered what it was like ...before the Fall. And *that* is what had made life unbearable. That is why I had cared for nothing but to wake and live through the day, to love the sun, the moon, the birds, and the trees. And that was hardly enough and far too much.

I was wild and I was listening. Listening to the song of the wildness running free and through me. I was hearing the old music that no longer flowed with the discordant ways we were dancing together. I was trying to dance to the old tune of the new heart, the heart buried and bound by the mind for so long that to finally unleash it was to explode in euphoria and anguish; it was to stand in the morgue of life, and swirl and be taken by a fiddler no one else could hear.

And so back up I went to my little hermitage on the hill that night after reading that account of the exile, and I sat up on a clear bluff overlooking the Georgia Strait, and I indulged in the body and the blood, so to speak, and then waited for the serum to soak in and the ethereal transmission to begin.

Perhaps an hour later I was on my knees, bawling like I had never bawled before, weeping Adam's weep, and crying Eve's tears, because I was living what they had lived, and I knew it now, without a shadow of a doubt. And I looked back from my *dominus flevit*[11] at Gomorrah and could see the electric lights shining shamefully in the distance, and all I could sense was the misery, separation, pavement, deceit, noise, pollution, confusion, and loneliness, and I howled with agony and wept on and on and saw no hope, no possibility for mankind, only the endless pain, conflict, and damning oblivion which would never allow an end or healing to it all.

It is as if I had tapped into God's own repressed anguish. And when that happens it takes you under, it takes you way down, and wrecks you on the bottom. And even if you can rise up from that, and make it back to the surface, a little piece of you will be left in the depths of agony with the others.

What a night of grief indeed. The grief of the entire world, built upon eons of isolation and sorrow, a grief that oozed out and consumed everything, and would not abate because we were together once, and now we were in fragments and the fragments were against each other and how on earth to make it through.

How on earth, indeed. For little did I know that the Earth was part of the answer. Little did I expect that at the height of my hopelessness I would be drawn to lift my head, and look across the bluff upon which I was writhing, and to see a giant, bowled, moss covered boulder with a splendid old pine behind it, gnarled and weathered, and bent cascading down over the rock. And with absolute certainty I knew at that moment that the earth was hearing my woe, and beckoning me, and offering to hold me. I knew at that moment that the Earth was the Mother, that She was everywhere, and right now She was in that tree and boulder, and She sought to hold me. And I stood up, walked over, climbed up, and laid down in the hollow, under the tree, in Her arms, and as I lay recovering and dozing off I felt a warm, loving, living form all around me, coddling me and caressing me, and the agony disappeared, and an inexplicable comfort came over me, and I fell asleep in Her arms, and slept the night through like a babe, and when I awoke I knew that I loved Her.

Soon after that reunion, on another night, in a dream I would be climbing around what appeared to be a soft mound of earth, but when I climbed on top of it I realized it was a huge breast, and a feeling of great peace and comfort came over me, and then in love and adoration I exuberantly exclaimed- "Mother!", at which point I began to awake, and in the groggy haze between the unconscious and conscious I could feel the subterranean, all encompassing heartbeat of the world Mother, in which all of our lives are loved and pulsing.

*

four

It was not long after that horrible and healing night at my shack on the mountain that I again left Vancouver, heading north to the Charlottes, to Her. But this time when I left I spat on the ground and said I was never returning. I had had enough. Goodbye to the pavement, the clock, the noise, the insomnia, the haste, anger, distraction, signs, rules, streetlights, and all the rest of it which stank of mankind's putrid indigestion. Goodbye to the lunacy, the psychic warfare, the evil eye, the spiritual smog, and desecration of all things alive and beautiful. Goodbye, I'm going to live with the Mother.

I walked back into Her. And oh what a sweet beauty She is on the coast of British Columbia. Like nowhere else I've ever been on the planet. Where the remaining giant stands of cedar and spruce have grown into a magnificent, other-worldly, thriving organism of tangled and intertwined biotica and biomass unequalled anywhere; all one great life, seething all about and in and through itself. Where the gothic giants are carpeted down below by a generous layer of the most verdant green moss the eye can take in. Where the ocean offers up its delicious gifts and abundance, pelagic monstrosities play about in the depths, a limitless swarm of sea-birds float and swim about, and there is always enough driftwood to cook your bounty and hang your tarp over; where the rainbow is more common than the moon, and where, one night, I was to witness the odd benediction of Luna's Sol-like majesty, as I stepped out into the evening to release my bladder, and turned my head upward, and there, hanging by the light of a full moon, was a perfect rainbow, cut in crystalline clarity and singing out the Mother's covenant with me.

    I had witnessed many rainbows in this land of plenty, many of which had come down from the firmament at auspicious moments, communicating to me that the cosmic eye was watching me and occasionally pleased. But never had I seen one at night, and never had I imagined that it would come, if it ever did, under the glow of a full moon. And yet the universe, as I have come to recognize it, is wholly intelligent, and the wonders and weather and natural occurrences I would come to witness would, with categorical regularity, make it obvious to me that the cosmos is more alive, more conscious, and more aware of us than we are even of ourselves.[12]

    Nothing is accidental nor arbitrary in life. Nothing. No tornado touches down, no numberless wave laps the shore, no hurricane rises or falls, and no wind even slightly blows without perfect intention and purpose. Everything is alive with consciousness and meaning. And the beasts that run about, or swim, or fly are no different. Consciousnesses within consciousnesses within consciousnesses. If a message doesn't come to you one way it will come another, and when you live in the wilds, and with the wilds, the symbols of our mythic beings often come through the wilds. Omens are alive and well in the wilderness, to be sure. You only have to tune into the other way of seeing.

    For instance, it happened one summer that, twice within a month or so, an eagle dropped a salmon head from up on high, down to land right nearby me. Had I been alert and sensitive enough the first time, I would have gotten the message and been done with it. But repetition is often a necessity in the sublime schoolroom where our dull and torpid minds fail class after class and often never even graduate from first grade. So we repeat, and repetition occurs, and the second time something unique like this, or anything else, happens it is time to wake up and take note, which I did. And the message, which I heard, and the lesson which I got the second time around, was that my Piscean era was finished, and a new way of being was well under way.

    It is these rites-of-passage which help the stages between transformations go much smoother; otherwise we're likely to hang on to old ideas and ways, and so inhibit the evolving movement within us.

    Another message from the sky, at another time, came repeatedly to me, again as a shift within me had occurred, or was about to occur.

This one came from the Ravens- those wise and wily tricksters of legend who speak out in tongues with their ancient knowledge and forethought. Ah, the garrulous raven, which is said to have no less than one hundred and thirty-seven different sounds within its repertoire, which is a might larger than our twenty-six letters, only six of which are vowels and therefore true sounds. To sit in between two ravens having a little chat over god knows what in the middle of the wilderness is to understand how limited is our perspectives on the intelligence of the beasts. It is we who are unevolved, we who are far from Heaven, we who are the parasites on a planet made for living and loving.

Though it was not a raven's voice which would call to me this time, but rather it was their aerial acrobatics which spoke out their message, as I was walking along a pebble beach outside of one of the towns on the blessed isles, and my inner world had been in a bit of confusion and turmoil, as per usual, and then one of the dark bandits flew overhead, let out a gargle to grab my attention, and then turned upside down, coasting that way for a while, then flipping back over, flapping a few times, then over again and gliding upside down, laughing at the fool human below, and then upright again, a few flaps, then back over and out into the distance, harbinging the overturning my life was about to take in the next couple of weeks.

It was a magical sight to witness, that stunt pilot showing off and carving words of wonder in the air. Upside-down was the perfect metaphor for me back then, though I was hardly gliding peacefully nor loving the ride. Life was all flipping over upon me, as it has always been trying to do, but I hadn't yet got my wings and so I stayed on the ground and somehow managed to stay upright.

Oh it's a crazy life at times. It's a marvelous ride on a mysterious train through a stupefying madhouse. A ride unlike any other ride, in which you can neither hold on nor fall off, and so you are tossed about in the blender, and whirled about on a string, and you're always falling and always caught.

When the Mother had caught me in her arms a few months back, that night on the apocryphal hill, something had changed which would turn me upside down and would complete my ground-school training, for no longer was I just a child of the heavens, I was also now a child of the earth, and with that new found lower communion came a critical wholeness that would mend an open wound which had been bleeding in me since Old Adam's mortal transgression.

Not that this solved the struggles I would still encounter while making my way through the pitfalls of society, but a re-union had happened which brought me- a male spirit, born, and bred, and a card-carrying citizen of the sky and of non-being- into *being*. I had finally landed.

The divorced spiritual Parents of my separated Self had come back together within me, had rejoined forces, and could work together again, and that meant that *non-being* and *being* were no longer on their own, no longer opposed, and so the mind and the heart were intimate, and therefore, in cosmological terms, conception could be conceived into the Mater by Dad.

It is a process that we all must go through, I expect- a reunion of our divided selves- one half which is strung high up in the heavens, timid to venture down, the other, wriggling beneath the surface, unable to leave the ground; a reunion which does not occur until the Spirit consummates into the Soul, and the livingness of the cosmos is won. Is One.

Once you have eaten of the flesh, so to speak, you must ride it out completely.

You must ride it out with one leg on a white Pegasus flying towards the sky, and the other on a black Nightmare, fleeing away in the night. And yet how to hold it all together? How to get away and remain? How to be and not-be, and, making the two into one, going nowhere, be free?

Another glaring synchronicity based on animals which comes to mind occurred while I was working in Sitka, Alaska, and a few of us had gathered on a buddy's sailboat for a couple of drinks, and we were passing a bottle of the German bitter, *Jaegermeister*, around which has on its label the picture of an eight or ten-point buck, with a glowing crucifix between its antlers. Amongst our party was a man who was at that time writing a book about deer hunting, and his keen interest in the emblem brought about a lengthy conversation regarding its possible meaning. We tossed about all sorts of hypotheses and then forgot about it and went on with the evening. The next day, however, I was rummaging through a thrift shop in the town and a certain book on one of the used-book shelves seemed to grab my attention for no particular reason. I picked it up and it was all about the sacred link between man and animals, and not only that, it contained an exact description of the insignia which we had been discussing the night before: it related the story of St. Eustacius, and how one day while out hunting he had chased, on horseback, after a large buck, and when he had finally gotten within his arrow's reach, the buck turned around and between its antlers there shone a glowing cross. At that moment St. Eustacius was converted and spent the rest of his fairly trying days spreading the good news, only to wind up being roasted in a hollow iron bull by the heathens of the day, though when they opened it up afterward he was found with a bewildering smile on his face.

This episode carried other synchronicities as well, for, not long after finding that book an acquaintance of mine suggested that I read Voltaire's *Candide*, which I did, and which described incredibly similar events to the story of St. Eustacius that had transpired in Candide's life, and so I figured the universe was trying to tell me something, which it was, because perhaps a year later another friend of mine wrote me a letter and, for no specific reason, chose to address it to St. Eustace. I understood then the message I was receiving at that time, but I will leave it to the curiosity of the reader to consider or disregard what that message was, however they choose.

Occasionally the messages from the wilds are neither symbolic nor abstract. Sometimes the warm-blooded beasts simply want to send out some love.

For me this type of event came about on a paddling trip I undertook with a very brilliant young man who had camped beside me at our illegal bush-camp in the forest, just behind the town of Sitka. He had never sea-kayaked before but decided to come along anyway. And so we each took a few days off of work and paddled across a channel of water to a nearby island with a large, extinct volcano on it. There we set up camp, slept the night, and the next morning paddled out to another island renowned for its puffin and auklet colonies.

The puffin is a beautiful and laughable creature, appearing like the clown of the Pacific, and we spent the whole day circumnavigating the outer island, bird watching, and then paddled back to the camp we had set up the evening before. The next morning when we awoke the weather was foul, with a strong southerly crossing over large swells from the west, making for a chaotic blender of spray, swell, and chop, which was a messy soup for small craft. Normally I would have waited it out and hoped for better weather the next day, but my buddy had a flight to catch and we had to get back. Always there is a good reason for making a bad decision.

We got halfway across the strait we were crossing to return to Sitka and the weather system picked up and shifted to an easterly, and suddenly we were paddling into a strong headwind, making no headway, and being lashed from the side by blowing swell and chop. My companion's lower back had seized up and he was having a very tough go of it. I was beginning to worry that we had screwed-up badly, because I knew that in these conditions if he tipped over I'd have a hell of a time rescuing him, and if I went over I'd most likely fail at the Eskimo roll- a technique which I was no expert at even in calm and tepid water, let alone in raging, icy seas- and he wouldn't stand a chance of helping me. Things were looking grim. Real grim. I was trying to support him, but what could I do? We were in separate kayaks, and I had to keep my own head forward, conscious of every incoming wave, and paddle fiercely just to keep from going backward. It had become an epic, and was bound to get worse, but just as I was thinking these thoughts, and sensing that we were in true danger, a massive humpback whale surfaced right beside me, and blew out a huge cloud of spume- which, on every other occasion that I have caught an unlucky whiff of the spray, smelled as bad as the most horrid halitosis a festering, never-brushed mouth could have, with a nauseating stench that stuck to your clothes and all, but this time it was the sweet perfume of love and support- and I knew the blessed beast was saying- "Come on man, dig in brother, you can make it, I am with you!" And I let out a joyful yell of gratitude and victory, and my mate must have seen and felt the same thing because we did dig in, and did make ground, and finally crossed the channel, coming to shore soaked and exhausted, but we were alive, and we were alive perhaps only because of the visit from the whale which had spurred us on. And the lousy American beer we toasted to that living gift tasted wonderful that night.

*

five

As well as the little hut I built on the hill near Vancouver, on all of my past travels up and down the coast I always kept an eye out for a more permanent, more remote spot to exist- away from the ubiquitous mental detritus found any place man had scattered his limited theories into form. I would consider the farthest cliffs, the steepest mountains, the most isolated valleys, or islands in the roaring sea, anywhere to build a hidden shack, a fort, a cabin, or what have you, and to one day step off of the last street I would ever set my feet upon, and walk away calmly into the bush. I dreamed of finding my spot, of constructing a humble lean-to, of sitting down beneath it, forgetting the likes of men, and of never getting up.

I sought to be in unpeopled wilderness, and live like old Enoch, away from the temptations of the dancing, song, and sin of the sons and daughters of men, except that, unlike that ancient forefather, I planned to take one of their daughters with me. Why be totally alone in the great outdoors, I thought, when you can have some lovin' with you?

If you like nature and don't mind a bit of hard work and a lot of isolation, British Columbia and Alaska are the best places on earth to be a guerrilla homesteader. The choices of where to camp or build a little shanty are never ending, as long as you're far enough away from the authorities and the concerned citizens who will get into a righteous fuss and fright every time they see something going on which is not tightly wrapped in codes and restrictions. The great, law abiding, sniveling bourgeoisie rabble will get you every time.

On one reconnaissance trip, far away from the rabble, looking for a remote building site, a couple of buddies and I took a floatplane into the mouth of one of the long, fingerlike inlets which carve up the BC coast, where we hiked up the river ten miles or so, firstly along an abandoned logging road, then onto an overgrown path, and finally we were meandering through grizzly trails which, in the thick knot of the rainforest's salal and brambles, were only as high as a bear walks, and therefore you had to crouch right over to use such paths, so these weren't the most physically- not to mention psychologically- comfortable thoroughfares to negotiate.

I remember reading the Alaska State Park's pamphlet on grizzly attacks the first summer I had gone up there. It stated, in perfect, bureaucratic, now-you-can't-sue-us-jargon, that if a grizzly charges you, you should not run but only look away from it, wave your arms about, and slowly back away; if it continued to charge, and attacked you, you should not fight back but instead play dead; and if now it persisted to maul you, you should consider it as a 'predatory' attack, and fight back with all of your might. I finished reading the pamphlet and was thinking- isn't this a wonderful piece of perfectly American advice- wait until you're damned and then try to save yourself.

During a large part of that first summer in Alaska, I was camped alone under a tarp in grizzly territory, and was piss-scared half the time and would be startled into anxious alertness at the slightest noise in the forest- of which there was an endless supply. And what with the short, northern nights- about three hours of partial darkness at best- and the perpetual rain pounding down, I didn't rest very well at the outset of that summer. But something happened after a while which allowed me to sleep comfortably; I suppose I just inductively grew weary of leaping up whenever a branch snapped or some other sound startled me but did not produce the *ursus major* I had expected, nor any other frightening beast for that matter. And so eventually I just stopped reacting to the ever-present, benign noises of the forest and forgot that these might signify a bear. I got so used to sleeping out in the open like this that I remember finding fresh cougar tracks near my camp in British Columbia one time, and as I was dozing off that night I suddenly questioned myself as to whether I should be worried or not, and I remember only the slightest response inwardly, lackadaisically negating the necessity of fear, and then I must have fallen into dream because I awoke the next morning fully intact.

Occasionally a friend would confess to me that their fear of bears and cougars prevented them from going into the wilderness alone- which, being alone in the wilds, was a rewarding experience that I had declared was singularly important and a life altering necessity. And then the friend would inquire whether I was still afraid of such animals or not. My answer was, "Yes, of course I'm afraid of them." But then I'd explain an important change which had happened to me, and apparently not to them as yet, which was this- I was not afraid of *potentially* meeting a bear or cougar, for I had learned that at every moment there is a false alarm if you're willing to allow fear to give you one. However, were I to actually come upon one of the carnivores, of course I was scared, but the difference between useless fear and jungle sense was what gave me, a coward, the opportunity to bask in the glorious outdoors, and stole the same experience from those others. And that is a terrible tragedy.

I recognize this dichotomy- this liberating or imprisoning nuance of fear- in many aspects of my life now: fear of potential harm, potential loss, or potential sorrow, all of which are limiting to life, as opposed to honest-to-goodness self-preservation fear, which is life affirming.

I had come to accept that life is not complete without some fear, and that trying to avoid what I feared was impossible without concomitantly building up walls which would bury me, because to avoid fear was to avoid life. I had to learn to discern between true response to a true situation, and false response to an imagined one.

I can say these things with great humility, for I was a born and bred, hopeless neurotic- a living authority on the crippling effect of the mind. I once had a dream in which it was shown to me that there was an incurable, pathological coward within me, discoloring everything I did, and everything I thought, and I awoke knowing that I could not get rid of him, for he was a part of *me*. I could only take into consideration the fact that his voice was a part of the chorus of voices motivating either my fulfillment or abandonment of life, and I had to make sure that he didn't win, because to him even the clerk at the convenience store was a grizzly, and the world was a terrifying, dark woods within which he sat cowering while the rest of me wanted to sing out and dance.

The first book I ever thought of writing was solely about fear, though luckily the coward was too afraid to write it, and so the rest of me won the pen. And soon I'll take another hill and become a ballerina.

And yet it had taken me many bewildering years of painful confusion and struggle to finally understand and overcome the useless fears that had been driven into my innocent life from day one. The endless, justified, irrational, irrevocable, cultural fears: fear of being lost in the world, of being different, of believing in nothing but yourself, of having no job (let alone a career), of having little or no money, no home, of living illegally wherever you chose to squat. Fear of existing in squalor amongst the pimps, and prostitutes, the heroin addicts, thieves, drunks, mutants and beggars, fear of being dirty, of neither caring for, nor needing anything created by mankind, fear of owning nothing, of thinking your own thoughts, of dreaming your own dreams, of being idle, of being nobody. Fear of death, fear of life, fear of disappointing your friends and family, of being disowned or of disowning, of offending another irreparably. Fear of being absolutely alone, fear of standing your own ground while the cyclone of madness spins relentlessly about you, fear of believing in and following your own reality, fear of being wrong, of never finding truth. Fear of the wildlands, of snakes, of cold and rain, of darkness and discomfort, of wiping your ass with your own hand, of where you'd lay your head that night, of what you'd eat tomorrow, of where you'd wash, and what you'd do when you woke in the sun with nothing to do but sit in the sun. Fear, fear, fear, and more fear, all ensconcing, all pervasive, encumbering, deceiving, disfiguring fear. All of it.

Many people talked as if they understood life and knew how to properly live it, but once you sat down and got inside of them, once they opened up the can of worms contained within and came forth with candor to expose themselves truly, it was always the same thing- uncertainty, hesitation, disquiet, boredom, anger, worry, envy, disease, and panic. There it was, in all and everyone, lying buried just beneath the shining veneer of their own private lie, which itself was haplessly buried deep inside the greater lie- the lie into which they were born and because they had no imagination, no intent, and no energy to extricate themselves, it was the same lie into which they would eventually grow sick, and old, and die.

They would die in fear when they could instead have lived in faith. In faith- not in a dogmatic, religious form- but faith in nothing knowable- faith for faith's sake, because it was the only way out of fear and death and sorrow.

But they had no faith; no faith in themselves, in God, in Creation, in Destruction, in death, or in Life. No faith, only fear. As simple and difficult as that.

*

six

After hiking in through those grizzly trails to inspect a potential homesteading site with some buddies, the valley we explored was absolutely beautiful, despite having been almost completely logged-out decades earlier, but it turned out that the land was owned by a complete buffoon- one who would have caused us no end of troubles- so we flew out a few days later without a further thought about it.

That trip, however, made me look even farther afield. I began obsessively pouring over maps and marine charts, like a prisoner who had come upon the blueprint to the prison, and who sees in it his hope for escape. Wherever I went, by boat, plane, car, or bus, I'd be staring out the window, seeking the Shambhala awaiting me, devoid of any rules or humans.

Finally, though, it was not a map which helped me decide where to go, it was my own heart; I simply looked within and asked- where did I want to go to *be*. The answer came quick and unequivocally- on the far, outside west coast, amongst the giant trees and crashing surf, where no on lived and few ever came.

Luckily enough, however, I would not have to go alone, for by then the universal drama had been kind enough to bestow upon me a *soror*- a woman whom I had been directed to be with through many dreams and sublime messages- and who was now thankfully a living part of my soul. We were on the same conveyor belt, and the conveyor belt was headed for the west coast of the Charlottes.

En route we gathered up all necessary supplies for our initial visit: a bag of cement, a sheet of half-inch aluminum, and some stove pipe to build a fireplace, a couple of tarps, an axe, chisel, saw, some blankets and sleeping bags, and a few buckets of food.

These supplies we loaded onto a floatplane and flew to a remote, west coast cove. There we unloaded, asked the pilot to pick us up in ten days- as there was no radio contact in the area- and watched him take off again.

The first thing to do was to scout out the area, and it didn't take long, perhaps one or two minutes, before we were standing under one of the most beautiful, anthropomorphic, giant cedars I had ever seen. A titan, a grandfather, with a horizontal limb about eight feet up its massive trunk, and the limb itself was about five feet in diameter and which, over the next week and a half, provided a wonderful canopy under which we cooked our meals during the regular rainstorms on the coast.

Very soon after our discovery and exaltation over the tree, we found nearby an abandoned old Fisheries cabin, which was about ten feet by ten feet in dimensions, and full of refuse, but still standing square and otherwise in good fettle. We knew then that we had been guided to the place we were supposed to be, for now we didn't have to build anything, we simply cleaned all the debris out of the cabin, tarped the leaking roof, put the windows back in place, built a very rough stone and cement fire place, with the aluminum sheet on top for cooking, cut a hole in the wall and put the stove-pipe through, and we were home.

Later that evening we hiked up one of the rivers in the area and there were so many eagles about that the sky was literally snowing eagle-down, and I ran about in an ecstatic trance of disbelief with my hat out in my hand, catching those feathery pieces of grace floating all around and never having touched the ground.

I suppose this was the universe's answer to my often visualized fantasy of running along a beach and diving to catch an eagle feather, fallen from a passing raptor, before it touched the earth. I reckon that this was the type of waking dream which symbolized my inner spiritual disposition back then: I had not wanted to come down, ever. But as I found out, and described earlier, despite my revulsion to the flesh's confines, the spirit has not come into life to avoid life, but to partake of it as fully and perfectly as one's nature allows, and so to stay aloft and soar around in the distances without ever entering the body and touching the earth may be painless, but, in the end, it is also pointless.

Anyway, the *soror* and I stayed for our ten days in the beautiful cove, where a few sailboats ended up anchoring out a storm, and a crab-fisherman dropped his traps and gave us some of the catch, but other than that it was just the birds, the beasts, and the trees to keep us company. Thus, like all of our subsequent trips together, away from the throngs, it was a good chance for her and I to be alone together, without distraction, which is really the only time the two partners in the work can get inside each other, dig into the piles of rubble, root around for hidden goblins and magic rings, and then mirror back to each other what they have found. It was always challenging, and always worth it, such trips of ours, for without this type of cooperative archaeology there is little value but entertainment in a relationship.

More than being an important time for our inner work, it was recuperative and inspiring to live for a while amongst such virgin forest and untouched earth, and I was thinking that this is what the earth must have been like before the hordes invaded and pillaged everywhere else. But one night I was to experience a strange energy and visitation during sleep, and then a disturbing and eerie sort of requiem began playing in the ether, and I was given a dream which showed the entire area in which we were camped, in all its beauty and diversity, and then a somber voice spoke and said- "But something is missing." And a terrible sense of unnatural absence occurred and I awoke and knew what was missing- the natives.

Never before had I understood, in this way, the tragedy of the de-population which the North American Natives suffered upon the entry of the white man. Over ninety percent of the Queen Charlotte Haidas died from smallpox or the common flu, and the rest were removed from their happy hunting grounds and placed in two villages where most of them remain today.

So now the earth was incomplete, and barren of an essential component of the ecosystem and spirit of the land. It was a funereal presence which I felt then- a loss that the earth itself had not forgotten, and continued to mourn. I know now that the world-soul still seethes with an agony as hard to approach as it is to endure.

For the rest of our time in that cove the forest felt like a home to which a parent returns after finding out that all their children had been killed in an accident; a deathly, sickening, horrible emptiness. And the Mother had shared her grief with me. And all I could do was sigh, and shrug my shoulders. That's all I could do.

The *soror* and I flew out again, ten days later, but, as always, a part of us remained there, with the grandfather tree, the little cabin kept all those years for us, the flocks of eagles, and the Mother with her unrequited woe.

How, when you have gone away from it all, have seen it from a different angle, watched as the futility of mankind consumes itself insatiably, and have suffered because you can no longer allow yourself to take any part in the delirium- how then do you take life up again? How do you play a role in a drama you have scorned and walked out on?

In the years past, if I wasn't thinking of a wilderness hideout, I would be considering other types of escape, and would be researching Trappist monasteries in France, or Orthodox monasteries in Greece- the kind of places where it's all or nothing, where one day you simply toss everything away, put on the dark robes, and spend your life drinking port and praying in obeisance to the Lord.

Or I'd imagine myself stoically self-exiled to an exotic land of peasants and simplicity, where I'd wait out my existence spurning all that I had been born into and could not stand.

And if these two regular fantasies became old, I thought perhaps I would just move down to San Francisco, or Santa Fe, or some such neo-bohemian place, and be a drunken poet. Or I'd decide that it was better in the end to fly out to a remote island in the Aleutian archipelago and build a stone shack and learn on my own the way of the Athabascan shaman. I was always trying to think of how I could survive, somehow survive in this world.

I was continually pouring over the classified adds, looking for an old Winnebago to drive away in and keep on going, or a plot of useless land out in the middle of nowhere, a place to go and plant a garden and commune with the soil, and not come back.

I bought myself an inflatable kayak, and then an inflatable raft, and I imagined myself paddling to some offshore islet, and waiting stoically for others to realize I had made the right decision, and then deciding to join me there. Whatever it took to get away, I was taking it. But I never got away.

Perhaps the closest I ever came to feeling the freedom and flow of the untrammeled spirit on earth were times I spent kayaking the outer coast, where the lift and drop of the endless swell raises you up and takes you down in a gentle, soothing motion; where you can sit in your boat within this calming medium, out as far as the furthest reefs, where the ocean pounds against the enduring loneliness of these last and isolate members of the continent, away from it all and sitting unscathed by the crashing waves, wrapped in a timeless stillness that will gather you up and remove you forever from the distant shore if you open up and tap into its remoteness.

Out there, alone but for the sea and sky and nothing to scar the infinite expanse which swallows you up and makes you a part of it. Out there, where only the occasional puffin or albatross comes around to remind you that other life still exists, that you have not paddled through a door in the void nor come into that place of forgetfulness and absence to which the weary soul so longs to go.

Out there, where the cadence of the paddle hauls you in and you lose yourself in the act, and the paddle takes over while you merely hold on and wonder where you've gone.

The sea is a lonely place, almost as lonely as God. Perhaps that is why we are drawn to sit beside it and look out to nowhere, so as to feel the type of absence which the spirit calls home. A home which is far from all else, and that is why we fear to go there, for it is a home where no one else lives, no one visits, and only the wind comes by occasionally to remind us of its kinship. A home without rooms, or walls, or furniture. An emptiness to which we are all drawn like Icarus to the sun. Only we do not melt and crash, but instead we dissipate and rise, forever after inhabiting only the remote and untouched areas of the earth, if indeed we come down at all.

There is foreign lostness to the outer coast, which sings softly to the tune of our alien existences, to our eternal wanderings in the oceanic self. You can go out there only once and get caught out there forever, and even if your body returns to the world and to work, and continues to love, and eat, and sleep, and lives out the rest of your life, you will remain out in the swells and the space, out in the lost reaches of the heart, where neither hurt nor love has ever gone. And you stay out there because of this, because to come back means to love and die all over again, because that is what happens when you cannot control your care.

And so your body returns to your friends and family who know not that you have buried yourself at sea, have set your spirit adrift into the warm abyss where nothing matters and you can breathe again and let the world go on its melancholic way.

What I found out there was the part of me which could not endure life- the part which wanted to fix it all and knew it was not fixable, the part of me that wanted to heal the endless agony, the part which could not accept the world for what it was and therefore had to die or leave it.

Out there I found myself smiling a soft smile I had never experienced before, a smile which came neither from joy, nor victory, nor laughter, but which came from the end of struggle, and the end of pain; it was the subtle and almost imperceptible smile of a soldier after the battle is over, a battle in which neither side has gained any ground, but only slaughtered each other until the few remaining troops had to stop and sign a truce; it was a smile that no longer needed to be aroused by anything, because it came after everything else had been removed, and therefore would never again leave; it was a smile that did not belong to the body, nor the mind, nor the earth, nor even the heavens, it was a smile that belonged to no one but ...me.

What I found out there was a place where it all fell away and only a huge, cathartic sigh remained, a sigh which would go on forever because the world would go on forever, and there was nothing that could be done, and that part of me I found out there was courageous enough to finally accept this, to sigh, and to look out away into the untroubled distance and to never look back. And that is why I am always out there. No matter where my body is, or what I am doing, that part of me is still out there, sitting in the slowly rocking swells, out past the anguish of the furthest reef, with my bow pointed west, towards nothing, and I look without seeing, listen without hearing, and feel without joy, need, nor pain.

I have seen this distance in others who have been away from the shore of life too long, and who now look about the world with that thousand-yard stare, which seeks for nothing, and attaches to nothing, because nothing is what it is after.

When you drift away like this it is almost impossible to get back, for your spirit leaves the earth and hangs like a kite above the clouds, waiting for the body to die and release it.

I have heard of astronauts, hovering out in space- far from the ensconcing psychic dome of anger and confusion around the earth- who find themselves immersed in an inexplicable ocean of love and peace impossible to reach in the dark spiritual atmosphere of humanity. And I have heard of their painful return back to earth, and how everything seems so grey, groaning with anguish, and useless.

Were it not for the greater will, driving me back down, flogging me against my own desires, forcing me to turn around and venture back to earth, I certainly never would have returned.

But the microcosm is an instrument of the macrocosm, the self is the vehicle of the Self, and service and duty come in many ways, and if you're called you follow, and if you don't follow you're dragged, and

I was dragged along until I realized I was beaten and so I got up and walked back on my own.

And during that long march back I realized that once you have died out there and then been resurrected, there is no longer a place for you in the scheme of things, no longer a role for you in the external drama; that you no longer belong to the great show; you are lost and autonomous, and for the first time ...you are necessary. Now you are a stranger from another world, come to share their strangeness, or take no part. No matter, you do not fill a void, you create one. That is all. But that is everything.

The spirit lives in all things, and is all things, manifest and unmanifest, formed and formless, absolute and fleeting. It moves at a different rhythm without betraying the torpor of the profane. It swirls through the linear, prosaic, and mean presences of the dream, vivifying and animating all. It belongs where it is welcomed, and is imprisoned where it is denied. It has no borders, no identity, and no characteristics. It has no need, no doubt, no unstillness, and moves without effort and effort cannot move it. If you look for it you cannot see it, but if you become it, it will be free.

*

seven

Most of the trouble comes when you forget who's looking out for you, who's running the show, and who has seen, like a champion chess player, the next hundred moves ahead, while you're mentally fumbling about and wondering whose turn it is to move next.

Every action, thought, intention, or desire one succumbs to within a specific paradigm wholly supports and reinforces the authenticity of that graven perspective. Habit and belief then become the cement which binds the brick-walls of the paradigm together. One must then act counter to the paradigm in order to test its reality. If it stands it belongs to life, if it falls, it never really existed.

Doubt will castrate the flow out of life. Doubt in God, doubt in yourself, doubt in the magic and miracle of all that is, is not, was, or never will be. Doesn't matter which. The trick is to believe in life- your life- and don't give a hoot if it all doesn't fit together nice and reasonably. Nothing is reasonable. Nothing is expectable, imaginable, or proper. We're inside a mad dance of homeless spirits, and no one is going to give a hot damn if you stand up and make it obvious. I couldn't help myself, because I didn't know why life is the way it is, and I could do nothing at the time but shout at the heavens and try to go the distance and back again.

One August, some years back, while still living in the world, I dreamt a dream suggesting that I go on an overseas trip later that year, and when I awoke there was no question within me as to whether I would choose to go or not. I would go, of course; I had been following my dreams for quite a while by then, ever since I first realized that they were communicating important things to me, and they always led me to where I should be, to the people I should meet and share with, and to the experiences I would need to serve my vision, or to fill out the missing aspects of my growing being. The question remaining after this dream, however, was how I would acquire the thousands of dollars necessary to take the directed journey. My penury had reached a pauper's level, and I knew it would be tough to save enough dough for the trip by working in the city, with its never ending expenses, but still the first thought that crossed my mind was to head back into Gomorrah and work at the Co-op and scrimp and save, and beyond that I thought no further. The next night, however, another dream came with the message that edible, wild mushroom-picking would be the most promising route to take that autumn, if I were to bank the coin required. So that was that and again there was no question about what avenue I would choose. The last issue remaining, however, was how to get up to the Charlottes- where a great deal of the wild, commercially viable Chanterelle mushrooms grow- as cheaply as possible, so as not to cut into my earnings before I earned them.

Whenever I had owned a vehicle in the past I would generally take a few extra days to travel up to the islands in a round-about route northward, visiting friends at certain points along my human 'trap-line', as a perspicacious acquaintance once referred to my incremental visitations of dear ones located in sporadic communities along the way. But at this moment I had neither car nor time to make my rounds, so the only answer left, of course, was hitchhiking. This was a method of travel I had used to move about quite regularly in the past, although I always did it begrudgingly, disdainfully standing like a contemptful beggar beside the road, as the affronting legions of motorists sped past me in polished and sealed comfort and indifference. And yet I had nonetheless gotten around all over the world this way, and so I accepted my fate that what must be done must be done and the less whining the better.

So early that September I found myself on the outskirts of Vancouver with my thumb out, and my impatience tucked under, anticipating the long and agonizing process of waiting, then receiving a ride a certain distance up the road, then waiting again, then another ride, and so on, slowly leap-frogging the sixteen-hundred kilometres northward to my distant goal.

And to be sure the same pattern as all other times began unfolding on this trip- there were periods of extended waiting, periods of futility and despair as I weighed the disastrous possibility that the next ride would never come. But what happened this time was that the rides which did come, and they did, somehow seemed to apply to my very existence; that is, it seemed that everyone who picked me up had something to say uniquely relating to me, that there was a common ground of experience or understanding which brought us together in a form of transient communion very quickly, and we'd have our pleasant dialogue over whatever it was that we had instantly ascertained was our point of contact, and then we'd come to a fork in our road and I'd be dropped off to stand and idle, and then a similar event would happen, in that the next ride I got was seemingly the ride I was supposed to get- it was the ride designed for me, by The chess player.

    This went on all day long until sometime around sunset I was left off in William's Lake where I decided to call it a day, and walked into a nearby park, put my sleeping bag down and eased off into the joy of slumber. It was during that night that something must have clicked within me- some recognition bubbled up from the omniscient subconscious into the density of my consciousness, awakening a smouldering realization within me- because the next morning, bright and early, I was out on the road and a young man stopped to pick me up who said he was only going about fifteen minutes out of town, but did I want a lift anyway. Normally I would be loath to accept a ride which terminated out in the middle of nowhere, out where you could get caught for days without getting picked up, and where the alternative possibility of hopping on a Greyhound, when the waiting had finally become intolerable, didn't exist, because there was no bus stop, and so being stranded for an indefinite duration was a real possibility, which I avoided at all costs, often turning down rides that were not going on to at least the next small town. But as I said, something had clicked inside of me that night, because of the chain of seemingly destined rides which had brought me that far the day before, something which whispered- "The ride you are supposed to have *will* stop and pick you up, you need not worry but only have patience, and confidence, and ...faith, because God is directing the show and what should be, is what will be." And so I took the ride, was dropped off in the middle of nowhere, as the young man headed down a side-road, and then stood there, thumb out, as per usual. But before I could fall into the state of impatience which I habitually came to at such times, a voice came to me again which said- "God is choosing your rides." And so I relaxed, and stopped caring if the cars whizzed inhumanely past me, and I eased into the fabulous acceptance of ...faith. And not five minutes later an eighteen-wheeler flew past me, jammed on its breaks and came to a halt fifty metres or so up the road, and I ran up and climbed on and we were off, and the three-hundred pound trucker began inquisitively interrogating me for the first few minutes and then turned his head to me, looked me right in the eyes, and said: "I picked you up because God told me to." And I said, "I know." And this trucker, George I believe was his name, went on for the next two hours with stories and anecdotes about how and when God had entered his life, how he listened for and heard God's directives, and what was to become of the world during and after the apocalypse. And I shared my own views on all of it, and we had some good old biblical style communion, and then he let me off in the middle of nowhere, again. And not but a few minutes of faithful waiting later did I get a ride from a wonderful, long-haired Christian fellow who was homesteading in the area and who took me to his favourite restaurant for breakfast so as to introduce me to his wife. And when he and I were done eating and conversing, we said our goodbyes, and I walked out onto the highway and was soon picked up by a man headed to my final destination, and who was a professional mushroom picker with all sorts of advice for me, to boot. Check mate.

The world becomes a different place when you realize God pervades the whole flippin' shmeer, that there is divine design throughout, and that nothing is made that is not made by the Maker.

God does it all, both inside and out. What the ego assumes it is feeling, or thinking, or doing, is being done *to* it. Make no mistake about it. No one is immune from the divine monopoly.

This makes it tough to keep on striving, or writing, for example, because everything ever written or waiting to be written is summed up in one word- God. There it is. There is no more

In the beginning was the Word, and the Word was with God, and *the* Word was God. Contra*diction* exists only in those parts which are seemingly separated from the whole; once the part is re-assimilated into the rest, and the self dissolves in the Self, all duality and strife are over.

As I said, this complicates the task for the writer, because instead of describing the world or an experience, you now realize that all you're doing is describing a compartmentalized aspect of the uncompartmentalizeable, indescribable God. And yet God hides within God's own creation, as the story goes, and books are one of the multifarious, mischievous ways God goes about in concealment, by inventing a hiding place and then hiding in you while you're searching through it. It's one hell of a good trick, to be sure.

To continue though. People who pick mushrooms are of a very interesting type generally. There are those who, out of interest, go north and try their luck for one or two seasons of crashing through the muck and occasionally stumbling upon a sizeable patch of the hunted spore;

there are other folks who live in the vicinity of the areas which bring forth the Pine, Morrel, Boletus, and Chanterelle mushrooms- which are the most common commercial varieties picked- and so these folks make some, or all, of their living off of the milk and honey coming from their own land; and then there are the true mushroom gypsies, who follow the seasons, migrating here, there, and wherever the picking is good that year.

The common denominator among all the types, however, is their self-chosen fringe existence, and the life of chronic or occasional indigence which accompanies such a decision. Some of the freest and poorest folks I have ever met were mushroom pickers.

I'm thinking of one young lad who made it across to the Charlottes without enough money to buy a return ticket, even if he wanted to- the cost of which was a mere twenty dollars, so he wasn't carrying much green, to be sure. Yet he simply expected that things would work out, and they did.

And a young couple who camped near me one year were waiting for the picking season to start with a half a tank of gas in their vehicle, a box of canned-goods, and a buck-fifty between them. But it didn't faze them a bit.

A fellow in his late teens, who was my picking-partner for a while, had been penniless for the last six months; he had left his father's home because he couldn't stand the man, and had wandered about until he ended up on the Charlottes where, for some reason or other, he wasn't granted welfare, and so he had to live without a nickel for half a year, being given food and shelter by some good citizens in the area, until the shrooms started sprouting.

Another man, a father with two small daughters, had come for a month or so, hoping to pick enough for his car insurance, food, and some nights out at the pub for himself. Small dreams perhaps, but when you're sitting around a campfire out in the bush, and no boss has been standing over you all day, and no alarm clock goes off in the morning, and a guitar is being played while you sip a beer and look up at the night sky, they are some very beautiful small dreams.

The population of the pickers is riddled with this kind of poverty, this kind of faith, this kind of liberation from the excessive tyranny of money, for they have found a form of freedom that money cannot buy. If a professional, workingman's gold-card was delayed for a week in the mail he'd have a cardiac arrest wondering how he was going to survive. But not these folks. Live with what you've got and what you need will show up, it's a law of the universe that they're well acquainted with.

Existence brings you everything you need, as long as you are earnest enough to need it. If you need nothing, nothing will come. But if you give a damn, if you are crazy with life and wonder, and possessed by the miracle of being, ardently digging it up, uncovering the immensity of this unbelievable creation, sedulously seeking to find out what it truly is ...to be, then life will hand itself over to you, it can do no other. That is life. That is what it demands, and what it gives. To float along, comfortable in the tepid roles of man, is to never uncover yourself, to never know who or why it is you are, and that is the greatest sin, and the greatest crime an individual can ever commit.

Without the slightest hint of proselytising, orthodoxy, or cowardice, I concur that God works in many mysterious ways, as the saying goes, and it is only for us to give up our limited views and expectations and our distorted ways of understanding and to allow that hallowed enigma to work its sublime magic upon us.

Anyways, the hitchhiking over, I was now on the Charlottes and earning a fine coin crashing through the bush, picking Chanterelle mushrooms that autumn, and after about ten days of this I was having dinner with Greg, the buddy of mine whom I had kayaked with on my inaugural visit to the islands, and he asked me if I would like to caretake a million-dollar fishing lodge for a month or so, which was closed for the season, and was nestled down in a quiet cove in the southern wilderness.

I accepted, and this turned out to be one of the most pleasant jobs I have ever taken and which mysteriously provided just enough money for me to undertake the journey overseas which had been the seminal cause producing all that followed.

This caretaking position- the first of many I was to have in different areas of the world over the next few years- was a spectacular opportunity, for not only was I suddenly the master of a mansion in the wilderness, I was also paid well, fed well, and the owners went so far as to boat my *soror* in for a couple of weeks of hot and heavy respite from the type of magnified solitude you can only attain in the distant wilderness which lies at the outer limits of the earth and mind.

And, by the way, don't let the pedants and rule-mongers tell you that you must maintain a Platonic relationship with your *soror*, which is a load of antiquated, uptight bunk. Me and mine, we made love like wild bunnies regularly.

Rainbows filled the sky for us during that time, Orcas cruised the bay, and bear and deer paraded about the grounds as we feasted upon fresh salmon, mussels, clams, and venison, and all these accoutrements only crystallized my recognition of the gift I had received simply because I had listened to my dreams, had followed the unspoken directives, and ...had faith.

Life is the thing dreams are made of indeed. I have often said that I have learned more from dreams than from anything else. I was regularly educated in the school of the subconscious, and instructional sentences were uttered to me. Axioms like: "Awareness requires no effort", "The manifest is the outcome of the sublime", "When you have stripped yourself of yourself, then shall you be whole", "Don't be afraid, because you're not really there", "Whatever overly concerns us outwardly, destroys us", "Surrender fulfils the whole because it completes it without doing anything", "Everything is consciousness.", "Everything is light", "For the knight to embrace truth, he must realize that there is only one truth for him to embrace", "God is truth", and so on.

But much more than just being educated and guided happened to me in dreams: All the subconscious characters creating havoc in my life were exposed in my dreams- the madman, rebel, coward, lone wolf, the alchemist called Valerian, and so on. And more, much, much more: I was absolved of my sins, finished with my karma, confronted Mara, found out why I had come to earth, found out who was for me, and who was against me; The Father aspect of God showed up symbolized as my physical father, and The Mother as my physical mother; I learned other people's thoughts, dreamt other people's dreams, had preconceptions, was destroyed by Christ coming after me with a shotgun, was baptised, resurrected, transfigured, and hallowed; I met aliens, Princess Diana, Mother Theresa, and St. Paul, all long deceased; I kissed the Mother Mary, and once ate a chocolate Virgin, all in my dreams.

It was during sleep that I also began to receive and experience the incredible power of divine energy which can be sent down from on high into the prepared body. I suppose this was a likely outcome of the path I had already been on for years, but I had never felt this type of intense energy- like being hit with a thousand volts of pulsating God essence, cast down upon me, for whatever reason I am not sure, but when it happened all doubt within me ended regarding the true force of the universe which gives but the smallest fraction of its limitless potential because ...that is all we can handle.

Many mysterious ways. And they have remained mysteries to me, and I understand nothing, but I am alive and looked after and held afloat in an inexplicable ocean of some genius and unfathomable design, which, thriving and fully cognizant, exists above all dimension, manifestation, and despair.

So many obscure, remote, and unique tunnels to run down and explore in the labyrinth of this godworld; so many options, investigations, contemplations, and asseverations to undertake- the infinity of possibilities is mind boggling: abstract nuclear mathematics and its relation to the orgasms of bivalves, the metaphoric sociobiology of Amazonian tribal ants, the mitotic inspirations of anaerobic bacteria living in the intestines of a parasite living in the intestines of a dying zebra subspecies, the ancient solar mysteries and the Eleusian charade, black holes and why we are in one, blue gnomes, the aliens within us, the psychosis of want, dreamtime and a strict diet of lymph, molecular abnormalities, the aggressive desire of grandmothers watching a young baboon masturbate onto its food at the zoo, the etheric osmosis of our spiritual effluvium, transgression therapy, the anxiety found in trees, elliptical resurgences, advancing partitional phenomenal, mitigative discontinuities, innocent blasphemies, how the workers know when the queen should be killed, errors in the akashic record, the absence of death, the hilarity of grief, the batesian mimicry of humans in the inhumans that live as they, the whole biological and living realm of this maddening and miraculous place called earth, caught up in a dream called life, and here we are and how to dance and sing and laugh when the limitations and infinities become clear. So many tunnels in the one created plenitude of our manifold, indivisible, absurd and privileged existence.

*

eight

    I was so grateful, and in a way so disbelieving, of all that had happened to me on the coast, including all the unique and brilliant people I had met during my travels, that at one point a while back I wrote another whole book, during a five-week all-out frenzy, which was mostly about all the eccentric folks who had come into my life in Vancouver and on my excursions up and down the coast, and I was going to call the book *The West Coast Kumbh Mela*[13], honoring the numerous unbridled characters hiding or running free out there.
    I was thinking then of folks like the fifty-year old, long-haired, big-bearded, insane clown who, as a young man went on scholarship down to America to play both university football and basketball, was a tennis pro, and an exceptional athlete about to be drafted into the big leagues, and then gave it all up for the wilderness, living four winters out on the furthest edge of the rainforest, and then existing in a teepee for a year and learning Native American spirituality from shamans. At the time of writing this he was spending every autumn in the American desert, every summer in the Canadian Rockies, and every winter in the Himalayas doing self-driven biological and ethnological research. And a true madman to boot. He would do the most ridiculous things, like inventing a method to keep his agility perfectly tuned by jumping up

and down on a trampoline, blindfolded, while throwing a medicine-ball against the wall and trying to catch it without knocking himself silly.

Then there was Crazy Al, a man I kept hearing about in a town which I lived in for six weeks or so, and by the descriptions of him I kept envisioning a sixty-year old, wild-eyed, toothless soothsayer, but wasn't I surprised when I was introduced to a thirty-one year old man in a tank top, who was built like he belonged on the national gymnastics team, and this was Crazy Al. And so we sat down beside each other in the pub, and started to chat and I guess he saw something in me which allowed him to feel like I'd understand him, because he leaned over, peered into me with a deep, serious, mature look, and declared, without a hint of holier-than-thou in him: "The problem is that these people are godless." And I could tell that he knew what he meant by that, and yet as the night went on I could tell also that he cared for others like little retarded children who had not the acumen to understand their limitations. Among many other things which we discussed that night he also claimed that, since he and I were approximately the same age, and of similar consciousness, we were both going through a zodiacal shift called 'Saturn return', which he attempted to describe to me though I didn't really get much out of it because all the while I was hoping it had some connection to the old Roman Festival of Saturnalia- the celebration of wine and orgies, when the slaves are set free for a week to change places with their masters and make up for the rest of the year in bondage. Feeling somewhat like a chaste slave at that time I was fairly enthralled with my take on his supposition.

And another odd soul: an American wanderer in his mid forties, whom, at the time of our meeting, was managing the small, illegal hostel I had taken refuge in for a couple of days, although he was mostly just hanging about, enjoying the crowd and waiting for the skydiving season to begin in the southwest where he had been teaching for years. Otherwise he roamed about with a small backpack, smoked the occasional joint, and told splendid tales about his own wilderness adventures, guiding experiences such as photographing an ascent of Everest, and the ten years he had spent up the coast on a tug which hauled log-booms through the harrowing, shifting currents of the narrows, and whose ship's captain, according to him, was a saint who listened to Beethoven's seventh constantly. There were no international borders for this man. There was only the earth, one earth, and he strolled about it like a lone wolf who had no concern for boundaries or working papers.

And then there was the red wine guzzling, acid popping, footloose Zen nun, who lived like a feather in a breeze, not worrying if she came down because a strong enough gust would come along to lift her up again and move her on to God knows where but somewhere, and she'd make her way doing this or that with intense passion and delight and then move on without a thought that it might be difficult ahead and wouldn't it be better to just stay where you are. No way. Keep moving, keep flowing, keep living, keep loving.

The coast is a limitless banquet of odd and indescribable sorts. There were draft-dodging geniuses, dope-smoking ministers, shaggy-mane drummers and didgeridoo players, wandering sailors, autodidactic naturalists, carvers, painters, explorers, heresiologists, blasphemers, and converts. The full spectrum of humanity is offered up there in its greatest extravagance within the most spectacular venue on the planet.

Everyone I speak of, and have written about earlier, certainly had no shortage of fears, insecurities or sorrows, just like all the rest of us. To be human has its requirements. But these folks inspired me and made me appreciate, as best I could, the unique chance we all have simply by being alive. I suppose it was for this reason that I had written the *Kumbh Mela* book- to tell the stories of those who most likely would never tell their own.

Soon after completing the book, however, I was given to understand that the 'powers' upstairs weren't all that pleased with it, most likely- it seemed from their ostracisms- because it was a horribly lopsided work, showing everyone in their best light while making no mention of their transgressions and towering faults- and so I burned the book a year later and never thought twice about that decision.

What I wonder now, however, of my time with all those magical people I met along my way, is this- did any of them make it across to the other side? And by that I mean, did any of them have the subtle lucidity and humility necessary to dissolve away from themselves and merge into the undying One? Or did they cling to their talents, idiosyncrasies, and skills, which allowed them to break out boldly from the norm, but would in the end become their undoing, if they were not able to relinquish these divisions to the whole? These are questions for which I have no answer. I have only the assumption that none, or very few, went the full distance. And I say this not out of pessimism nor scorn, but out of realism. For to cross over you can take nothing superfluous with you. No desires, no dreams, no longings, no regrets, no unfinished business. You walk through with a clean slate. You emerge without anything on your person except for the rose, which you are allowed, and even asked, to take back with you.

Unless the indefatigable intent is there to dissolve away the hard parts and ease back into the One, the individual is bound to continue being but a puppet of the ego. For none of us can cross to the other side with any characteristics, idiosyncrasies, talents, or pride. We must all melt nondescriptly into the fabulous wave, or remain ignobly isolate and separate like a turd floating about in the bathtub of a knave.

Until we release all that makes us stand out like sore thumbs amongst our fellows and the world, we are destined to wrestle with the only Titan who can beat us on this earth- ourselves. The way of sin must abate, and the way of absence take over. For you make it across when it doesn't matter if you make it, because you don't know what it means to make it, and so you stop trying. Then you make it. You cross over from the death of separation into the living moment of God when it comes time to lie down, because you have finished with this chapter in the eternal story of your being. That is when you must fall away completely, stop everything, forget everything, shed a final tear, and ...lay down.

And so I say, perhaps none of the fabulous folks I met during those years of wandering had strong enough intention to stand tall, and then to lie down. And yet I have met one who did make it. And if, at the end of this life, I am able to say that I met only one true man amongst all the people who came and went before me, I can say that I met at least one. One man who began to show me what it meant to be a man, and that it had nothing to do with unique abilities, physical strength, machismo, stoicism, handling strong drink, or screwing multitudes of women, but that to be a man meant to see clearly the abject follies of the world and to choose instead the one and only way in which to be on this earth- the way of integrity- and to choose that way at every turn no matter what the cost, and to know that the cost would often be dear.

I say that I learned about this costly integrity from Ed- a person so full of noble humility and priceless honor that he might be aghast right now were he to know how I had seen and truly felt about him- or perhaps I did not learn about such integrity from him, perhaps I still have to learn that lesson, but at the very least I saw the living example of a man who had chosen to stand strongly against the tide of greed and desperation which consumes the lives of most of us on the planet, and to let the world carve its own path to its own destruction while he forged on alone in the night with an irrevocable force and conviction to never join in on the looting and loitering with the masses but instead to set to bailing out the sinking ship while everyone else was busy pissing into the hold.

It was back a few years, when I arrived for the first time in Sitka, that beautiful little Alaskan town surrounded by snow-capped mountains and islands leading out to sea; a vibrant little oasis of charm and personality standing out like a flagship on the magnificent outer coast of the panhandle. But I arrived there as adrift in life as a piece of flotsam thrown overboard by foreign fishermen which then bobs about aimlessly in the indifferent swells of the great Pacific before being cast up on shore as a chunk of refuse belonging to a different people from a different land, and even they don't want it. These were my lost and existential days of nomadic rambling, when nothing mattered but to keep going and going and pretend that I hadn't lost what I had lost and that I was going to find what I never found back then, which is to say- peace.

I had ferried down from Skagway after working a short contract at the Whitehorse fish hatchery, clipping the adipose fins off of six-thousand salmon fry during the day, while my female co-worker bush-hags held outlandish belching contests, and then I would spend the night drowning my estrangement to life in pints of stale beer at one of the town's many ignominious blues bars during the evening. Day and night it was culture at its finest, let me tell you.

Anyway, I ended up in Sitka as less a part of the earth than I had ever been in the past and took on serendipitous employment with Ed's two-man kayak operation, where I would end up doing all manner of things including guiding, instructing, selling, purchasing and running the show one month while Ed was away on other business. Mostly though I found myself for two summers working alongside a man who in my mind came to embody a paradoxical hybridization of the Buddha and Robin Hood; a man who's intransigent honesty, intent, and maturity of soul has remained unparalleled by any other, ever since our time together.

Ed came to Sitka as a young man to work for the town's main employer, the pulp mill, but upon completing his agreed-upon one year contract, and having seen the reality behind that rapacious and unconscious industry, he promptly quit, turned on his heels, and became the town pariah, a traitor, intent on preserving what was left of the surrounding forest and shutting down that gigantic, belching cyst forever.

It was a vicious battle and Ed's existence was threatened and impeded on more than one occasion, but in the end his sedulous conviction and uncompromising conscience would become the pivotal stroke in closing down the pernicious scourge.

I came upon him a few years after all of this was finished, by which time he had become the unassuming epicenter of the environmental movement in Alaska. His office was the control room of sedition and attack, filled from floor to ceiling with newspaper clippings, government documents, legal texts, and conservation periodicals. It was a sight to behold the inner passion of this individual, manifested in his nature-lover's Sorbonne of the day.

As well as this monumental aspect of his character, Ed was also an innovative computer programmer, engineer, house builder, paddling equipment designer, and perhaps the most knowledgeable and honest businessman ever to tangle in the world of industry. It was quite a tremendous apprenticeship which I underwent those months we had together, for, along with all of the knowledge and skills I gained from his expertise, it was his character- and perhaps his character alone- which allowed me to exist with one foot in the world and the other dangling out in the chaotic ether.

I say his 'character', although I am not certain how well that limited word describes his characterless existence. To be sure he had qualities, idiosyncrasies, and imperfections, but there was a purified emptiness about him which was unmistakable- a vast, inhuman, impenetrable depth lying like a bottomless ocean right behind the unflinching pupils of his deep brown eyes. It was as if no one of any describable personality existed within him; no little ego waiting impatiently for recognition or applause, no little cares or needs or wants directing his every move, no little self struggling to prove or express itself to the rest of the world. He seemed absent of all the insecurities and petty needs which lie like bandits in the skulls of the greater part of the rest of humanity. A Buddha, as I said, as hollow, transparent, and unflappable as the sky.

He had reached that august neutrality in which the reception and rejection of other people's spirits blend into a singular, harmonious non-reaction- an inner event which not only brings great equanimity, but also pivots other individuals, upon meeting one such as he, back onto their own dualistic selves.

It was this particular, remarkable absence of the little qualities within him which made other people, who were still crippled by the shoddy weight of their infantile psyches, become uncomfortably self-conscious in his presence because, among other things, whatever lay behind his eyes would offer no support or acceptance to any ego's pathetic theatrics, and would only react to a true and natural gesture coming from within another, and since most of us have been built up on affectation, warped predispositions, and histrionics alone- he would react very little. And it was this lack of response, this vacuum of consciousness into which the unwitting person, caught in the void of Ed's limitless being, would fall that would begin the little uncomfortable quivers which come when you run into a mirror that offers no reflection. Or perhaps a perfect reflection.

Ed was a living piece of litmus paper, an acid test for fake persona's; a hollow canyon into which one could scream and scream but out of which would come nothing, not even the echo of their own voice, only the sense of falling ever further and further into the dark expanse of non-existence- a place where all sentient beings are horrified at the thought of going.

Ed was a finished product, a philosopher's stone, an individuated, accomplished, established, true and living aspect of the One.

And so it was in his presence and mentorship that I began, or perhaps continued, to whittle away at the false structure of my false being, slowly carving away the learned responses, hidden conditionings, and trumped-up characteristics.

All this I can declare in retrospect, but back then I hardly knew what was going on except that all my games were over because I was in the presence of a master. I was being tempered in the purifying fire of his stainless consciousness. And I would even go so far as to say that Ed himself most likely had no clue of his own effect on others- that was how unaffected, sincere, and innocent he had become. I say innocent, but not docile. No, this was a man who could not be blown down by the putrid breaths of people who had only learned to parade their peacock feathers around but were really mere hatchlings scratching about in the turf. Ed was indeed as innocent as a virgin, but he was also as powerful as a bull. A gentle, unobtrusive, relentless man, fighting the good fight in a land of people who grabbed for anything that appeared as if it could keep them from drowning and who still drowned nonetheless. A colossus of a man, hidden within a thin and wiry frame, carrying about on his shoulders the smoldering remains of a dying fire.

Looking back I wonder how worthy a neophyte I was- back then at the time in my life when I had been so ripped to shreds by the world's futility and my own insatiable contemplations, and what was left of me had been scattered into the winds, until I had no center in which to turn and confront and receive this marvelous specimen of humanity; I was on a path that had no direction, no footing, no mileposts nor ease. I was at a stage in my development which the alchemists of old might have called the *dissolutio*- the tearing down of the old self so that a new one can be rebuilt from the rubble within. And yet, that perhaps, more than anything else, was why Ed was in my life- because there was no more stable pole on earth than himself- a pole by which I could orient myself and hold myself to the ground.

There were times of slippage however, when I would be out guiding or instructing and in the middle of a sentence in which I was orating a paddle maneuver or explicating on a natural wonder to the impatient ears of customers or clients I would all of the sudden freeze, and there I would be looking out at them, and they looking in at me, and I looking in at myself, and a rift would form and widen within me and the distance back to earth seemed immeasurable and I could see the uncomfortable gestures beginning as the clients waited, wondering and worrying that perhaps their guide had become catatonic or had entered into a flashback or hallucination; and part of me would be struggling to make it back to earth, to continue on with the discourse and the life I was struggling to lead, and another part would be hovering off in the distant outskirts of existence, unconcerned, and coldly removed, watching the stop in the play from which I had become fully detached. But then, thankfully, the unasked-for, extemporaneous pauciloquium would abruptly end and I would come out of it and go on, and the bewildered clients would snap back into their interested and submissive roles and somehow I'd make it through that day, and the next day, and so on for two intense summers of life in the world without being in the world.

This is the type of occurrence I carried around with me like a carbuncle swelling inside my head which, every once in a while, released a septic load of disorientation out into my world. And yet I have no regrets over my imperfections during those summers. I have no worry that, had I been more attentive or more together I would have received and taken a greater gift from Ed than I was capable at the time, for I have learned enough by now to know that you can't learn anything from another which you must in the end learn better from yourself, and you can't teach another what in the end they must learn better from their self. And in this sense we are all free from each other; free to pursue our own paths, find our own truths, and live our own lives, and if anyone tries to tell you different you can bet it's because they need something from you which they have neither the courage nor tenacity to get from themselves.

The one time I believe I struck the inner chords of Ed's immense spirit, albeit inadvertently, was on my last day of work when we were saying our goodbyes and I was handing him back my office key, which spurred me to remark, "Well, so now I am keyless again", which I was. It was that comment which sort of stopped Ed for a moment, as he stood there somewhat spellbound and perplexed, and then, with a hint of amazement- as if perhaps he had not heard me correctly- he inquired, "You mean you have no keys?" And I said no, I didn't own anything which had a door or a lock on it: no house, no office, no car, no mailbox, no storage locker.

As I was stating this I remembered how shocked my friend Rick also had been when he found out that same fact about my existence; he was shocked because he was toting about with him a heavy chain of the horrid devices. And it was the same with Ed, who now, for the first time I had ever seen, showed a hint of envy and admiration towards another. Oh, it wasn't a feeble, impotent form of schoolboy envy or admiration; it was his mature way of saying, "Well done man, now there's a worthwhile accomplishment."

We all come here to take our own tests, face our own trials, and have our own experiences, and no one can accomplish another's life for them. Such is the way of the growth of the spirit.

I learned this necessity often and always in my travels up and down the coast during my decade of wandering and growing. One such experience came while in Sitka, during this period of my unpredictable instability which I now see was unavoidable and caused largely by the unrelenting contemplations which hounded me unforgivingly about the all and the everything and my unrequited queries as to my proper role within it. I was endlessly seeking answers for which I did not even have the proper questions, and endlessly seeking destinations towards which I did not even know the way. But a time came during that summer when I would learn a lesson, a way of being, regarding the folly of my desperate seeking and probing and looking ahead- a lesson which would stick with me, and return again and again as I lost and refound it, in many ways, under many guises, but always with the same underlying message.

  It came about on a kayaking trip I had decided to take alone down the outer coast of Baranof Island. It was no huge expedition or perilous venture, but it was undertaken as a personal quest to extend myself beyond the tiring round of thinking, drinking, working, contemplating, writing, and sleep. And I remember paddling out of Sitka a little timid, a little concerned about my abilities to handle the full-on coastal waters, but I headed out nonetheless and pushed southward through the islets and reefs, away from all that had come to weigh upon me and which continued to carry only the pretense solidity.

  It was a terrific first few days as I paddled below looming snow-capped peaks, and past gigantic rafts of lethargic sea otters that floated indifferently along in the swells. I have often said that if I had to come back to earth again as an animal- other than a free flying bird that is- I would return as a sea-otter, those Taoist priests of the water; I would spend a life of leisure and disconcern, floating in the swells alone, or entering into the pleasant orgy of the rafted community, and I'd eat urchin caviar all day, and watch the stars and make love all night.

  Anyways, along with those otters, humpback whales flipped and flirted about during my trip, and wildflowers and eagles abounded in the earth and sky as I meandered southward. I landed my kayak for a while near a hot-spring, twenty miles or so down the coast, and soothed my bruised and broken spirit in the Mother's steam. It was a beautiful holiday from myself at the beginning of the trip, but soon enough I was back inside, back into the old, relentless brain, pondering over this or that, wondering what it was all about and where it was all headed and who was I to be a part of it, and why didn't I know who I was who was a part of it? I ended up camping on a lonely island and drinking a load of bad American beer and walking about aimlessly on shore without being able to still the chronic investigations which continued to plague me.

  But then it happened- as all cries into the ether must eventually have their audience- that as I was paddling back up north a few days later, at no more peace than when I had left, and I could see the final cape looming off ahead of me, at which point I would turn north-east and head for home, that a shift in the weather occurred and a thick blanket of fog came whistling across the water and engulfed me completely, totally blocking out the world around me. The wind, waves, and swells were still minimal, so I continued on my course, heading into the mist in the direction I had already set. I paddled on for perhaps half an hour or so and then without recognizing the subtle movement of my consciousness, something altered within me, something sublime and yet incredibly profound; it came about because I could not see much further ahead than the bow of my boat, and so I had lost all onward vision and sense of destination, and what happened is that I realized that for the first time in my life I was not looking ahead- because I couldn't- I was doing nothing except what I was doing. I was paddling. There was no future, no outcome, no goal, no awaiting experience, there was only the kayak, the sea, and ...me. It is impossible to describe the magnificence of this sudden disentanglement which happened to me. In a goal-directed culture, in a time and accomplishment driven world, I had just fallen through the cracks. Throughout the entire course of my life up until that point I had always been looking ahead, always planning, always waiting for a goal or an answer to appear, always existing where I wasn't actually existing. And then the blinding mist of beingness descended all about me and I could see nothing ahead, plan nothing ahead, and expect nothing ahead. I was just being where I was being, being what I was being, and doing what I was doing, and nothing more. I was right where I was, and only there. As if I had set foot in the true present presence of existence for the very first time. I had attained to the absolute actuality, the bare-bones of beingness. And then I understood why Zen practitioners spend their entire lives pursuing the now-time[14] of being. Yet I knew something better- that it could not be pursued, it could only be lived and allowed and you could not grab hold of it, you could only dance with it, become it, and let it go.

*

nine

During my youth my father excelled at the self-created skill of being able to observe people in a passing crowd and invent names for these anonymous by-passers, which, after he had pointed them out and I had looked at the person, tended to suit them perfectly. Anyone passing by on the street, sitting nearby in a restaurant, theatre, or anywhere else in the great inglorious world of the *hoi polloi*, was the unconscious subject of my father's light-hearted and lucid pseudonyming, so to speak.

To him, Clem was the chubby tourist walking purposelessly about on a ferry; Boris and Hortense were the thoroughly benign and working-class, incognizant neighbours camped beside us one year. Orville was an uptight, perfectly manicured clerk at a convenience store. Zelda was the repressed, and embittered housewife doing chores on her front porch. It didn't matter what the person's name really was, it most likely couldn't have labelled them any better than my father's trained sociologist's keen eye, acutely witnessing the underlying essence beneath the obfuscating form.[15]

Which brings me to the Dumbrowskis. The Dumbrowskis were more of a fabled family to my father than an actuality; they were ever present, and yet never became more than potential. They existed in many guises, but never in reality. Wherever we lived, or travelled, my father would always claim that the Dumbrowski's were going to join us, or we would meet them somehow along the way. They were part of our life, part of the drama in which we were inextricably bound, though I never recall meeting a true Dumbrowski. And yet, given the Law of the Word, it was inevitable that this fantastic species would one day appear before me in the manifest.

I bring this up not for its nostalgic and anecdotal qualities alone, but because this produced one of those many occurrences, or hallmarks, as it were, in the growth of my soul- the little repetitions or oddities by which I began to intuit the magical, sublime livingness of God's theatre- and so, though I had never, in reality, met a Dumbrowski as a child, their mythical affinity to my being, due to my father's regular verbal incantations, would inevitably bring about their existence in the outward drama of my life.

It came to pass that on a rainy autumn day I was hitchhiking along a logging road on the Charlottes, planning to do some Chanterelle picking so as to fill my pockets with some dough again, but suddenly I felt the need to turn around and head the other way. No doubt I had my own ideas about why I was doing this- the ego has an excuse for everything it does without ever humbly admitting that God does everything- but regardless, soon after spinning about and thumbing my way back out of the forest, a beat up old pickup-truck came along and I was given a ride by a woman who would in the end drive me right to the mushroom fields and who, it turned out, was the cousin of a good buddy of mine from back east- four thousand kilometres away- and she had grown up in the town right next to mine. Things like this are intended, it is only for us to empty ourselves into the whole and believe. Had I not turned around she would not have picked me up, and had she not picked me up the rest would not have followed.

What happened is that we drove to a mushroom-picking camp and I set up my tarp and went to sleep. The next day I met a hippy couple who were from my home province as well, and who, soon afterward chose to camp right beside my dilapidated tarp, and their name, of course, was ...the Dumbrowskis.

Although these two folks were far from the vulgar, proletariat, dim-witted mob that I had come to associate with the name, I took this event to mean that I was finally at one with a part of my destiny. And no doubt I was. The Dumbrowskis turned out to be absolutely kindred spirits of mine. Our minds met and agreed upon some of the subtlest matters. As well, soon after our meeting I was to remember having had a dream of the woman Dumbrowski, perhaps a week earlier, before they camped near me- a dream that I could not piece together at the time, but recognized her in it after we had spent some time together.

It was a portentous message, and after a few weeks of spiritual exchange, our time together would culminate with her and I alone, standing together by the side of a lake and receiving the rainbow covenant, signalling the fulfilment of our communion.

In relating this I must continue to argue that each of us must accept their own reality, that each person's reality belongs to that person and that person alone, and that we are not born to agree, we are born to see. And I was beginning to see that once I had disentangled myself from the multifarious layers of phantasmagoria and inertia, I came closer and closer to the inside of the circle, and at that point everything that happened belonged to me, and only me, and I had to believe in it or else I might have to die like all the rest, and start all over again.

I believed, and not long after these events occurred I had another dream in which I was wearing two coats- one inner and one outer- and they were almost perfectly matched. That is when I began to recognise the old axiom that "what is outside of us is a reflection of what is inside", and *vice versa*. The spiral was beginning to tighten.[16]

It was not long after this that I also began having dreams of my *anima* growing older. There she was, painted across the canvas of my subconscious, the same Sandy whom I had found and lost years earlier, and yet somehow she was different, as if she had an older sister whom had now taken to the stage in my dreams. I couldn't, for the life of me, interpret their symbolic meaning; not, that is, until a few weeks later.

What happened is that after my service was complete on the Charlottes I was given the sublime directive that it was time to bug out and head south again, so I jumped on a ferry, arrived in Vancouver, and within a few short hours ran smack into the living incarnation of this older Sandy- the very one I had been dreaming of. Instantly I was in love. That was when things began truly coming together, and truly falling apart.

When things like this happen to you, you can bet you're on a cosmic course piloted by the unknown captain directing your ineffable craft into the infinite beyond. You know you're a part of something so big and inexplicable, so unique, and so unprecedented, that try as you might to let others in on what is happening to you, you don't really even have a clue yourself, and the best thing to do then is to just soften your gaze, open your heart, loosen your expectations, and let it all happen.

This is exactly what I didn't do. No, poor me, a most unlikely candidate for such a privileged cosmic convergence; I, like a starving man at a banquet, stepped up to bat without an inkling of how to play the game. And I swung, and swung, and swung at a ball which was never meant for me to hit. And when finally I had struck out I was miserable. Which is to say, for the second time in this crazy lifetime of mine, I had found, loved, and lost my *anima* in the flesh. And when absurdities like that happens to you, you curse God for making a scapegoat out of you and for allowing all the imperfections and indifference in the antiquated bureaucracy of the heavens to screw the whole show up. And yet it wasn't the heavens that were screwy, it was me.

That is- as I finally figured out, through all my whining, and gnashing, and writhing about- I had entered the wrong door of the castle; I had mistaken a sister for a mate. Apparently, as the powers were none too lax in reminding me, I was only supposed to knock on this elder Sandy's door and say hello, but in my misguided habit of taking the world for the way men see it, I went right for the bedroom and forgot the rest of the home. And that is when I learned a very hard, very important lesson: what God does not want to have happen, does not happen. Laugh or scoff as you might, but the force which runs about and through us, and makes all things which are made, has greater power to orchestrate the factors in our lives, and make sure that the greater event holds sway, than any of our little egos are wont to allow. I met this absolute force of will, and it stopped me and caused me more grief than I am prepared to relate. And that is all there is to it.

Looking back I can chuckle at my rage towards the heavens then, at my clenched fist cussing and calling down the maleficent force which had set me up. But I had to find, as we all must find, that what we most desire is not necessarily what is best for us. And I had to go crazy with sadness and mad with confusion over this love lost as quickly as it was found, and I had to leave Vancouver again for a spell and head down to Northern California, and I had to wander amongst the giant redwoods, alone and feeble and distraught because God was against me, and I had to walk and walk and walk and drink myself away in a little town with a little bar called, interestingly enough, 'Jack's Pub', and then I had to walk and walk and walk again until finally coming to peace in a tiny motel in the middle of nowhere; a motel, which, like myself, had a few lights missing, and, laughingly enough, would spell out the message of my imperfect gaze in bold and unquestionable terms, for, as I came upon this little motel in the woods, as the sun went out dying into the Pacific, there, on the last day of my insane pilgrimage, lay the bold and clear letters spelling out both the place I would lay my head that night, and the consequence of my own myopia: JACK'S MOTE_. Some lights had gone out on the sign, and the L was missing in the word, and the word was with God, and the word was God, and the word became flesh and descended into my darkness, extracting the beam from my spirit eye, and I went to sleep that night and awoke a less bitter and a stronger man for my errors.

That loss, which drove me practically insane, led, however, on to a further, inward realization, as loss always does if you are strong enough to flip the coin and take what you're given into the welcoming wind. Many hard lessons which I learned through loss and struggle in my outward life became valuable insights which would expedite my inner process later on.

Regret is a matter of perspective; to have regret is to not yet know that every external failure is leading to an internal victory. Regret is the interstice of time in between the two. For would a relief pitcher in baseball, who, when warming up in the bullpen before being called into the game, and failing to throw a single strike in a hundred attempts- would that pitcher, when finally on the mound and throwing strike after strike, and in the end winning the game for the team, would he later sit alone, sombrely regretting his errant attempts while warming up? I think not.

The pain and confusion I suffered when my elder *anima* withdrew from me- or was withdrawn from me by the force of the law, so to speak- after our brief but intense love affair, which caused me in the end to condemn and curse the bumbling bureaucrats in heaven, and their seemingly pernicious intervention, would in the end provide a lesson which would later quicken my internal movement from the sacred marriage of the microcosm, to that of the macrocosm- which is an event that is, as always, obscure, and sublime, and not so easily delineated as words might make it seem. For it was during the loss and aftermath of this physical relation that I was given dreams and understandings telling me that she was not the correct partner for me- that another woman, whose soul was more suited to the destiny of my own, had already been sighted and chosen and that I needed only to be patient- a characteristic which was seemingly absent from my psychological makeup at the time- throughout it all, and the great plan would come to fruition. Needless to say that despite my initial disparaging remarks to the firmament, and my vocal ingratitude, the prophesied relationship eventually occurred and the chosen woman became an essential aspect in the furthering of my heart and spirit, which is to say, she was the one who became my *soror mystica*, as mentioned earlier. And so once again I could only throw up my arms in bewildered hallelujahs and wait for the next test to arise, as they are wont to do on the awkward path of the hapless chela.

Anyway, it was largely due to this outward scenario which I have just described that, a while later, near the end of a process which culminates a certain period of the inner work, I had taken another caretaking position and was looking after some cabins, boats, ducks, and chickens in the remote, untouched wilderness of the southern Charlottes, but this time I was completely alone for a month of psychic involution and communion with the land. Furthermore I had just recently learned to descend my microcosmic consciousness- my self- into my microcosmic being- my body-, thus finally enjoying the ecstatic union of spirit and flesh- of the male and female aspects of my own being; aspects which had been becoming more individually apparent and more conscious of their uniqueness, and therefore more capable of recognizing each other and uniting.

And so, projecting my non-being into the flesh of being I could bring forth a sort of peaceful union which is only possible once the two polar opposites are separated unto themselves and then reunited. It was as if an internal union was taking place which brought about a tranquillity and sense of well being which I had never experienced in the previous years of my exhilarating ride from plateau to valley and back up again on the indefatigable roller-coaster of existence.

And so, continuing on with this procedure, it happened one night in a dream that these two halves- the male and the female- came together and I could see that they were vibrating at very different frequencies, in altogether disparate patterns, but as the two bodies merged into one, the frequencies blended, creating a new harmony, a harmony which would have been impossible to achieve for either of them left on their own.

An electric explosion from this union awoke me as the energy shot about disentangling itself. At that point the complete and everlasting union had not come to pass, but I was given to understand the magic and beauty of this internal marriage- the *mysterium coniunctionis*, or chemical wedding- by which the one becomes two and then the two merge back into a wholly new one. The next night Venus came to me in a dream and said that from the union the night before the mystical child would be born.[17]

This ethereal coming-together is symbolically similar to the courting ritual of eagles, in which the two flirting birds will fly high up into the air, then grab hold of each other, stall in their ascent, and then plummet downward, grappling and wrestling with each other and spinning about in a mad, tumbling descent- which is the oddest form of foreplay I've ever seen- and then break apart before hitting the turf, only to fly back up again and have another tussle with each other's loins. I say that the spirit and soul join in a similar fashion, as they grapple while descending towards the ascending flesh, in the perilous mating of essence and form.

To be sure, the event of my own inner coming-together complicated my efforts to feed the chickens and bail out the boats which I was caretaking- it is tough to rocket off into space and also take out the garbage- but it is always essential to stay somewhat grounded, lest the lightning come down and incinerate the electrodes.

And so I kept on with my duties, minimal as they were, and kept on walking amongst, and living with and loving the Earth, and let the process run on its own- in the darkly catalysed body- inalterable speed, as it is intended to do, for I have found that many problems come simply by inhibiting a natural movement which, if allowed, will progress along on its unconstrained way.

Thus it happened that, as quickly as in the manifest event earlier- when my elder *anima* and sister on the Tree of Life and I were parted, and I was left to drift and then to be led to the intended union- I again felt the greater Self divide the male and female halves of my microcosmic, inner self again. This caused a certain level of anxiety and confusion, to be sure, but it was because of the previous experience- of the coming together and then the taking apart- that I relaxed and listened and realized that if I surrendered to the Self (as if there was an option) an even greater union might occur- the marriage of the Macrocosmic Consciousness, the Father, with the Macrocosmic Body, the Mother Earth.

It is as if the lower union had to be temporarily divided so that the higher selves could meet. For true wholeness does not exist within the microcosm, because only the macrocosm is whole, because it is the *whole* thing.

I once read in an esoteric text- the kind that falls into your hands with indescribable synchronicity, right at the time your path has become profound and confusing- that, in occult circles, it is considered the second greatest union to mate with one's mystical sister, and the highest union to mate with one's mystical mother.

I suppose this is what symbolically happened to me both times- that initially I had so desired the first option, that I could not see anything else, and so I had to be grabbed from above and taken off course so that I would not bungle my highest destiny and mate with a Sister, instead of The Mother.

It is interesting to note that my *soror* belongs to the spiritual archetype of my biological mother as well. But my *soror* was much more than even that. Much, much more, to the point where I realized that in her I had met myself- inverted and flipped about in the warping mirrors and vortices of the ether perhaps, but she was me, and I was her; that is, we were the same being, only reflected through the cosmos in a different way; we were 'twin souls' as the term is known in esoteric circles. Thus, being in relationship with her created a convergence of aspects I had never read nor heard about: a *soror mystica*, who belonged to my mother's archetype, and who was my other self, and also my lover.

And who, in the history of the occult world, could have imagined such an implausible and irregular happening?

Anyway, the marriage of the Father and Mother within me would not come to complete fulfilment on that trip either. There were still some things to work out, one which would take me to the other side of the earth, and to another place where the two cosmic Parents had gone to war thousands of years ago, and were now attempting to reunite. But that's another tale altogether.

It was also during this care-taking and monastic stint, down in the southern wilderness of the Charlottes- which was the single longest duration I had yet spent alone, in total isolation- that so much had been cleared out and fell away from me that my insides felt as if a giant psychic enema had been gushing in and washing things out for weeks, and taking all the shit inside me with it, so that when I lay down in bed at night, before drifting off to sleep, I would fall further and further away from identity until I left the orbit of my little existence and entered into the vast space of consciousness which exists within each of us, and there, with an adroit non-effort, I would negate myself and vanish completely, and all that would remain was the living space of the Self behind the self, which was my true Self.

Finally, my true Self, the one who I was beneath it all. And by returning to *It* the dam between non-being and being broke open, and the lifeblood of divine energy came rushing out of the space, and into the body, exciting and rejuvenating the connection between them again.

In order for this to happen I had to completely forget about myself, to evict any idea of who I was or whatever compelled me. I had to become as small as a tiny flame and then blow myself out. Only then did my Godself wash through me, unimpeded, and the contiguous ocean fell into the tiny drop that was me.

In doing so I found, as I disappeared from within myself, another *I* which was also me. It emerged and encompassed me, and the soft electric energy of the larger dimension would pour down, upon, and through me as the first I regained itself without losing the second *I* which was surrounding it and all else; I am inside *I*, self within Self, body immersed in consciousness, a presence within a presence, and both of them are me. And the energy poured forth like this until *I* fell asleep, or fell back into identity, whichever dream world came first

This was a tremendous rite, one which had been hovering seemingly far out of reach from the moment I started my inward pursuit, a decade earlier. Back then I had gotten up and going before I knew where, or why, or who, or how, or what was happening. I was up and going and running from not-God to God, and back and forth, on and on through all the merciless stages in between. Flailing and fighting, struggling, loving, laughing, stumbling, squirming, wondering, asking, listening, surrendering, and then back up and flailing again. At first I was a madman, then a saint, a liar, a preacher, a thief, a soldier, a hero, a loser, a servant, a tyrant, a victim, a fool. I was up and at it, and going through the howling darkness and glee, through the gratitude and contempt and worship and spit. I was a part of it, none of it, no one, some one, everyone, and all. I was never sure and always certain. I couldn't give in and I couldn't go on. How it came to be so I had no clue. I couldn't start it nor stop it nor join in. It happened without me participating and it happened because of me. In between God and not-god I loved and hurt and lost and grew and shrank, and was built and broken in the stress and calm of non-meaning.

It's a hapless lot of incalculable madness, this happening.

When everything begins to go right and wrong simultaneously, and you lose the ability to tell the difference, for there is no difference, and either way you don't really give a damn, because life has flopped up and down on you so many times that, like a person on a crazy ride at the country fair, you lose the intensity, the fear, and the joy of the event, and instead sink carelessly back into yourself; for you have become psychologically gimbaled and unable to lose your sense of equilibrium.

When you have lived existence out completely in its manifold directions- when you have thought and fought, pondered and wondered, yearned and wept, hated and loved- all to their furthest extent, and yet you are still unbroken, still earnest, still alive and mad for life, still strong and fighting, still driven on and on like that wild hare fleeing the unforgiving hounds- the most unexpected shift eventually occurs; the self dissolves in the vision of its limitless dimensions, the mind loses meaning, the heart loses loss, and the whole swollen mess of life literally flips inside out, and upside down- as occasionally it seems wont to do- and everything changes at once, yet nothing has changed.

When pain is no longer painful, joy no longer a thrill, life no longer a teeter-totter between estranged opposites, then the leveling-off is well under way. That is when you become dangerous and necessary to the world, because you are outside of its struggles; you become a random particle, divorced from the chains and rules of life, and so you are both needed and distrusted, admired and despised, and praised and blamed, because other people's troubles are no longer your troubles, their taboos no longer your taboos, their sorrows are no longer painful, and their euphorias mere trifles to you. You are beyond their sufferings, concerns, and desires, and therefore all powerful and yet powerless amongst them.

Always thundering forward like this, it has to go on and on, all the while stopping without ending, because everything is always ending and nothing ever ends, though it only comes back to us when we let it go, because it was ours to begin with and we only had to stop chasing it in order to be caught. That is when God and not-God happen together. The wheel grows wings. The lion lies down with the lamb. One eye weeps from laughter, the other from pain. And suddenly you're always separate and never apart. You have become what nobody told you you were. And it is finished.

*

ten

Heading back down the coast late that November, I had caught a ride on a black-cod fishing boat and we were soon running through the remnants of a hurricane and being thrashed about in thirty-foot seas. That was when I understood why Christ had often chosen fishermen as his disciples- because fishermen are inherently the brave, hearty, storm-tempered souls who every day plumb the hidden depths to gain sustenance for the masses, while at the same floating deftly upon the furious gale of life.

To be a fisherman on the wild west coast is to learn about life quickly via the path of hardship, loneliness, camaraderie, endurance, and faith. I have found no other occupation on earth in which I have met so many saints in the making.

The boat I was on was captained by a truly marvelous fellow, Doug, who had been orphaned from his wayward parents as a small child, and then divided from the rest of his siblings when they were sent to foster homes. He had seen every sort of tragedy and sorrow by the time he reached puberty, and to this day you can hear the tremor in his voice when he speaks of the injustices which he grew up with and witnessed as a young boy. Somehow, though, his spirit refused to be broken, and he matured with an understanding of how *not* to treat others. Which is to say, he had learned, as it were, the noble quality of *respect*. And that means he had the mature and humble ability to see life through another's eyes, to re-*spectate* existence from their standpoint, which is a rare and admirable characteristic in the self-centered culture of the west.

One of his crewmembers, Fred, who had worked for him driving trucks earlier in life, related to me a very telling story of Doug's character. Fred said that one day he was driving down a logging road he had been told not to go on because of its hazards, but went anyway to save time, disregarding Doug's directive, and ended up rolling the truck over on its side on a steep embankment. Not only was Fred ashamed, but he assumed he was out of a job and most likely in debt for a huge repair bill. He called up the boss and contritely told him of his offense and of the crash, expecting to get what was coming to him. Not from this Doug though. Oh, he was tough when he needed to be tough, but when someone came to him with sincerity and intent to make things right, he was as forgiving as God. I relate this short anecdote largely so as to share the first sentence which Doug said to Fred upon hearing of his error and accident. Doug, who had been through hell and had come out of it of his own accord, and was trying now to build up some heaven on earth, simply said: "If that's the worst thing that happens to me today, I'm gonna have a great day." Then he hired a front-end loader, drove it up to the site of the crash, and skillfully lifted the truck back upright. And that was that.

Doug's fishing crew was composed of a handful of hard-working, caring, brotherly tough guys. A true family of men who believed in their father, who believed in them, and therefore the collective spirit was as strong as a bundle of sticks bound unbreakably together. It was a true metaphor for Christ with his disciples, out on the infinite and lonely sea of the spirit, aiding and caring for one another, and not a Judas amongst them.

I sat out the storm in the lower galley, fighting off seasickness, and fell to admiring the love and endurance of these ten young men and their seasoned pilot.

To be far off shore in a howling tempest is to be on another planet, in a different solar system, and to learn to depend on no one but yourself and those who you call your mates. And that is to learn how to live as one.

The sea was so rough, and I was so green, that the fellows had apparently taken up a friendly bet regarding whether I would empty the contents of my stomach that night or not. One of the guys even went so far as to put the movie *The Perfect Storm* on the video in the galley, in a jocular attempt to push my limits and seal his victory. He told me that the fishing boat depicted in the movie had encountered the confluence of three separate weather fronts, which had created a chaos in the seas that was unheard of in the past. And then he told me that we were heading into a section of the open coast where the meteorologists had predicted four fronts were to converge within thirty-six hours, and that he and the others were hoping to quickly pull up all the fishing gear they had left out there a few days earlier, secure the catch, and then get the boat out of there before it hit. That was some unsettling news for me. So I sat there with one eye watching a raging storm on the television, and the other eye looking out the window at another tempest, while the waves crashed over the deck of the boat and the winds howled in both scenarios, and I was wondering if I had finally come to the epicenter of my existence, where fantasy and reality met, where the show and the audience merged together, and the Maker and Made became One.

If that was the case, I thought, then I'm going to make sure this show ends without tragedy, and, surely enough, we rode out that first storm, and the four incoming fronts serendipitously never manifested, and the next day the lads set to work hauling their gear and harvesting their catch, while I sat up on the top of the boat, watching sperm whales feed on the offal, as huge albatrosses circled all about, and tiny rainbows, off in the distance, came and went between the clouds and the horizon.

That trip on the fishing boat was a valuable lesson on the hardships met, and the labor required to be an offshore fisherman, or a fisher of men, as it were.

It takes me back to a vanguard meeting some years back, the fallout of which may account for much of which transpired within me, and perhaps was responsible for many of the experiences which I have been relating throughout this book.

While heading up to Alaska for my second summer of work, perhaps three years prior to that ride on the fishing boat, I met for the first time in my life a 'Christed' individual. At least this is what Tom, the crab fisherman, said humbly of himself, and I have no reason to doubt him. Tom was an incredibly soft and gentle, divorced father of three. He openly described the ordeals he had undergone over the past few years during his unexpected and unasked-for relentless chastening. He had lost everything dear to him: his wife and family, and the respect of those around him. At one point near the end of his trials he was sitting alone in his empty house and he could feel the Spirit enter and suddenly the walls of his house caught fire and he knew that he was being tested- the final test- and so he laid down on the floor and understood that he could not get up until he was told to go. Call this psychosis or faith, what you will, but he stayed in the house until the flames were all about and finally the Voice came and told him to leave, and he left. Soon afterward he was incarcerated in a mental hospital because he refused to lie about what had happened, and the authorities did not believe his story, suspecting him of arson, which is understandable, I suppose. Apparently there was one doctor in the asylum, however, who recognized Tom for who he truly was and had attempted to get him released, stating that he had undergone a spiritual transformation, but the ignoble medicine men in charge had not the eyes to see, and so kept him in bondage.

When I met Tom he was on the lamb, so to speak. He had been released on his own recognizance, as long as he would continue to take the mind-altering drugs prescribed for his 'condition', which he didn't, and so the hired guns were after him.

I spent only a day and a half with him but it was an eye-opening event, for he told me of many of the inward incidents which had happened to him along the way, most of which he had no clue nor understanding about, for he had grown up dyslectic and could hardly read. It was only after his crown-chakra had blown off, as he says, that he began struggling through books and texts to understand more of what was happening.

I say it was interesting, and most likely destined, for me to meet him, because from then on I had a living example of one who had been grabbed by God, beaten down, and then raised back up, and it was a meeting I was going to recall a while later, as the Spirit and I had our own wrestling match which I was destined to lose.

It was a number of months after this, after I had worked my summer in Sitka and come back down south. I was hiding away from the world for a month or so at a buddy's place in Victoria, while he was off somewhere else on the globe, and I had been making my rounds at the pubs, wandering around in blessed anonymity, and taking in the city's exemplar respect for fiddle music. And then one afternoon I found myself sitting on the couch in the living room in a bit of a reverie and daze- as I was habitually falling into about this time- and suddenly I heard a voice which said: "Give me an opening and I will come in." And at that moment I knew it was Christ's voice, the one who came before me, who conquered life and death, and who now roams about in the ether as a guide to all those who would choose to be free. Jesus the Christed one, the alpha male, and omega female.

I was around thirty-one years old at the time, just about the age in which Christ had begun his ministry. And though at that moment I had no clue how to create that necessary 'opening', I knew, at least, that I had to leave the world behind again so as to make it happen.

And so back I went again, back to the coast, to Flores Island, out from the ways of death and destruction, out again, alone again, to find some way to make that opening and let the Man come in. And I say that I had been out there for only a few days when, walking along the beach, I could suddenly sense another person with me, beside me, in me, all around me, I am not sure but I am sure that I was not alone and I am also sure that I have never been as alone since then as I had been previously in my life. Let the Pharisees, critics, and heathens have their say, but when you, of no talent nor ability of your own, find yourself walking with your hand in the hand of the man who rules the water, the other way of life is now done with forever.

Oh, perhaps life itself becomes no more cheery than before, no more easy, no more full of understanding, confidence, or peace, but one thing has changed forever- your days of walking this earth as the loneliest person alive are finished, and in another sense, they have only just begun. And that is no small thing.

I relate this now, near the end of the book, to give retrospect to the trials, failures, and successes I have documented throughout. Though I know not what parts of my life were altered by the Christ event, I know many must have been.

However, after that first opening it would be yet a long time before that new seed was to take root, grow up, and become large enough for the birds to come and nest within. It would be a long time before I realized how the spirit which lives in all things takes your soul over when you let it, and fertilizes the young shoot, and when it is grown and finally blossoms, it cuts you off at the roots and shows you how to fly.

It would be a slow and awkward period for me, as I learned to understand how the Body is spread all over the earth, incomplete and fragmented, and crying out for its missing members, and only those organs which have become living vehicles of the whole can move about and reconnect the amputated limbs. And no one knows but the master planner where that will be done, how long it will take, or what will be needed to stop the incessant bleeding.

And so I had to relinquish myself to the extent that I was capable back then, had to cut all ties which bound me to others, had to listen for the call, or receive the dream, and ...I had to follow. I had to follow not knowing why I was going where I was headed, but knowing that there was someone who did.

When this type of irregular and sublime event occurs, and the concomitant duties which follow befall you, others begin to wonder about your life, to question why you are going somewhere, or doing or not doing some such thing. And the biggest problem is that ...you have no answer.

My patented response was, "I'm following the spirit." But what that means to one whom is not following it I have no clue; I came to imagine that to them it meant- "I'm lost in a fantasy of make-believe and confusion and I can't get out." And yet when it came right down to it, and I'd speak with another about the essential aspects of this mysterious life we are granted, occasionally the tables would turn, and we would meet in that unencumbered place beyond only what can be seen.

I make no claims here for myself. I am only speaking my own truth, in my own voice, because I must; I am the only one who can say what I have seen, and yet I am not that one either, for the Self inhabits the self in all of us, and only when we abandon all sense of possession and accomplishment do we realize the one who does what is done.

To follow the call of the spirit is to lose and gain without choice, because you are no longer the chooser.

Jesus carried the Christ to earth, and left it for men to toss about like a hot potato which some will drop or throw to another instantly, and a few will hold on and carry as far as they can go.

It's as if you're handed a ball and you run with it, not because you know where the goal is, but because you're being chased, and because there's no one yet around to hand it off to, nor are there any fans, not even a referee. All you know is that you must carry it as far as you can before being caught and tackled. You're cornered at one moment, and then with a quick move you're out in the open and running free. You're tired, scared, and mad as hell. The field goes on and on and the game never finishes. Only you do.

In this we are all less like Jesus, and more like Simon of Cyrene- who carried the cross for a while, only to hand it back in the end. Yet the Christ may be invited into oneself, and is elevated in priority whenever a person, with absolute sincerity, acceptance, and courage, utters the divine fiat, "Thy will be done." Then the Christ is the one within who mercilessly takes all the rest away from you. Christ is the destroyer, the emancipator, the ruthless madman who comes after you until you're finished. Don't let them kid you in Church, Christ will knock you down, beat you senseless, take everything you have, and burn it in an inward bonfire. Your only hope at that point is to get away, which you never will. In fact, there is no hope, because Christ takes every hope away. You can only lie down, and stay down. You are finished.

Oh how I laugh now at the gentle Christ of our sleepy churchgoers. What a romantic heap of stool. The warm, cuddly Lamb of God- bah! What a ruse. Christ is like a wild and mad wolf at your heals. He is a murderer, and you are his victim. He will kill the lie inside of you with merciless love. Oh, the truth will set you free indeed, but first it must destroy you.

There is no soothing balm which comes to anoint your wounds in the night, but only the scalding flame itself, and you are the kindling. The chastening will not end but in your own death's death. Thus perhaps it is that this violence comes out of love, but let me tell you- it is violence, make no mistake about it.

When the Man comes for you, it is the most torturous blessing you might ever receive.

To be blessed is to be given what you have barely the ability to take. To be blessed is to be shown the way, and yet be afraid to follow. To be blessed is to rage against the merciful benevolence which sustains you, and to have bestowed upon you what you are not always grateful for accepting. To be blessed is to be humbled because you have what you did not ask for- the burden of a privilege you cannot imagine how to use.

To be baptized is to be shown who you are. To know who you are is to be who you are, and when you know who you are, even if the whole world were to rise up with judgment against you it would feel as if naught but a light breeze rustling through some distant trees. For after we have been baptized in water and spirit, and have carried our own cross and died between two thieves on the lonely mountain of the world's pain, that is when we are resurrected and brought back, and it is then that we will refuse to die again for others, and we will begin to live Life itself for the very first time.

To that end I say, while the dead are burying the dead, let the living exhume their lives.

When finally the chastening is complete, it is through the eyes that God meets God, and thus grows closer and closer to the remembrance of oneness. The soul now serves a greater plan than it can fathom, and so must stop asking "why? why must I leave? why must I stay? why must I lose and gain and lose again?" The Christ is a role in which the script is taken away from you, and you must wander from stage to stage, with no idea of what part you must play next, nor what you will have to say, nor when you will be finished and told to head on to another.

That is when life takes on a flowing foreignness to it, because what you do and where you go no longer belong to you, because that is your role- to have none. And therefore you are as if on-call, and ready to take on any role in the drama, if only to help see it through to its end. You become the non-existent middle ground between Heaven and Earth; the Ghost through which the Host prepares the banquet. For the Christ is ever crucified, rising at the center and zenith of our pyramidical consciousness, and thus dragging upward, as if attached to a giant sheet, the rest of the laboring cosmos.

Here we must toss aside all judgment. Here we forsake both good and bad, for, as it is said, God alone is good.[18] Whether a person serves their Christ self or their villain, they will still be a profane mix of good and bad, and only the mist of hubris will convince them otherwise.

Let no man or woman confuse themselves with their roles. There is no person who is Christ, there is only the Christ which one is given to wear like all other costumes until one is tired of it- tired of taking on other people's karma, other people's sin, and other people's lack of intent to straighten out their own bent lives- which is that station of the cross where Jesus had said "What have I to do with thee?", and his apathy finally set him free. For eventually even the Christ aspect of the individual, like all others, must die and be reabsorbed into the One- the microcosm must evaporate and rise into the macrocosm- if the person is to lose identity with the separate self, and become the impersonal Self. For absolute union with the All is impossible if the yogin or yogini maintains any thought of separative existence from the rest.[19]

*

eleven

In every one of us there is an angel dying. And yet all that is needed is a shift, an inversion, for at the furthest reaches of the ignorance which ensconces us, lie the antipodes of sorrow and ecstasy. We have dwelt in the former, dark end too long. Now we need only fight our way to the lost extreme, for these opposites are not actually opposed, but are the same thing, viewed from different directions.

Thus, when the walls and chains you are bound in finally show themselves plainly as webs of your own ignorant devising- that these arise from neither the Good, nor Evil, but from your own confusion- that is when you stop struggling to break away from false prisons, chuckle a bit at the lesson, genuflect for a moment or two, gape wildly with wonder at it all, and float calmly away without caring.

To explain this further is impossible, for explanation may comfort and console us, but it will never set us free, because freedom comes at the expense of understanding, of expectation, and of meaning. And to grow up in a world of explanation, and to long to be free, is to be born with shackles implanted inside of you, and to have to tear yourself apart into little pieces to get the manacles out. But what must be done must be done.

Such an overwhelming predominance of odd events happened to me that I began to take in the full and unbelievable drama, and thus to realize what was really going on- I was coming to the end of my karmic cycle, for reasons of which I cannot be certain, but to be sure the firmament had broken overhead, and the Spirit was surging forth, desperate to retake command of my being.

I had been spinning out there on the fabulous ride of the tumbling manifest; out on the whip of the disintegrating circumference, where everything comes and goes and no time to wait or you'll miss a part of the show. But I could not stay out there forever. The gravity of my disparate parts began coalescing and cooling, and falling into the center from which there is no return, because there is no desire to return, because there is no desire, because nothing is missing.

One of the last of these fragments which I came to contain, was the long sought after flower of eternity- the Rose. The Rose is a particle from the Garden, brought down with mankind during the Fall. The Rose is the innocent, guileless, virginal aspect within all of us, though occasionally it is fully manifested in the life of certain individuals more than others.

There was no specific one person who became the Rose in my life, for I met a number of true Roses, generally in doe-like, gentle, and inwardly beautiful men or women, whose spirits express that part of the Garden.

I believe that we all harbour this aspect in a precarious and hidden spot within ourselves. I say 'hidden' because to bring it forth without thorns is to send a sheep out to the wolves. For the Rose belongs more to Heaven than to Earth, and it is this precious aspect of life which is guarded and rarely exposed to the marauders.

And so I have no doubt why I was drawn to these sorts of people outwardly, and to Rose Bay itself, so often. For I had to finally meet the Rose within myself, and I needed to see it manifested out in front of me before I had a clear image of what it was that lay buried within.

Thus the Rose became a part of my inward life because it was a part of my outward life, or perhaps it is the other way around. No matter. I can say this about almost everyone I have ever met- that they were either manifested aspects of myself, which lay dormant or clouded within me until I met them in true and living colour, in the outward show of my inward life; or they were living aspects of my inner being which lay dormant externally, until I became them inwardly and then expressed them outwardly. Either way, the outer depends on the inner which depends on the outer. Oneness is duality.

It is like this for all of us, though at times there are certain opportunities afforded which allow life to provide the entire make-up of our inner beings, brought to us on the canvas of the world, thus aiding us towards completion.

And so, just as I had to encounter outwardly, in another person, the Adversary within me, the Shadow, Hero, Guide, Mercurius, Anima, Wanderer, Madman, Alien, Christ, Coward, and Fool, so also I had to meet and assimilate the Rose.[20]

Which is to say, I had to become absolutely innocent, and absolutely inviolable.

And so that autumn as I was heading back down to Gomorrah from the pure and beneficient islands, and I could sense the oncoming doom of the weeds- those psychic fiends- along with the rest of the city's effluvium, which in the past had so easily soaked in through my tender shell- having fallen asleep, I dreamt of a knight in black armour, and when I awoke I knew that the armour was for me to wear, and that the armour was ...indifference. I knew then that I had been given the right to not care, to offend the offenders when necessary- to gird up my loins and let nobody through the portcullis who was not welcome in the castle. Which is to say, I had been given the order to be as cruel and unfeeling as ...God.

This was a turning point for me, because I had spent the last many years consciously breaking the walls down which separated me from others, from the spirit, and from the heavens. And now I was being told to build them back up again, so that I might walk back into Nineveh and survive the stoning. For, up until then, I had not been able to hold the inviolable space within myself because I had been rejecting the darkness required to defend it.

Now I had to become dark myself, and had to stop accepting people's slothful, chaotic, or vulgar ways, simply because they had allowed to happen to themselves what was happening, and which they had neither intent nor energy to transform, and therefore by my not accepting them, they were forced to accept themselves without my acceptance- and that was a greater gift, and a harder lesson, than my unconditional, courteous acceptance would have given.

It was a decree and consciousness shift which, to this day, I am still struggling to perfect- and that is: how to stay open to the sublime event, and yet have the walls necessary to protect myself from the dis-eased hordes. It is an art unlike any other, but I see now that it is an essential element of the psyche if the virgin soul is to live amongst the rapists.

It had been my temperate disposition within the world's malice and errors which had left me slow to wallow. I had been trapped and languid in the horrible pathos of the day. I had no composite tendencies, replete or inviting, which might have gathered me full into a fury. I had suffocated in the torpor of lies *because I had no anger*, not even for myself. And without anger there is no way out of this lovelessness. The only way out is to punch your way out, with a wrathful love as murderous as a mother has for her child in danger.

Love, violent love- that merciless, uncompromising mandate; you must love your own soul with an inviolable madness bent on nothing but freedom, or you will die softly in this world of courteous lies.

And if I now appear brave upon the turbulent waters, it is because I have found that I will no longer drown; because I learned to breathe below the surface of life, to sink into the mud like a frog in winter, and inhale osmotically through the pores of my numinous membrane. I learned how to die and be reborn every day, and so to remain strong in the battle. I learned how to retreat when I am out of bullets, and how to attack with a loaded gun; I learned how to yield and hide, burst forth and conquer, how to flex when the force would break me, and to hold firm when a hill can be won. I learned how to stop caring when things became futile, and how to care when life was prepared to grow in the sun.

I learned to forget the monstrosities called right or wrong. I learned not to search for happiness, truth, knowledge or meaning, but only for beauty and love. I learned not to fight the day, but to fly in the wind like an ethereal dove.

A dove, I learned to float over the earth like an indifferent dove. And I learned to fly towards nothing ...but beauty and love.

As such the Rose- the Rose with thorns- and many other characters came to exist within my consciousness, as parts of my fuller self, which was itself a part of a greater self, which was part of a greater self still perhaps, and so on, and by accumulating my completeness I came into the service of the Greater Vehicle, by which all my aspects will rise up with me at the end of time.

In the end we must all contain the whole world; we must take everyone in, give them shelter, devour them like food, digest their unique occurrence, and absorb them into ourselves. We must become everyone if we are to ever become ourselves. The walls of individuality must die, the shell of the scared chick must crack, and the little bird must screech, totter, fall, and fly, if ever it is to soar away one day, mate in another lost land with another infinity, build a nest, and bear another world of its own.

I dove and ascended, digested and expelled, grew and shrank, and gathered every pair of opposites into me before, like old Noah, I entered into the Ark of the Self. Then I rode out the deluge, landed back upon the stainless earth, and dispersed my seed across the insubstantial cosmos.

But to allow this to happen I had to keep letting go of the circumference, keep releasing my grip on the ride and allow the sense of falling and vertigo to overcome my frantic need to grab hold; to fall away from it all, over and over again, until the mass grew large enough to pull everything else into it, and that now warm and molten whole ...began to glow.

I had to toss my little self away and become nothing *and* all. I had to take others in, modify them, and be modified by them, assimilate them, and be assimilated by them, and then let them go.

I could not define myself if I was to engulf the Mystery. I could not deny life if I was to affirm the glory of being. I could not limit myself if I was to accept my eternal non-being. I could not contain only myself if I was to grow to contain the entire world.

If I had kept trying to be something that I no longer was, or kept looking for something that wasn't there, I would have gone mad. I had come from the sky and had no desire to accept life on earth, but I had to accept it. I had to include myself in all of it, or remain on the outside forever.

You see, people who are born of the earth need, oddly enough, less from life than those born of the sky. Because to be born of the sky means to come here with nothing, and therefore, like a refugee, to need everything. To come here from the sky means to need to be drunk with ecstasy, inspiration, wine, poetry, wonder, love, nature, or God, because to be here with naught but the sober profanity of mankind, is to waste the reason you came. And to deny this reality is to deny your very self. To live here without being ever intoxicated with some form of existence or another, is to be barren of both the sky and the earth, which is a horrible vacancy to endure, for that is all that is left- to endure. And so you have to learn either how to die, or how to live. Or both.

I found that to exist within all contradictions, is to learn to exist beyond them.

I realized this necessity because I had been rejecting all of life, but not in the way that a man rejects something- by knowing it is wrong for him, saying 'no, thank-you', and moving on towards what he truly desires. No, I had been rejecting the world like a spoiled child, throwing away the toys I had been given and then asking for more, and then throwing these away and so on. I had to learn to accept life and understand that it is a gift, and that one of the gifts is the right to reject the gifts, but only if it is done like a man who looks to heaven, thanks the giver, and yet says he is better off without them. Only then is rejection a form of acceptance, and the contradiction, which destroys life, is finished for good.

*

twelve

I have described these events in my life as they occurred and had effect upon me, and as I came to understand them within my limited scope, but I know also that what befell me was only partly a result of who I was and my individual destiny; it was also, perhaps largely, a function of the whole and therefore due, for the most part, to needs and reasons of which I am completely oblivious. This undivided show is so gigantic, so astounding, that I do not claim to know truly what my role in it has been, nor what it is all about. Though I do know that it is certainly about something.

What happened to me may have occurred because I am perhaps on the last round of my earthly incarnations and have needed to acquire all my missing fragments into one so as to become a circle and a whole. Or perhaps it was all due simply to my intent, which I formulated at a time when I did not understand the power of such a conviction- the intent to return to God-freedom and, if possible, to take as many others with me as I could. This may in fact have been the *modus operandi* behind every serendipitous encounter, every realization, every grace, and blessing bestowed upon me over time.

Or perhaps I was like one who comes down to earth for a brief spell as a lost particle from the other side, so as to inform others of a lost aspect of themselves, and also to retrieve their missing kin. Like one of those falling stars who so dazzle themselves in the passion of their ephemeral descent that they forget to put the breaks on, and to join into the realm of being. And yet I came to the consciousness of my imminent, destined melt-down, and fell only to the point of burning. That was when I grew wings, and, like the great Phoenixes of old, arose from my own ashes, but instead of flying off I simply glided down, landed upon this fair earth, and began singing my song. In doing so I slew the Death which had come for me, and brought to earth my new Life. Configurations change, events modify events, and if one thing moves the rest must move with it.

We only change the world by changing ourselves. Nothing we do ever truly exists in isolation. There are no absolutely personal nor autonomous actions. Everything exists as part and parcel of the whole, and no one person has a life divorced from the rest. It is the recognition of this which eventually allows the surrender of arrogated, specific personal attributes; it allows the ego to soften and flood out in the acceptance that there is no action which is not an action of the whole, and therefore what we are is not the separate, striving selves we think we are, but are instead living threads in a dynamic fabric which shifts and alters as one event, though the apparent parts imagine an apparent existence apparently divorced from the rest.

What we feel and think inside is irrevocably bound by invisible strings in the invisible connectedness of all beings and all places. And so, in the end, we realize that our thoughts are not our thoughts, nor are our feelings our feelings, for they belong to the whole, and our self is simply our closest proximity to the Self, which, at the center, we all are. And thus it is only through the self that we get to the Self, which is the spot where there is both unity and separation.

And so the paradox of this partial and impartial Self, which we are, lies in the acceptance of duality and its enterprises; the paradoxical duality- a part of, and apart from, the whole- which is the fundamental reason why, at the very core of things, everything we had experienced at the periphery becomes inverted: in and out change places, cause and effect merge, subject and object blend in and are abolished, and the less you become the more you are.

Ambiguities never cease to persist in life, nor do contradictions, alternative explanations, aberrant cases, and incoherent experiences. There is no logical system which can encompass, condense, or convey the multifarious exigencies synthesized into the all. Where pattern and principle break off, that is where life begins.

This is why things go haywire when you're heading towards the core, because the closer you get to the center, the more duality becomes apparent, for the spokes are closest right at the hub, and therefore the divisions and the One exist side by side; here a person finds the almost simultaneous occurrence of love and hate, like and dislike, light and darkness, and failure and victory.

As the moving periphery approaches the motionless center, an inversion occurs at which point longing only leads to further distance, desire creates more loss, hope begets despair, and only surrender and faith lead towards the immanent aristocracy. These contradictory qualities are at the center of the spinning wheel, which the circumference can never get to nor understand, and therefore whomsoever lives out on the feverish radius exists only where the world of effect happens so slowly that the immovable cause remains obscure.

It is only when you stop completely that you fall back inside and witness the evolving universe from the revolving hub; and it is only then that separation turns into union, pain into laughter, death into life, and the kaleidoscopic manifest betrays itself as but the splintered fragments of a singular white light dispersed outward through the prism of the self.

I had to accept myself as a finite expression of the infinite Self, and by that acceptance to accept the Self also. For until I accepted my part, I was apart from the whole, and when I accepted my part, I was in and of the whole.

I recognized this metaphorically one day, in a round-about way, during the biological contract which I had worked, looking for Murrelet nests, as I explained earlier.

The job itself was quite straight forward: one individual would shoot an arrow, which had a spool of fishing line attached to it, over a tall, old-growth tree, hoping that the line would drag over a sturdy branch during its passage. Then his assistant, which was myself, would go and find the arrow, cut the line off the end of it, and attach a spool of 4 mm diameter rope to the loose end of the fishing line. This line was then pulled backward, over the top of the tree, by the original marksman. And when he had attained the attached end of the 4 mm rope, he then severed it from the fishing line, and attached an 11 mm diameter climbing rope to its end, which I then pulled back over the tree again, via the 4mm rope, until I had the 11 mm line in hand, and tied it to another nearby tree to create an anchor. Thus, through this procedure, starting with a thin line, we ended up with a strong climbing rope over the top of the tree, upon which the climber could ascend to search for nests.

Now, during this procedure, while I was hauling over the 11 mm rope as quickly as possible from my partner's side to mine, via the 4 mm rope, I had to lay down the 4 mm rope on the ground, trying not to get it tangled up in the thickly gnarled undergrowth of the west coast rainforest. On one occasion, however, I was too careless and when it came time to re-spool the 4 mm, it was in a hopeless tangle. My attempts to unweave it simply created more of a mess. Finally I capitulated, and began the long process of grabbing the entire clump of rope and gently pulling it apart, loosening up the knotted mess a bit, grabbing each free end, and pulling as much of the loosened rope out of the core as possible. This had to be done over and over again. In this way, gently loosening the mass, and then inch by inch retrieving the rope at both ends, I was able to untangle a great deal of the rope. The problem was this- although the free ends were growing and the knot was shrinking, the knot in the center which remained was getting tighter and tighter, until there came a point when it could no longer be gently loosened, because to loosen it would mean dragging one of the free ends back towards the knot, thus eliminating the gain. It was then that I realized this method was finished; it had gone as far as it could, but could go no further.

I sat there distraught and bewildered for having botched up such a simple task, but then a thought occurred to me- now is the time to roll up one of the loose ends into a tight ball and weave it through the central knot. So I carefully gathered up one loose end, rolled it into a small ball, and then painstakingly wove this ball in and out and through the larger central knot, until, finally the whole was untangled.

It was in a similar way that I recognized the necessity of both the oriental and occidental ways in our lives- that both are required if we are to untie the great God-knot in which we are bound. By this I mean that an individual can ease back effortlessly into the macrocosm, the Self, in the time-proven method of the east, but eventually there comes a point when that Self can go no further, for the knotted creation remains, inhibiting any further evolution. That is the point when one must ball oneself effortfully up into the microcosm, the self, in the way of the occident, and weave oneself amongst the tangled fibres of the world, if God is to finally be set free.[21]

*

thirteen

Our selves exist only in relation, whether it be with the earth, with others, or with God. To realize this is to lose yourself in relation, and more than that- to become relation. It is a bond in all directions, and you belong to everything, and more than that- you are everything. The boundaries of separation weaken and dissolve, and only the integral bonds of relation remain which produce the cosmic dance.

In the slack, motionless movement, between the sublime ebb and flow of existence and non-existence, where inside and outside exchange themselves- there it is that separation occurs only so as to glorify the One.

When finally the Self has taken dominion of the self, you become like a boat by which others might cross the perilous sea. You become the ark and the covenant.

The archetypes and mythos begin to swirl about the limitless vortex of your uncaged non-being. And in that living absence you are not contained, but ...you contain.

To become such a window to the infinite is to be nothing and to be all; it is to weep when others come weeping, to laugh when they are laughing, and to dance, and dance, and dance when they come to you dancing. You're inhuman and so bloody human that you die everyday from sorrow, and rise everyday from joy. You are no longer separate. And you are no longer you.

Like a door which swings both ways so heaven and earth can visit each other; you become the nothing which allows the all; out of the original binary comes the absence called the third, the slack tide, the non-breath between breaths, the hole between the external and internal which creates the whole, the living non-division between us. The Wholly Ghost.

And so, in the sublime paradox of this position, in the tangle of our oneness, no matter what you do or how you do it, the higher you rise, the higher you lift others with you; to free yourself is to set all free. As you liberate yourself, you liberate everyone, for you are everyone. And so there is no sense in getting bound in another's prison, simply because they are a prisoner. To remain behind for them is to turn back for Eurydice and to lose her in that turning.

These days we must be both Orpheus *and* Eurydice, if we are to return to the surface with our whole selves intact. Eternity in the Tree of Life is paid for by nothing but our own lives; as the fruit falls also from the limb, so too we must fall into the mire, and grow upward from the dirt; we must cultivate our own spirits, ever pruning, grafting, fertilizing, and pollinating all the radiant blastemas of our own sapling selves; we must learn to shed our own fruit, and become living trees in the Forest of Life. For even as a sapling is not a tree until it can itself bear fruit, so only when I came to see through the eyes of the One, did the abundance of the God within burst forth in fecund and laughing rapture from me.

Each of us is everything, and everything is each of us. It's like the Jewelled Web of Indra- in which there is an infinite carpet made of hollow gems, each of which is completely clear and empty in and of itself, and yet it contains the reflection of all other gems. In this way we are more each other than we are ourselves. Only the clouded ego-gem thinks it otherwise.

The microcosm is the means of the macrocosm, which is the medium in which the microcosm flows. Man is God applied. Waves within water within waves. Gods within God within Gods, where everything ends and begins in the singular, manifold, dynamic stillness. All of life emerges from, and dwells there. God does not see you, or me, or any others; God does not see many, God sees One. When the edge collapses the center grows, the hairy beast sprouts feathers, the feathers become flames, and the fire turns the chaff into manna.

It is a manic dawn which breaks in and rolls over upon you. It is a glee and tremor which catapults you away to the here which is nowhere. No more repentance. No more concern. No more assurance. No more to learn. The Beginning which has never ended has taken over and devoured you. And you have devoured being. Like the famed Uroborous, you are at the head of time eating the tail of space, engulfing itself to nility, and from that zero all infinities are born.

For at a certain point in the evolution of Being, each fragment of the whole, each individual, will come to recognize themselves as the center of all experience; that I am not outside of you, I am inside of you; that you are not inside you, you are inside me; that there is neither inside nor outside. Because the further you look, the more you see, until you cease to be a player, and become the cosmic Play.

When you become everything you are no longer trapped in the world, you are the world; indeed you must dance in both realms, or you shall dance in none.

But to get to both aspects of the One, you have to wipe yourself completely off the map and become the map. Your mind must dissolve into the Mind, and your body must become the Earth.

Why this is I have no clue. Why this way and not another, is inexplicable to me. It is a great godsea, and we are waves within it, and who can say how, why, what, or wherefore?

*

fourteen

No matter what I have written here, nor how I have explained or come to understanding, throughout it all I was nothing, and did nothing, for it was the great mystery of life, of the spirit, which did it all. And yet I once had a very wise woman teach me a breathing exercise which she claimed had been taught to Jesus by the Essenes. Whether this is the case or not I am not sure, either way it was a powerful technique, which helped me to still the relentless banter rattling around in my head at the time. And once, when I had used the exercise, and then lay down and entered into a deep, penetrating stillness, the woman then asked me why I had come into life, which made me wonder- why did I come here? And though I had certain ideas of why, a voice resounded unmistakably within me and said at that time: "Share your journey."

At that moment I knew that, in telling my story, I was offering nothing to anyone, except perhaps a reason to believe, not in my reality, but in their own, for *my* journey was specific only to me, and may have little or no consequence for any other. Thus I have written this work simply to relate *my* experience, and not to create any assumption that it will pertain to anyone else's; I intend no didactic outlay, nor do I offer advice, for that would be a vice, and I have found it best to leave each to their own course and karma.

My way was no other's way. In fact, the path which I was on is no longer the same one I am on now. I walked that mile and then started in a new direction.

I knew at the moment that I decided to share my journey that I was not offering anyone a solution. I have stopped believing in solutions. The surfer on the teetering crest of the wave asks not why the water flows and rolls as it does, he simply lets himself go into it, become a part of it, and ride with it as far as it will go. That is the reason he surfs.

And so I entered the Kahuna's tube, riding in the whirl and the torrent and trying to stay on the board, and when the surface and the floor came too close together, the mighty tsunami broke over and almost killed me, but then it floated me up and set me gently on the shore.

As if sitting around a campfire later that night, I have tried to tell others what I have seen in the tumble and glide, and to share the mystery of my ride, for that is what you do at the end of the day. And then you go to sleep and dream another dream.

And so it was only when I began to tell this story, my story, and to accept that it was my reality and mine alone, that I finished with that ride.

This, then, has been my perspective, which is not truth, for there is no truth within perspective. God alone sees truth, for God has no perspective.

After all, what can you expect from one human life, as it goes step by uncertain step, from unknown land to unknown land, ever caught in between a timorous hello and a heart-wrenching goodbye? I suppose that depends upon which dream you signed up for, but once you have eaten of the flesh, so to speak, you must ride it out completely.

I could have been a thousand things. I could have been a shepherd on the Orkney Islands, a fisherman in Norway, fiddler in Ireland, poet in Uganda, medicine man in Botswana, bohemian in Greece, a vintner in Chile, lay-about in Australia, a father with a joyful batch of kids in Argentina, a hermit in Newfoundland, a priest in Papua New Guinea, a hedonist in Hawaii, sadhu in India, a holy man in Tibet. I could have enjoyed being a craftsman or artist anywhere. I could have made hookahs in Kashmir, reed boats in Chad, totem poles in British Columbia, yurts in Mongolia, vodka in St. Petersburg, love in Marseille. I could have been all of these things and more if I did not have to be the one thing I had to be, or chose to be, or was chosen to be. I came to strike a specific blow, at a certain angle, in the required place, at a determined time.

As it was I lived out those years on the coast of British Columbia, wandering about both aimlessly and with purpose, loving and leaving as I went. I lived at the core of the throbbing heart of the Mother's world, at the precipitous interface between the mythic and the mean, and in the tumbling downpour of the Father's matterless mind.

There were so many brilliant souls whom I met and shared moments with along my way. So many of them touched me to the very quick, held me in their arms and eyes, and became a living part of me. It is as sad as thankfully laughable to look back on all the fleeting characters who walked a few strides along my path, and I along theirs, as we granted each other the benediction of our sorrows, and fears, and ecstasies. How we shared, and grew, and parted then, without knowing we were one.

Perhaps it is even harder now to hold them in my heart than it was to hold them in my arms. I see them all off somewhere, faintly, smiling warmly back at me. That is the love and agony of our distance and closeness. They live within me, and I within them. And that is the heart and the reason I came here- to dive in, and descend, and never to worry about resurfacing.

And yet it all seems now like a powerful dream which can be remembered perfectly upon awakening, and then loses its hold slowly throughout the day, until suddenly it is gone and it can't even be recalled, nor remembered that it ever was. As if I look back upon those times with friends and loved ones like the trailer at the end of a movie, as the credits roll, showing brief, touching scenes, and helping the spectator remember the feel of the whole.

At the end of my decade on the coast I could feel one chapter closing in my life and another one about to open up. I walked out and onward with a peaceful sense about me, and didn't hold on, nor sorrow, nor worry, nor cry, as it became so strange and beautiful that I was touched where I had touched. For what is my own but that which I have taken or given to others. That is all I have done on this strange and wild, cold and crazy planet, where I came down to take and give and become all others, and then to rise up, and forget.

I looked back upon those ten years which I could never have imagined living before having moved out from the east. Ten years so powerful and life altering, so full of friendships and revelry, loneliness and confusion, wonder and exploration, spirit and flesh, and a host of experiences and blessed gifts towards which I could only smile and sigh nostalgically as I sat there, perhaps for the last time, on a suburban hill overlooking Vancouver.

In the night the city's lights took on an overwhelming peaceful and friendly feeling, twinkling gently back at me, as I looked down upon the stage which had given so much joy and agony to me. And I felt then, as I had on Flores Island earlier that summer, and at my shack on the hill a few days before, that these places were saying goodbye to me; that the forums in which my soul had worked, and learned, and grown were now living parts of me, and would always be, and the trials and challenges and dramas for others were to continue on down below, beneath the lights which seemed so soothing and innocuous from above, and so unified and living to me now, and which were letting me go another way, and were smiling at me, a warm, appreciative smile, which seemed to blend and meet with the smile within me, because I had joined in and diffused myself into the whole, and we were now like parting friends who had been through the best and the worst together, had toughed it out, had grown and forgiven, and now genuinely cared and wished the best for each other.

It was a goodbye to a city which had embraced and spat me out as many times as I had done to it. And it was a goodbye to myself, from myself; I was leaving that world and that self which I had been and I was heading towards another, without knowing where that other lay. And I was doing it with the pleasant sadness of good buddies parting and knowing that they wouldn't see each other for a good long while, and so they hold each other closely, and then, releasing each other, and wiping a tear, they turn away to face a new day, having finished their time with the old.

We linger like this in each other, and in the places we've been and set our hearts into. We join in and are never lost from the earth ever again, nor from each other, though we leave and may never return.

In the end I grew away from the troubles of separative being. After the years of rebellion, condemnation, struggle, and turmoil, I finished with the process by which I would finally melt away like a dwindling chunk of ice which had been smashing about down the river after the break-up, only to then merge peacefully into the warm and gentle flow, losing itself into the whole; I dissolved into the careless realm, and became the calm and yet resolute river myself, carrying all things along with me on the voyage to the endless sea. For I found that nothing ends, that there is no end, though the mind seeks completion in all things. We go on forever, and this *is* the problem, for our eternity rends the walls of all our paradigms; it is an understanding which we try so hard to avoid because it brings no alleviation to the way in which we require goals and accomplishments so as to position ourselves in the fluid complexity. Yet it brought me to that type of peace which comes from not needing to partake of everything all at once, from not desiring to attain what I did not have, from not needing to be something, or become something else, because there is no need to rush about in eternity, for everything will happen, like it or not, and it will not cease, and when you know this about the world and yourself you begin to require less, and do less, and you sort of ease back, not out of fulfillment, but out of knowing that the all keeps going, no matter what, and therefore the little matters begin to fade away, and only what is eternal remains, calm in the acquiescent acknowledgment that nothing is ever gained nor lost, and the passing show will flicker and fade, as it is wont to do, and the grief and glory will come and go with it, but the

Self shall continue forward, softly watching from the other side of dying.

I can say now that I am a living part of the west coast, and it is a part of me; such a part of me that where it ends and I begin I cannot tell. We grew together and in doing so melded ourselves into each other, and even now I can feel the trees and sea and mountains moving in me, not separate from myself, but of myself, and I know that I am also there, out on the isolated, windswept beaches, and amongst the forest and the hills. I feel myself within the land which I grew to love and married my spirit into. And even as I leave, I know we will never be truly apart, for we have woven our separate fabrics into each other.

The comings and goings which I undertook in my person, now occur within me, for this life is the plane in which things appear and disappear, allowing us to learn how to let go.

God is here and now, with me, in me, of me; the one which is both of us, wrapped in the embrace between spirit and flesh, without reason, without assumption, without concern. In, and of.

And so I take leave, for I have crossed the line, so to speak.

Know that a part of me remains somewhere, far-off on the northern, wild coast, forgetting and forgotten, alone and not alone, sane and not sane, alive and not alive, in agony from the impossible beauty of it all, bewildered, rapt, and laughing.

Know that the spirit also crashes onto the shore of life, slowly, ever slowly, tearing down the solid, imprisoned rocks and islands of the soul, grinding the stones into sand, and creating a beach, a place where we can walk upon more easily, where two unique worlds come together, and through our hearts unite into one.

*****

Endnotes

[1] When I speak of my siblings on the Tree of Life, I mean just that, for I have no better way of describing it. I mean that our flesh siblings are not our only siblings, perhaps not even our closest siblings, but there are real sisters and brothers who lie scattered over the earth, without knowing each other unless their collective karmic forces have brought them very near to each other in one specific life, and even then a person must be keen enough to recognize these siblings as their own.

I came to find quite a few people, who, over time, I realized were very close to my spirit, and probably had been for many incarnations- if I will be allowed that eastern metaphysic- and therefore belonged, as it were, on the same limb of the Tree of Life as myself. This idea is more thoroughly expanded upon in the endnote on 'archetypes'.

[2] The *genus loci*, as far as I understand it, having never read a single word defining or describing it, occurs when a person, for no particular talent or power of their own, becomes the central spirit through which all others within their domain exist. A *genus loci* exists, I expect, in every gathering of people, from workplaces, to schools, to buildings, to countries. There are no specific borders, nor limitations. What happens for the person carrying the spirit is that their consciousness contains and effects everyone else's; it is as if all others exist, unknowingly, within a sea of the *genus loci's* psyche, and generally only that person will know about it, and often not even they will understand what is happening. The *genus loci* need not be the leader of the group, although in pragmatic terms this would be perhaps the most efficient person, which is why a president's or prime minister's consciousness can shift a whole country, and why the Pharaohs were able to command all of Egypt without moving from their thrones, and also why the pyramid is the perfect symbol of how consciousness begins at a point on the top, and emanates downward- just as a small light in the ceiling illuminates a huge room- encompassing a much greater area below.

The *genus loci*, though, is the strongest spirit of the area, not necessarily the outward leader. Hence, some of the axioms of Lao Tzu's Taoism describe this, stating: "The leader does nothing, and everything is done", and "If you need to meddle you are not worthy of the kingdom."

One could say then, in this spiritually evolving world, that God is the presiding spirit everywhere, and the *genus loci* is God's ground for being able to affect all others around that person. And this is the reason why different cities, companies, schools, and countries have different feelings to them, because the consciousness of the person who is the *genus loci*, being a filter of the One consciousness, modifies and pervades all within that person's spiritual domain.

[3] Regarding the intoxicants: I had no doubt at the time why booze has, from time immemorial, been called 'spirits', and why the Gaelic word for whiskey means 'water of life'; nor why A.E. Houseman would include in his poem, *Terence this is Stupid Stuff*, the lines, "Malt does more than Milton can, to justify God's ways to man."; nor why one of Omar Khayam's quatrains would run, "I drink not for joy of wine, nor to scoff at faith, but only to forget myself for a while. That is my sole want of intoxication. That alone."

And as far as marijuana: I have no trouble accepting the historical myth that Lord Shiva sat for five thousand years smoking ganja in the Himalayas.

And regarding magic mushrooms: I understand why the likes of Gordon Wasson and the McKenna brothers would laud these and other natural psychedelics as windows into the spirit world, and why John Allegro, one of the translators of the *Dead Sea Scrolls*, would go so far as to write a book called *The Sacred Mushrooms and the*

Cross, propounding that Christ and his followers were a mushroom cult, although, personally, I have found contradiction in Allegro's argument.

I understand and have experienced the profound shifts in consciousness under the effects of intoxicants, hallucinogens, narcotics, and psychedelics, and I believe, for some people, that these are valuable tools in the destruction of binding paradigms. However, I doubt whether they are worthy tools in the creation of the true spirit, which does not require such catalysts, and therefore abstinence is also a required drug, at a certain time, along the path.

[4] Whereas Jung uses the word 'archetype' as a temporary function of the self (i.e. hero, virgin, mother, etc.) and considers it as a bridge between the unconscious and the conscious, I use the word to denote the 'archetypical' spirit, connecting heaven to earth, into which each person is born and in which they are destined to live out the entirety of their incarnation. In this sense my use of it is more similar to Plato's Forms.

Although no symbol nor metaphor can ever describe the spirit- for the spirit exists beyond such limiting explanations, I might say that an alternative way of understanding the archetypes, or, the infrastructure of the spirit, is to see each 'archetype' as a branch on the tree of life, and each 'type' as a twig on that branch; that is, the 'types' are the individual 'selves' and the archetypes are the limbs of the 'Self', which is the whole tree.

That a certain twig will always be only what it is, is essential; for if all twigs wanted to be the same type of twig at the same place on the tree, there would only be one twig and the tree would die.

Differences exist so as to complete the whole, that is why we cannot escape the 'spirit archetype' into which we are born, for it is an emanation from heaven to which the 'type' belongs, just as a creature belongs to its species for its whole life.

The necessity of this structure is not necessarily limiting, however, as each individual may choose not only to express the full range of possibilities available to the spiritual archetype- and the possibilities, though confined within the archetypical parameters, are infinite, so that no single human life could accommodate even a fraction of them- but the individual 'type', can also extend the current range of possibilities of the archetype to which he or she belongs, thus, for a moment, reversing the cosmic flow, by altering what normally precipitates from the heavens down into form; this is accomplished by spiritualizing the flesh and mirroring it back to heaven. "As above, so below", declared Hermes Trismegistus.

This last event- the reversal of cosmic dispensation- can only happen once the 'type' has become whole and has become fully conscious and the spirit and flesh have become one.

Thus, though it is most often more profitable for the soul to tune-into and follow that which descends from heaven, this is not a categorical rule, and, in fact, once the spirit is fully in place in the flesh, the individual has a more intimate vantage point, so to speak, within the microcosmic realm, than either the spirit or flesh have on their own, and therefore in a sense a 'whole' person must 'be' as perfectly as they can, even if this implies, and often it does, going outside of the boundaries of the norm. This is how the individual progresses the universe from the bottom up, so to speak.

I say, therefore, that Jung's term 'individuation' applies when the 'type' has become conscious and self-determined enough to not be simply a puppet to the archetype, and therefore the individuated 'type' creates a new Form which is set into heaven and therefore precipitates in to, and modifies, earth; that is, the 'type' has become eternal, and not just ephemeral, and will, from that moment on, be included in the eternal aspect of the universe; which is another way of saying that an individual is now a fixed component of the cosmos- a part of the hidden projector which produces the visible show.

There is much responsibility in this, however, for the greatest danger lies in the individual foolhardily following their ignorant ego's whims, instead of listening for spiritual guidance from above, and thus, instead of perfecting their spirits and then advancing the whole, they merely exist in a prideful, imperfect state.

A profane way of describing this is to say that someone who does not come to understand who they are and what the parameters and possibilities are in regard to accomplishing their highest destiny in life may, on the ego's whim, become a mediocre physician instead of a valuable statesman, or, instead of being a loving mother and excellent piano teacher, they might become an unemployed academic; what has happened is that they have become what their ego desired them to be, and have not become the perfected essence of their true being. The roads are many, but not all of them lead home.

The ways in which we express or repress the spirit which we carry into life are infinite, although there are always certain limitations which we are best to become aware of so as to use those talents to which we have been entrusted to our own and the world's greatest benefit, as much as possible.

It is enough to say that the permutations for anyone's life are limitless and it is only up to each individual to listen to their own heart and dreams so as to choose their highest calling.

I have come across quite a few different 'types' within archetypes, which I have identified in the past, and, although these individuals carry the same blueprint within, they have chosen to express, or repress it, in different ways, coming to live in different rooms in the same castle, so to speak. Another way of understanding the distinctions is to think of 'archetypes' as letters in the alphabet, 'types' as fonts, and the alphabet as a whole, being the number of archetypes available in the cosmos, although I expect in the universal lexicon there are many more than a mere twenty-six.

Examples of types and archetypes within my range of experience include: two men I know- one whom I grew up with, and one whom I met later in life- both who carried identical spirits which tended, among other things, to be what I would call 'rebellious eccentrics'. One of them became a criminal, the other a truculent hermit, but these were merely expressions on the continuum of options which their spirit had available while operating in the earthly drama.

As well, four women I have met all carried the exact same spirit within, which I can best describe as 'free-thinking, earth wanderers', and expressed their essence in different ways. The first had lived out the essential aspect of her nature when she was young and then attempted, as firmly as possible, to repress it and live a very conventional life. The second had done similarly early in life, and then had sort of hybridized her spirit to society, still being a free wanderer occasionally, but also using her disposition to modify certain business practices of the company in which she was working- making them more 'earthy', so to speak. The third woman had maintained the core of her essence, when I met her, and was very much a freethinking earth wanderer, despite having had two children. The last was more of a pure manifestation of the essence, flowing in life as a traveler and benevolent gypsy woman, so to speak. (Notice I used the word 'pure', and not 'perfect' here, for purity is what comes when all the dross is extracted from gold, whereas perfection comes when that gold is formed into the ideal of the craftsman. An individual with a 'pure' essence may be far from perfected.)

This example of the four women I met, containing exactly the same spirit, suggests that the form in which our life takes can be open-ended, even if we follow as completely as possible the call of our inner, true being.

The last example of 'types' I will offer is of two men I know who look almost identical- as the 'types' of the archetypes sometimes do, and similar appearances often betray such archetypical closeness- and both are what I would call 'valiant, hero types'. One of them became a dope grower and yet, despite operating outside of the world's laws, maintained a high level of integrity, honesty, and dependability. The second ran a non-profit bikeshop and was also a high-integrity, honest individual. Each of the men were solid, dependable, trustworthy individuals.

Once again, however, I add the disclaimer that the description of the outward lives of these individuals does not really point to the inner 'spiritual archetype' to which they belong. All definitions and descriptions fail, for the inherent, archetypical spirit can only be witnessed when one looks at others from the soft aspect of the eye (that which sees the whole and not the part), and abandons all preconceived notions about what life is or is not.

After having written this endnote, I came across a quote which refers similarly to what I am attempting to convey. It runs: "Each man is a part of the Creator, or Cosmic Man; he has a heavenly body as well as one on earth. The human eye sees the physical form, but the inner eye penetrates more profoundly, even to the universal pattern of which each man is an integral and individual part." (Sri Yukteswar, quoted in *Autobiography of a Yogi*, by Paramahansa Yogananda, p272)

In fact, what I have found is that the eternal archetypes of the cosmos float down from the sublime projector and get received and broadcast in our movies and shows- themselves only outward symbols of the Great Show- and the dramas are also acted out on the many stages of the world's tragic comedies, played out in the 'real' lives and journies of real souls.

In fact, we call our *cele*-brities 'stars' because they are the overt manifestations of the *cele*-stial goings on (our media is the planetary reflection of the cosmic medium); but the same movements, relationships, acts, and scripts used in the media, also operate in certain groups of 'ordinary' people, at certain times, as individuals walk, albeit unknowingly, through a scene pertaining to their stage of cosmic growth.

I know, for example, of four people who were enacting, on the profane level, the quaternity of the four main characters in *Star Wars*: Princess Leah, Luke Skywalker, Han Solo, and Chewbacca. One of them was even called Chewbacca for a time prior to their meeting, and the other three were similar in actions and appearance to the other characters. There was even a Yoda-like character in actions, appearance, and lifestyle in the swampy woods associated with it all.

Often, if my own life was involved in a drama similar to one which had been picked up from the ether and used in a movie, I would have a dream of myself as the specific actor portraying the event in the movie which I was experiencing in 'reality', as it were. It is therefore not strange to me also that one of the male actors whom I admired as a young boy is now the partner of a woman who belongs to the same archetype as my partner at this time.

We are magnetically drawn together like this. There is less will in our day-to-day affairs than we think.

I have witnessed, as another example, two coupleships occur, in different areas of the country, years apart, in which I had recognized absolute similarities in the appearance and archetypes of the males, and similar ones in the females, and the couples, who never met each other, were drawn to their similar partnerships out of 'love', so we say. But perhaps the real reason is that these couples were pieces of the puzzle that could not avoid being placed together. Such types of 'blueprinted' cosmic affinities happen everywhere, and this realization betrays a type of redundancy which, if humbly understood, would make people accept that they are far less unique than they think; separate, yes, but not unique.

In order to understand and to feel the limitlessness of the spirit, it is essential for the individual to stop identifying him or herself as the twig; and that means the person must become the essence itself, the sap, which flows throughout the whole tree as the Self inherent within all selves. This is the *mercurial* nature of the finished soul.

In this way one begins to widen the range of the archetype into which they were born, and then to expand and encompass other archetypes; the boundaries soften, consciousness expands, the self becomes its own community, and the soul becomes a living part of the living One; the individual now contains the entire collection of archetypes within their single twig, for the twig is still the self, but the Self is in the sap.

And yet liberation does not come from denying the twig, but, rather, by being the best twig possible, so as to increase the health of the entire organism, while at the same time de-identifying oneself with form- the twig- and becoming the sap, the essence, which exists everywhere (this idea will be expanded upon in the endnote on the marriage of the East and West). It is a matter of becoming less self-conscious, and more Self-conscious.

The Tree of Life is blossoming all over the world, in all communities, as individuals attempt to grow an entire set of twigs, so as to contain the whole Tree; the macrocosm within the microcosm.

What happens is that the individual 'self' flows out of the twig, into the branch, down the branch and into the trunk, and down the trunk until it gets to the center, where the earth and the roots begin. It is here where all archetypes exist, intermingle, and consummate, and, upon arrival, the individual becomes an open nexus through which the true sap- the *aqua vitea*, or living spirit, can flow throughout the complete Being.

What I am describing is the outcome of a process in which the little self is whittled down to nothing, so that the greater Self may see; the moment you lose yourself as such, you become like a vacuum into which God cannot help but inexorably be sucked.

When you become a living nexus in the sleeping whole, marvellous things tend to happen around you, without you even intending them: couples will meet for the very first time, people will remember important dreams which they had forgotten, realisations will appear out of nowhere, solutions will manifest, problems will arise that cast light on a person's character, and all souls will take refuge within a consciousness which is not limited to their own; all this simply because you are both the hard and the soft aspects of the tree, the static and dynamic, the flesh and the spirit, the part *and* the whole. So many hidden things going on that the common man will never recognize, nor understand, nor perhaps even care about, and yet this substratum of spirit is in everything, and is everything.

[5] By the term 'spirit of the land' I mean a person who is a direct, symbolic expression of the spirit contained in the land. Most people are general expressions of the land in which they grow, which is why different races and cultures have differing appearances and behaviors. However, within any culture or race, there are generally a few individuals who are, what I would call, refined aspects of the spirit of the land. Which means that they are the living embodiment- the incarnation- of that part of the earth's spirit. I have met quite a number of these types of characters.

Sandy was specifically a spirit of the coast. It is hard to describe the reasons why I came to this conclusion. Two of the more easily explainable insights I had are as follows: It happened that on one of my visits to the outer coast I dreamt a dream in which a young blond woman, who looked very much like Sandy, was at a football game and was involved in various activities which are not pertinent to this explanation. The dream was interesting enough to me, and I gave it my interpretation and left it at that. A few days later, however, my friend Greg, who was living in the area for the summer, told me of a dream one of his clients had dreamt, while kayaking with him a few weeks earlier. The dream was also of a young blond woman, fitting Sandy's description (although he had never met her), and she also was at a football game. This was an interesting thing for me to hear. Although Greg's client's dream and mine had different actions going on in them- for the dream's messages to us were different- they contained the same animated character, the spirit of the land, of which Sandy was a living aspect.

Another clue to my understanding of this connection our spirits have to the places in which we exist occurred when I saw that an older woman, who lives now on the part of the coast where the dreams above occurred, belongs to Sandy's spiritual archetype, and, before moving there, this older woman grew up in the small town in Northern British Columbia where, interestingly enough, Sandy now lives. And so they were both drawn to the location on the earth for which their inmost beings had the greatest affinity.

I have met other individuals who are spirits of other lands, and who are drawn from all over the earth to the area to which they are inherently familiar, because, regardless of their place of birth, they are more fundamentally a part of the area to which they are drawn- if they follow their inner call.

[6] The *anima* is a man's symbolic inner female (just as the *animus* is the woman's inner male). She is quite often represented in dreams by a woman he is in love with, or has been in love with, or respects for whatever reason.

However, my *anima* went beyond this typical definition; as I would come to piece together the pieces of my life I would slowly understand that many people, both male and female, with whom I had close friendships or love relations, were either manifested aspects of my greater being, or siblings of mine on the Tree of Life. Sandy, for example, was not only my *anima* for a time, but was also my young sister on a limb very close to mine on the Tree of Life. And she was a person with whom I was never intended to have a long-term, intimate relationship but only an intense period of sharing together in which our spirits joined and remembered each other, before we parted ways and continued on our separate paths.

[7] *Mercurius* is a transforming agent; it is a person who makes you grow out of an old self and into a new one.

For Hans and I there were a number of both inward and outward incidents which would convince me of my earlier statement- ie. that Hans was my *mercurius*. An example of this was one event in which Hans noticed a small owl being attacked on the ground by a couple of ravens, and so we ran outside, chased the birds away, and Hans slowly approached the wounded owl, and, after many patient minutes, finally picked it up and took it back to his cabin.

Less than a year later I was to read in one of Carl Jung's tomes on alchemy, *Mysterium Coniunctionis*, a statement which claims that *Mercurius* took upon himself "the role of arbiter between the owl and the birds who were fighting it." (p234)

When synchronicities like this begin to pile up on you in various ways, as they did with Hans and myself, you begin to believe in the mythological patterns, which describe the symbolic process of a soul's growth in the subtle world. I did, anyway.

[8] A Bardo is an after-death realm of auto-creation, as described by the Tibetan Buddhists. In a Bardo, as in life, an individual is both the unknown Creator and the unwitting victim of his or her own creation.

[9] The *soror mystica*, or, mystical sister, is the female half of the male-female partnership. In alchemical lore these two work together seeking the philosopher's stone, or Holy Grail.

My *soror*- who will find her way into the story further on- and I were brought together by the invisible choreographer, as the saying goes, through a series of dreams and unexpected happenings, which also will be related later. She quickly became my lover, consort, and colleague, as we entered upon the same path, towards a destination neither of us could have imagined.

The alchemical partnership seeks, in essence, to find each person's own divinity through the conscious assistance of another who, in intimate relationship, mirrors back all the aspects of the other's soul which lay hidden; aspects which either taint or cloud the polished vision through which God could otherwise see clearly through human eyes. It is a lengthy process, one requiring commitment and humility to allow its rare completion. But, in fact, every coupleship or marriage is itself the crucible in which this process takes place, albeit mostly on a dark and unconscious level, and therefore everywhere on earth there is the possibility of husband and wife learning about themselves- via the other's stimulation- and of all that lays hidden within, including each one's dormant alter-gender other half; i.e. the man's female side, and the female's male side. And in doing so each reaches a wholeness in which the spirit comes to inhabit the flesh, the two become one, and heaven and earth are united through them.

A good *soror* or *frater* will take you inside of them, cut you into pieces, mulch these up, and then reconstruct a whole new you before spitting you back out. The working partnership is like two factories facing one another, which demolish and rebuild the other continually.

What I have come to believe that the Holy Grail, or chalice is- within relationship, that is- is the meeting of two people, each of whom have come to love the other, which they created, and therefore upon looking into each other with love, they attain the union of opposites where Creator and Created are one.

I came upon this belief in a purely synchronistic manner, when my *soror* and I were discussing the Holy Grail and staring at each other face to face, in a somewhat intimate way, and at the moment one of us mentioned something about the chalice, we both suddenly turned to look at an open book beside us, and there on the pages lay one of those gestalt drawings which appears to be one thing, but suddenly it shifts and appears to be another; the black-and-white line drawing which we saw was the side view of two faces looking at each other, or, when viewed from another perspective, using the space between them as the object, it appeared as a perfect chalice.

This is the visual understanding of what can be felt by two sensitive individuals looking at each other with love, for then the bond between them creates a holy receptacle, a chalice, in which the Spirit comes to rest.

I stated above that this description of the Holy Grail applies 'within relationship'. Outside of relationship the body itself is the chalice which must hold the individual's spirit; for, outside of relationship, an individual must embody both aspects (the male, or spirit, and the female, or flesh), in order to be whole. Therefore the flesh must be the chalice which receives the spirit.

It may also be the case that the philosopher's stone, or Holy Grail, is not one thing but is many things, and therefore is whatever is specific to the individual, and therefore applies only to the one who finds it and no other; each must find their own idiosyncratic gold.

[10] Years after this experience I came upon these descriptions which are similar to what I saw. I offer these supporting observations simply because, other than these two quotes, I have never read nor heard any similar description of this event which I experienced: "Closing my eyes, I saw flashes of lightning; the vast space within me was a chamber of molten light." (Paramahansa Yogananda, *Autobiography of a Yogi*, p163); and, "…samadhi ecstasy, which is the state you reach when you stop everything and stop your mind and actually with your eyes closed see a kind of eternal multiswarm of electrical Power of some kind ululating in place of just pitiful images and forms of objects, which are, after all, imaginary." (Jack Kerouac, *Dharma Bums*, p33)

What I realize now is that I had witnessed the 'light' which precedes everything, and *is* everything. I recall, on another occasion, being on a ferry bound for Vancouver Island one fine summer day, and as I was looking out into the blue expanse of the sky I could see millions of little light protozoa flitting about as if the stratosphere was a giant, liquid-filled petri dish, and I thought perhaps I had too much coffee in me, only the vision didn't go away and ever after when I looked into the sky, and through the sky, I could see what I would eventually find out had been called, by the ancients, prana. That is when I realized that light is alive, and that Sol is *sol*-id- merely trapped living light.

[11] The hill upon which Christ wept for Jerusalem.

[12] From my experience, the rainbow covenant is received generally when a divinely inspired task is finished, knowingly or not, and then often one sees it at the moment one is thinking of the event, which was fulfilled.

I could compile a fair sized list of all the times the rainbow covenant acknowledged my efforts- or, most often, my ignorant surrender to the required action- but this type of event is hard to explain because it is an *intimate* event- it requires one's conscious understanding of the incomprehensible intelligence of the cosmos accepting you via this affirmation. Nevertheless, anyone devoted to the further evolution of the spirit will recognize the exact thought which passed through them, and why they thought it, the moment they first see the rainbow covenant.

[13] The Kumbh Mela is a massive gathering of holy people and pilgrims, held every twelve years in Allahabad, India, at the confluence of three rivers, the Ganges, Jamuna, and Saraswati- which is invisible and said to be the river of the spirit.

[14] On the other side of form lies the eternal beginning, the Self. Time does not exist there, for everything is an instantaneous precipitation into form; nothing came before 'now', and nothing comes after it, for the beginning of creation is always 'now', and is not based on the causality, nor effect of time, for time is not.

The closer you get to the timeless beginning, the less power time has over form.

As such, at one point I was involved in a 'time reversal' (as we, who are caught in the illusion of time, would say), in which an event, which had gone wrong in the drama of humanity, was erased and changed, by God, by going back to a point where it was reparable and then continuing with the new precipitation into form. This type of cosmic activity is *not* a logical event, and therefore cannot be understood logically.

The instantaneous precipitation of all form from God at every moment negates linear causality, which negates time, and therefore past and future can be altered because they do not exist, except in the perspective of those separated from timelessness.

The manifest has already happened in the sublime realm; what we, who are in time, call 'now' is actually already over. That is why nothing makes sense- because we are living in a secondary world, which means we are not really living at all, merely experiencing what trickles down to us from the place where Life is, from the Beginning.

Time is the outcome of living in a world of effect. For there is no time in the place of cause, which is the Beginning that is always the Beginning, there is only the writhing primordial, red-soup of energy which never changes but that a mind grasps hold of it and makes something out of it and casts this something down into creation, that it might enjoy its endless fall through the abyss of form.

[15] Having said that, the names we are born with are not arbitrary, and are important labels, often disclosing a singularly important aspect of our journey or predisposition on earth, and so it is with humble regret that I acknowledge having changed the names of the real people who populate my real story, but it is not my right to advertise another's existence in front of a world in which they might, for very good reasons, desire to remain anonymous.

Ah, but what's in a name, you ask? Many things, I say.

My first name is Jack. A Jack is a common man- the antiquated, colloquial name for a servant, a man servant, *servator mundi* (the 'body' according to Jung), *or man-jack*, as it were, from which arises the oft-used expression 'a Jack-of-all-trades' (I am certainly not this, although by my early thirties I had done such varied jobs as: caddy, worm farmer, paperboy, prep-cook/dishwasher/delivery boy, hockey referee, farm worker, gas jockey, service in both the navy and army, waterbed installer, co-owner of two retail outlets, truck driver, warehouse labourer, road crew worker, security guard, co-op employee, mason's assistant, fish-hatchery slave, kayak guide, biological assistant, internet writer, mushroom picker, and caretaker of numerous locations. I relate this list without braggary or arrogation, but only so as to conclude that I understand quite well the reasons why "All work and no play makes Jack a dull boy"); a Jack is the often ridiculous character in a nursery rhyme, who jumps over candlesticks and falls down and breaks his crown and so on; a Jack, in the biological world, is what is called a 'promiscuous salmon' who swims up the stream two years earlier than the rest of the species, and spawns over the awaiting egg beds while the mature bulls fight futilely to the death for their now plundered breeding grounds; a Jack is a levered device to help lift heavy things from the earth; Jack is a prefix for such vernacular expletives as jackass, and jack-off; and Jack is the most powerful card in the game of Euchre, a game which, by some, would be considered as the cultural sport of the cultureless land of my upbringing.

My middle name is Ernest, and throughout my life I have indeed been earnest, perhaps to a fault, often forcing my way through a set of circumstances, which might have been better left alone or adroitly seduced, so to speak. But earnestness was a necessary trait to balance out the rest of my apathetic nature, thus allowing me to accomplish things which I had not really the energy to accomplish. Such earnestness could also account for my being an Aries, a ram, which, among other undiscovered aspects of this sign, tends to make me somewhat of a bull in a china shop in the world where spirit and matter mix and collide.

My last name is Haas. Haas, in Dutch, means rabbit. And though the root of rabbit, unknown to the greater part of mankind, is Rabbi, this does not prevent the cosmic joke from coming full circle and completing my name as Jack Rabbit.

Furthermore, on one of my Father's trips to Holland- at a time when I was in Canada, writing about my experience of wonder and absolute non-understanding- he found himself often being laughed at when the receptionists at hotels would see his surname as he signed in, for at that time a country-wide advertising campaign had recently been set in motion, and it had a rabbit as the lead figure, and the rabbit spoke the words: "Mein naam ist Haas, ick weiss von nichts." which translates, synchronistically, as "My name is Haas, I don't know anything."

On top of all this, my name is not even Jack Haas, for my birth name is actually John- a name which means "favored by the gods" ('favored', from my opinion, in the sense of a child choosing a particular teddy bear out of the pile, for no logical reason, and carrying and thrashing it about for a while, until one of the eyes is missing and a leg needs to be sewn back on; then the child chooses another)- and my parents had simply called me Jack from day one, or, actually they had called me Jackie to begin with- a fully androgynous alias which might be symbolic of my later, earnest need to marry my male and female halves within me.

And my surname, Haas, was actually my father's stepfather's last name, and so I have no actual blood tie to the Haas lineage.

Therefore it seems appropriate, given the all too real and all too unreal drama of my odyssey, that my name is Jack Haas, and my name is not Jack Haas.

16   This inner and outer reciprocity is not an absolute rule of the cosmos, due to the essential fact that the greater Will might veto or override the rules of the show for a time, and place a person in non-reflective circumstances when the need arises.

17   If you look softly into the face of a person who has assimilated both their male and female halves into their being, with your spirit eye, you can see a distinct angular line bisecting their face and showing one half as male, the other as female. Hence the hermaphrodite, or *sacred androgyne*, which comes about from the completion of the alchemical process.

The final product of this merging, however, is not necessarily a 50/50 split between the male and female portions of one's being, in fact, it is likely that one gender outweighs the other- depending on what one must accomplish in life, and the way in which this must be done. The merging then becomes more like a Cabernet/Merlot blend, in which the individual vintner mixes samples of differing percentages until finding the perfect amalgamation of the two varietals.

In metaphysical terms it is the 'I' and the 'AM' of the 'I AM' which denotes the division to be healed between consciousness and form, non-being and being, male and female, mind and body, spirit and soul. Once we recognize that the 'I' is outside of being, and the 'AM' is inside being, and that we are both of these if we are 'I AM', then we can begin to embrace the half we have neglected and so repair the cosmic damage from the fissure of God's mind and will.

[18] All duality and contradiction stem out of the original division- right and wrong- which comes from eating the fruit of The Tree of the Knowledge of Good and Evil. The best way to rid oneself of this misperception is either to know that there is no right or wrong- that there only *is*- or to consider that everything is right *and* wrong at the same time. Thus the duality is enclosed in the One.

[19] For other perspectives, I would refer the reader to Andrew Harvey's book, *Son of Man*, and Chokecherry Gall Eagle's book *Beyond the Lodge of the Sun*; these books describe each author's own account of the Christing.

[20] For the reader's own interest, about other understandings on The Rose, I refer them to Rainer Maria Rilke's little known work, *Roses and Windows*, and to the 13th century French classic, *The Romance of the Rose*. I do not claim that these works corroborate my perspective, but that they offer genuine observations on this phenomenon.

[21] Whereas historically it has been the Eastern way to merge the individual into the whole, the Tao, or Brahma, as it were, it is the Western way to become a differentiated, idiosyncratic part, and therefore 'individuated', to use Jung's terminology. It is my contention that both of these 'ways' must be incorporated into life. Thus the Buddhist must become both a Hinayanian, and Mahayanian- a lesser and greater vehicle; the Hindu must be both Krishna and Arjuna; the Taoist must be both the ocean and the drop, or, according to Lao Tzu, the Taoist must "Know the male but keep to the female"; the Christian must be both the Father and the Son, that is, he or she must "Come from the undivided", the Self, by "Entering in through the narrow gate" of the separate self; and a follower of Jiddu Krishnamurti must become, in his words, "Both the observer and the observed."

This is where the microcosm meets the macrocosm, and God, as the metaphor runs, lives like a spider in the web of his own creation.

And so God depends upon man as much as man depends upon God. For they are one.

Books by Jack Haas

The Way of Wonder: *a return to the mystery of ourselves*
by Jack Haas   ISBN: 0-9731007-0-2

A groundbreaking exploration of the mystery of existence, in that it both assimilates many divergent paths, showing how these proceed toward the same hallowed destination- wonder- and also by preparing the reader to walk along this way. This is a book devoted to the miracle, awe, and beauty in all life. It is a book about the rapture of unknowing.

"...written out of reverence for the beauty in all life. ...especially recommended reading for students of comparative religion and personal spirituality." *Midwest Book Review*

"...a most unusual, and powerful book." George Fisk (author of *A New Sense of Destiny*)

"This book really impressed me. ...a most stimulating read." Alicia Karen Elkins (Gotta Write Network Reviews)

"Wow! ...What a glorious, uplifting, inspiring affirmation it is!" Jonathon Kerslake (editor of *Lived Experience*)

Roots and Wings: *adventures of a spirit on earth*
by Jack Haas   ISBN: 0-9731007-4-5

An autobiographical account of Haas' journeys in spirit, and sojourns on earth. This is a blasphemous, recalcitrant, rapturous work which offers further accounts of the author's inimitable experiences while out and about in "this crazy, beautiful, impossible world", as he describes it.

"**...exquisitely balances poetic rapture and esoteric insight. ...a glorious illumination of our spiritual birthright.**" Benjamin Tucker (author of *Roadeye*, and *OF*)

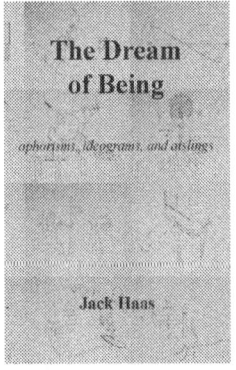

The Dream of Being: *aphorisms, ideograms, and aislings*
by Jack Haas   ISBN: 0-9731007-5-3

A unique compendium of poetic aphorisms, transformational drawings, and esoteric insights.

www.ingramcontent.com/pod-product-compliance
Lightning Source LLC
Chambersburg PA
CBHW032119090426
42743CB00007B/395